INTUITION
— and your —
SUN
SIGN

About the Author

Bernie Ashman has been a professional astrologer for over thirty years, having discovered his passion for astrology while reading Dane Rudhyar's *Astrology of Personality*. Since that time, his astrology practice has expanded to include writing, lecturing, and counseling clients from all over the world. He is now a recognized authority in the astrology field, and his writings have earned accolades from his readers and peers alike.

"I see astrology as a wonderful blueprint in assisting individuals to more clearly define their life choices," says Ashman, and his person-centered approach to astrology has made him a favorite with his readers. Ashman is known for his ability to make even the most complex topics accessible to the novice astrologer.

Ashman is the author of *SignMates: Understanding the Games People Play* (Llewellyn Publications, 2000), *Sun Signs and Past Lives* (Llewellyn Publications, 2010), *Astrological Games People Play* (ACS Publications, 1987), and *Roadmap to Your Future* (ACS Publications, 1994; reprinted by the American Federation of Astrologers, 2000). He has also written articles that are posted on the Llewellyn website, and his articles have appeared in several magazines and journals, including *Dell Horoscope, Astro Signs, The Mountain Astrologer,* and *Welcome to Planet Earth*. His insightful interpretations have also been used for astrology software programs used worldwide, most recently by Cosmic Patterns.

Practical Methods to Unlock Your Potential

INTUITION
— and your —

SUN
SIGN

Bernie Ashman

Llewellyn Publications
Woodbury, Minnesota

First Edition
First Printing, 2014

Cover art: iStockphoto.com/23728529/Marina Zakharova
Cover design by Kevin R. Brown

Llewellyn Publications is a registered trademark of Llewellyn Worldwide Ltd.

Library of Congress Cataloging-in-Publication Data
Ashman, Bernie.
  Intuition and your sun sign : practical methods to unlock your
potential / by Bernie Ashman. — First Edition.
      pages   cm
  ISBN 978-0-7387-3894-9
  1. Astrology. 2. Intuition—Miscellanea. I. Title.
  BF1729.P8A84 2014
  133.5—dc23
                                                            2013050727

Llewellyn Publications
A Division of Llewellyn Worldwide Ltd.
2143 Wooddale Drive
Woodbury, MN 55125-2989
www.llewellyn.com

Printed in the United States of America

Other Books by Bernie Ashman

Sun Signs & Past Lives: Your Soul's Evolutionary Path
(Llewellyn Publications, 2010)

SignMates: Understanding the Games People Play
(Llewellyn Publications, 2000)

Astrological Games People Play
(ACS Publications, 1987)

Roadmap to Your Future
(ACS Publications, 1994; reprinted by the AFA, 2000)

Contents

Introduction
WHY READ THIS BOOK?

It is my belief as the author of this book that each of us is intuitive. One of my goals in writing this book was to offer you a user-friendly approach that gives information so you can more effectively make use of your intuition. You don't need to have an in-depth understanding of astrology to make this book work for you. All of the information is conveniently laid out for you in your own sign chapter. Astrology is a unique system that can facilitate your understanding of how to better utilize your intuition. It offers you a way to put this energy into practical use. In reading this book, you can see how the planets assist or guide you to trust your intuitive instincts, no matter your astrological sign.

In reading your own Sun sign chapter and its meridian discussions, you can increase your intuitive awareness. Each meridian discussion is designed to help you expand your intuitive awareness. If you are a reader with more advanced astrological knowledge, you may try to use the information in connection with your Moon sign or the placements of other planets in your chart.

You can increase your communication ability with others by reading their sign chapters. This will allow for greater understanding of how to tune in to each other's needs. Reading other sign chapters will help you get a better understanding of how a lover, child, friend, or business associate functions on the intuitive level. It can facilitate mutual understanding with others. There is a lot of unspoken language that occurs between people. By reading this book, you can gain insight into the inner workings of someone else's mind as well as your own. You will be able to learn how intuition interacts with your consciousness on the mental, emotional, and spiritual levels.

It might prove informative and fun for you to compare a relationship planet like Venus in your own sign chapter to the Venus of someone else in their sign chapter. This will give you some clues as to how each of you intuitively approaches relationships and what you might seek in romantic and non-romantic partnerships. You could use this technique with each planet. By reading Mercury for you and for someone else, you can get information about each of your communication patterns and needs. The Moon reveals how you express feelings and what you seek in a home. The Sun describes how you desire attention and seek creative self-expression. Mars shows how you can be assertive and push for your own needs to be met. Jupiter lets you see how you can travel on the mental and physical levels together. Saturn gives you a glimpse of your mutual desire for ambition and serious plans. Uranus gives you a preview of how you could each seek freedom and unique goals. Neptune lets you peer into each other's romantic desires and idealism. Pluto gives you a sneak peek into each other's emotional intensity, passion for life, and even business instincts.

Another reason to read this book is that each of us can experience an intuitive block. A past or current experience may be causing this interference. When you read the planet descriptions, it might help you transcend the origins of why you feel intuitively stuck. Whereas the astrological signs offer the possibility of discovering a deeper intuitive awareness, the planets activate intuition into a pragmatic reality. Realizing what might be causing this interference with your intuition can go far in releasing your intuitive flow into clearer expression. Your intuition could be experiencing an obstruction due to a fear of failure, a past rejection, or simply confusion about how to solve a problem. Through reading the pages in your sign chapter, you may experience the catalyst of inspiration you need to forge ahead toward a more fulfilling future.

The Benefits of Intuition

There are many benefits to developing your intuition. One is it raises your self-confidence and has an empowering quality. You find you are more decisive. This allows you to experience less anxiety in making choices that best suit your purposes.

You also find that you have greater insight into the thinking of others. This allows for clearer communication and less tension in your relationships. Harmony is easier to achieve when you are able to tune in to why people think the way they do. You gain awareness into the actions of others, and it becomes easier to hear what someone else is saying rather than reacting too fast to their words. Intuition guides you to attract the love and abundance you hope to find.

Another benefit of intuition is that it allows you to be more resourceful in researching information. This is great for problem solving. Your perceptions become more expansive, allowing you to see situations from more than one perspective. Your reasoning power intensifies into a creative force.

Intuition can be beneficial for your mental and physical health. It allows you to relax more and not speed through life. Timing your actions and knowing when to take a time-out helps you avoid getting burned out. Intuition rests your mental faculties and recharges you to be that much more alert. It helps preserve your inner strength, keeping you centered as you live your everyday life.

Your creativity is energized in a big way. Intuition makes it possible to explore your creative potential in exciting ways. It allows you to tap into energies you did not know existed.

My Own Intuitive Experience

I am an intuitive who became an astrologer. I began to study astrology at the age of twenty-four. People often described me as a sensitive person, but I never really thought of myself as intuitive. In learning to master astrology, I became that much more intuitively clear. There is something about the psychological and spiritual experience that astrology gave me that helped develop my intuition. My practice of astrology grew immensely over the years, and I eventually began to trust and believe that much more in my intuitive ability. I still was not so sure I was that intuitive when I first started doing consultations for people, but my clients kept telling me that I was and they have continued to come back for more consultations over the years. I continued to hear that I must be an intuitive, because how could I know so much about a person before hearing much about their life story? It could not have been their astrological chart alone that gave me all of the information.

Learning to meditate was one technique that worked for me in becoming more intuitive. It helped me relax into the experience. Taking peaceful walks and spending time with my favorite people increased my intuitive awareness. Learning to slow down helped my energy build. It was intuition that told me it was vital to know when to push into action and when to pause. I became aware of an inner voice trying to guide me. It wasn't really anything mystical. For me, it was tuning in to what my intuition was trying to tell me. The reward is priceless for taking the time to become more intuitive. It is my hope that the material in this book will inspire you to increase your own intuitive awareness.

Light, Shadow, and the Dawn

In the sign chapters, you will notice that each planetary meridian is described in three ways: light, shadow, and dawn. The light describes your strengths in how you benefit from tuning in to a planet's meridian symbolism intuitively. The positive payoff from using this planet energy is explained in this section. The shadow, or challenges, describes what occurs if you are not in the flow with a planet's best offerings. This might be due to resisting what it can do for you or simply not knowing how to channel the energy productively. The dawn, or maximizing your potential, explains the highest manifestation of using a planet's gifts for you intuitively. In this section you will read about the evolutionary intuitive synchronicity that you can experience in the meridian being discussed. This is a special intuitive insight you can develop. The sign chapters open with a meridian dashboard summary for your sign. This will give you a quick scan of what it means to put all of these powerful intuitive planetary messengers to work for you.

The Four Elements

The astrological signs belong to an element: fire, earth, air, or water. The fire signs (Aries, Leo, and Sagittarius) are fast to act on intuitive impulses, making the world respond quickly to their goals. The earth signs (Taurus, Virgo, and Capricorn) prefer to proceed with caution. It is as though intuition is a stabilizing force leading to pragmatic and focused planning. The air signs (Gemini, Libra, and Aquarius) have a tendency to reflect with their intuition. Why? To ensure that their mental insights are filled with logic and polished with clarity. The water signs (Cancer, Scorpio, and Pisces) have a natural ability to tap into intuition but are not always fast to act on it. This is because they want to process what the energy means before putting it into action.

My friend and fellow Llewellyn author Sherrie Dillard wrote a wonderful book on intuition called *Discover Your Psychic Type*. She identifies four psychic types: physical, emotional, mental, and spiritual. When reading the book, I felt that the physical psychic type corresponds to the astrological earth signs, the emotional psychic type is linked to the astrological fire signs, the mental psychic type is associated with the astrological air signs, and the spiritual psychic type is related to the astrological water signs.

The psychic and intuitive forces of the universe are alive and well in all of us. It only takes a bit of awakening to our inner potential to receive the gifts this miraculous energy can deliver to make our lives more fulfilling, healing, and enlightening. When we make use of intuition, we can experience what the great psychologist Carl Jung called *synchronicity*, or a meaningful coincidence. Synchronicity can confirm that we are tuning in to the messages being sent to us by intuition.

In my 2010 book *Sun Signs & Past Lives*, I discuss how the four functions described by Jung—emotion, intellect, sensation, and intuition—correspond to the four elements. Emotion is similar in nature to the fire element, intellect fits with the air element, sensation is very much like the earth element, and intuition is linked to the water element. In my book, I describe how your day of birth is an intuitive doorway back into your past-life patterns and how you can transform these impulses into growth-promoting expression.

Think Positive

Positive thinking attracts intuition. Could it be that simple? It may not be the total way to become more intuitive, but when you don't dwell on negatives, you will find intuitive paths easier to access.

When reading your sign chapter or that of someone else, don't feel bad when reading a shadow description. Remember that nobody is perfect. This book is intended to help you make better use of your intuition. Enjoy reading *Intuition and Your Sun Sign*. Think of the reading material as a convenient guide to help you glide more smoothly in the world of intuition.

Ordering Your Own Astrological Chart

If you would like to have your own astrology chart, go to my website for instructions on how to do so: www.bernieashman.com. You will be shown the best way to get this done.

— *Chapter 1* —

THE PLANETARY MERIDIANS

In East Asian philosophy and especially in the practice of acupuncture, there is an energy known as *qi*, pronounced "chee." This is the life force or vital energy that flows through the human body along channels known as meridians connecting all of our major organs. It is interesting that in the meridian system, there are twelve major meridians related to the major organs in the body, just as there are twelve astrological signs. The ten planets rule these signs, with Mercury and Venus assigned rulership of two signs each. The planets travel along intuitive meridians not visible to the naked eye. These energy highways can allow our consciousness to bathe in harmony. When we don't flow with the positive or constructive movement of these intuitive meridians, or pathways, we can experience discord or a lack of harmony. When we make the right connections, our life is a wonderful and creative reality.

The Planetary Meridian Orchestra within You

It is important to remember that it is possible to activate the meridian energies at any time in your life. Each of us, in my opinion, has reached a point in time when we can move into what I call an "evolutionary intuition." There is an orchestra of intuition within you, as symbolized and powered by the planets. Think of yourself as the conductor of this orchestra. You can call on a planet, or more than one simultaneously, to accomplish your goals.

Each of the planets in astrology acts as a catalyst to guide us into using our intuition in a particular way that corresponds to its symbolism. It is as though each planet knows it is on a special mission to attract our interest in intuition. Each has its own scent to get our attention. Try to think of a planet as entering into a partnership with your Sun sign to lead you into greater intuitive awareness. Or you might want to think of it as your consciousness aligning with the intuitive messages the planets may be sending. The planets act as gatekeepers and even portals that lead us to deeper experiences of intuition. Each is a type of electrical circuit or activator that stimulates greater intuitive awareness. The astrological signs respond to the intuitive currents that planets send them. This will become more apparent as you read the sign chapters. There is a constant interchange of energy between these two great agents of intuition. The planets stimulate the signs to receive their energies. The signs in turn try to become allies to refine the intuitive messages sent by the planets into even clearer expression, allowing us to more accurately translate this energy into practical use.

Let's take a look at the planetary cast of characters.

Sun Meridian

Purpose: Creative Expression

Element: Fire

Sign Ruled: Leo

The Sun meridian is a strong force to activate your self-expression. Though the Sun is the closest star to Earth, it is commonly referred to as a planet. Just as the Sun in the sky defines the very solar system in which we live and gives its light and heat to sustain life on Earth, likewise the Sun meridian denotes your central life force and ability to energize and define a creative self. Therefore, the Sun sign represents your core identity or ego. The Sun symbolizes a need to exhibit the ego strength or willpower to shine in the world. It is a driving force to point the way to demonstrate your talents confidently.

In astrology, the Sun rules the heart of the human body, and in a sense it is the heart of your creative expression. The Sun meridian shows the particular path or life direction that you must recognize to manifest a true display of your creative power. The Sun meridian represents the colorful manner through which you make choices to define and expand your internal and external worlds. It is important for you to manifest your Sun energy in order to properly energize your psyche.

The nature of the Sun symbolism is similar to the cellular structure of the human heart. It denotes your need to fall in love with the creative process and life itself. There is feeling and emotion pumping in your heart as much as blood. Lined within these heartfelt feelings in the Sun meridian is pure golden intuition. As you will see in the sign chapters, it depends on your actual Sun sign as to how this meridian might manifest for you.

Moon Meridian

Purpose: Creating a Home and Expressing Feelings

Element: Water

Sign Ruled: Cancer

The Moon meridian is there to help you find your way through life by tuning in to your instincts. Though the Moon in the sky actually contains no water, the sea-like images or craters upon its surface, which are especially visible at the Full Moon, correspond to astrological symbolism rich in emotional and intuitive water.

The Moon denotes your innate drive to establish roots, family, intimacy, and a sense of security. How might this work with your Sun meridian capacity to embrace intuition as a vibrant creative force? The Moon guides you to trust your feelings. Expressing emotions as a way to create clear communication is connected to the Moon meridian. You may not necessarily have a solid logic when riding your Moon frequency, but you may still be on target in pursuing a goal. The Moon coaxes you to let go and ride waves of intuition to secure your present and future. Your subconscious is represented by the Moon's symbolism. Even your moods are stimulated by this planet. The Moon is a key player in allowing you to feel nurtured by your intuition.

Finding the home that best matches your needs is influenced by the Moon meridian. The intuitive side of the Moon can guide you to create a living space that allows your intuition to work more harmoniously. Think of this as creating the right feng shui or sacred space in your residence that stimulates your mind and spirit to channel intuitive power more smoothly.

Mercury Meridian

Purpose: Mental Insights

Elements: Air and Earth

Signs Ruled: Gemini and Virgo

Each of us has a conscious mind, or logical left-brain hemisphere, as depicted by the Mercury meridian. The winged messenger allows you to be curious about life. This planet is a multitasking giant, showing you how to juggle more than one activity at a time and still maintain your sense of direction. It sends you forward to drink from a multitude of life experiences. Mercury helps you sift through ideas to see which might best meet your needs and lead to the desired result.

This is the planet that rules communication. It is the part of your intellect that may make you a great networker in relaying information to others. This mentally restless heavenly body weaves its insights into your own thinking. Perception is the hallmark of Mercury. Your ability to be adaptable and accept change is increased by Mercury's influence. Resisting change may limit your growth. Mercury tells you not to fear acquiring new knowledge to keep your brain sharp. Staying young in spirit is easier when tuning in to the Mercury meridian terrain full of its exciting mental networks.

My friend and fellow Llewellyn author Diane Brandon wrote the very insightful book *Intuition for Beginners.* She describes how we don't have to choose between using our logical left brain and our more highly attuned intuitive right brain. Ms. Brandon says it is a mistake to think you must be either logical or intuitive. She makes a great point that our brains are designed for the two hemispheres to work together in harmony. I totally agree with her.

Mercury shows that a certain degree of mental toughness is needed to reach your creative intuition. The Mercury meridian works with you intuitively in that you can evolve into experiencing an altered or shift in perception to gain new insights.

Venus Meridian

Purpose: Relationship Tendencies
Elements: Earth and Air
Signs Ruled: Taurus and Libra

Relationship-oriented Venus guides you to find harmony in your people connections. There is a social drive in this planet unlike in any of the others. You want to reach out and touch someone. This love goddess meridian can send you intuitive messages on how to seek a soul mate. Venus inspires you to find like-minded peers and a suitable partner, whether in romance, friendship, or business. There is an innate need to search for those with similar or at least compatible values. The desire for companionship and social stimulation comes under the domain of this smooth-moving planet.

Venus can fill you with a love of the arts. Your aesthetic talent can blossom when you respond to the muse-like intuitive wave of energy sent by this planet. When connecting with Venus, some people excel in design, image consulting, art, music, or even cooking.

Another side of Venus is a desire for peace and comfort. Learning to relax and recharge your battery is part of the Venusian experience. Venus guides you to balance action and rest, to push or pause. Finding the correct balance keeps you healthy and happy. Learning to reward yourself for doing hard work is wise.

Some people respond to the Venus pulse by starting a business. Balancing a budget comes naturally. Knowing how to market skills and get that message out to the public can be shown passionately and with great wisdom. Being a diplomat in negotiating with others can become a talent.

Mars Meridian

Purpose: Initiating Action

Element: Fire

Sign Ruled: Aries

The Mars meridian pushes you to be more assertive and courageous. Mars is connected to expressing anger. When you are being direct in what you want, then you are more than likely pulling from Mars energy. When you are impatient to get your needs met or at least feeling strongly about this, then once again, you are probably expressing this fiery red planet. After all, in mythology, Mars was the god of war. Learning to become patient or less impulsive is a Mars issue. When you get better at tuning in to Mars's intuitive energy, your ability to act quickly on an idea becomes sharper. Knowing which battles to fight and which to bypass comes with intuitively tuning in to a clearer expressions of Mars. When this planet becomes your friend rather than a nagging adversary, you find a dynamic energy expression at your fingertips.

Identity is a Mars keyword. You gain a greater sense of your self-image when understanding your emotional intensity. As you evolve into your higher self, your actions symbolize this growth. People respond with cooperation when they get the idea that you are trying to create win-win situations. Self-absorption is the shadow side of Mars, meaning you are only looking out for your own self-interests. The shadow turns into light when selfishness is converted into seeking harmony through your actions with others. Where or how does intuition come into the picture to remedy the problem? It is when you allow yourself enough time to take control of a situation. Slowing down your reaction or response time is a sign that your intuition is being used to solve a problem or help find a solution to a question. However, if you are being too passive, this fiery meridian will push you to speak your mind. Mars challenges you to slow down into a rhythm to capture its messages. If you are moving too slowly in your life, this planet can inspire you with intense waves of motivating intuition to move faster.

Jupiter Meridian

Purpose: Expanding Knowledge

Element: Fire

Sign Ruled: Sagittarius

Jupiter is the largest planet in the universe. Astronomers say that all of the other planets could fit inside this very large planet. The Jupiter meridian represents fiery enthusiasm. When we make use of the intuition provided by happy-go-lucky Jupiter, we attract good fortune through optimism. Jupiter rules the liver in the human body, which is the largest organ. The liver filters out toxins. When you manifest positive energy, you are deleting negative thought patterns. This cosmic gypsy can lead you to travel on the mental and physical levels in exciting ways. The intuitive waves this planet sends to you will inspire you to learn and seek knowledge. You might become inspired to teach what you know to others. People may perceive you to be an excellent counselor or advisor.

When you make use of the Jupiter meridian, you can attract good luck. Thinking positive thoughts creates successful outcomes and makes for a more enjoyable ride through life. A bit of moderation is required at times to make sure you don't become overexpansive and bite off more than you can chew. Exploring life in an eclectic way keeps you energized and mentally stimulated.

Saturn Meridian

Purpose: Career and Ambition

Element: Earth

Sign Ruled: Capricorn

The Saturn meridian is lined with focus and pragmatism, offering you a reliable grounding wire. Seriousness saturates this planet's meaning in astrology. Yet astronomers say that if Saturn fell from the sky, it would be light enough to float on an ocean. This means there must be a way to alleviate the worries you face when feeling overwhelmed by responsibility and work. Ambition is stimulated by Saturn, and career goals are encouraged by Saturn in a big way. This meridian targets your mind with an intuitive strategy for success. When you utilize the intuition manufactured by Saturn, you can accomplish goals that require your greatest effort.

The challenge in making use of the Saturn meridian is not fearing to take that first step toward a goal. The magic comes when you move forward, even in the face of adversity or obstacles. Saturn asks you to create a structure for intuition to manifest through you. Just don't become too rigid. Make a plan, but stay flexible. Moving beyond the rings of caution that surround this planet can take some courage and determination. Adaptability and accepting change are the lubricants that allow Saturn, the cosmic chiropractor, to guide you to make the adjustments necessary to become a success.

Uranus Meridian

Purpose: Future Goals and Inventiveness

Element: Air

Sign Ruled: Aquarius

The Uranus meridian stimulates you to think in terms of new, exciting goals. Uranus was the first planet discovered in modern times. It was first spotted in 1781, between the American and French revolutions, hence its symbolism connected to freedom and individuality. Another theme is this planet's association with new technologies and innovative thinking. The social media being used by people all over the world to connect with each other and share ideas is definitely a Uranian idea.

Uranus orbits on its side, while the other planets travel in a straight up-and-down, more vertical posture. This unique planet is capable of exciting your nervous system and mind like no other. Uranus can send your insights in new directions at the speed of light. The Uranus meridian will tempt you into spontaneously changing direction and perhaps reinventing yourself. Thinking outside the box is the essence of Uranian intuition. You can develop a sixth sense of intuitive vision that allows you to see the world through new eyes. This can make it possible for you to have new perceptions about your potential and bring a surprise or two to your door. Don't fear marching to the beat of your own drum when this insightful planet comes calling with its bolts of cosmic lightning.

Neptune Meridian

Purpose: Creative Imagination and Idealism

Element: Water

Sign Ruled: Pisces

The Neptune meridian excites your creative imagination. Encouragement to believe in your ideals is inspired by Neptune. This planet quietly guides you to still your mind in order to sense its intuitive footsteps. The Neptune meridian is the hero of the collective unconscious, activating your innermost being to tap into the ideas that will best arouse your higher consciousness. Neptune sends intuition into your mind, taking you out of your usual routines and normal ways of operating so you can become recharged. In astrology, Neptune rules sleep and altered states of consciousness, such as what can be achieved through meditation. This planet encourages you to seek ways to relax your mind. Healers, artists, and those with psychic ability respond enthusiastically to this planet's meridian influence. Neptune stimulates a transcendental or magical type of energy in us when we fall in love with a person or get inspired by a beautiful experience of nature or a heartfelt life mission. Anyone can become more intuitive by entering the corridors of this meridian and walking along the same path with this magical presence. Neptune, the cosmic dreamer, lends an intense idealism and romanticism. It encourages your search for spirituality and a sense of unity with life. Escapism is the shadow that can surface when running in the wrong direction with Neptune energy. Faith and belief in yourself leads you to a clearer use of Neptune's intuitive gifts.

Neptune guides you on how to slip into other levels of mental awareness that take you out of ordinary time and space. The Neptune meridian puts you into a magical world, as though you are finding the door through the mists of Avalon from the King Arthur legend. It's as though your inner voice guides you to this place when riding on the Neptune meridian thruway.

Pluto Meridian

Purpose: Personal Empowerment and Passion

Element: Water

Sign Ruled: Scorpio

The Pluto meridian sends intuitive power that allows you to penetrate with laser-like intensity through any obstacles in front of you. This planet infuses your creative passion powerfully. A sense of personal empowerment blossoms to increase your self-confidence. The survival instincts connected to Pluto really have no rival. Business savvy is another Pluto theme. Rebirth and personal transformation may become your reality when tuning in to Pluto magic. Pluto takes you deep into your psyche. The intuition offered by this planet has a cleansing effect that rids you of self-defeating thoughts so a new dawn can manifest. Self-mastery launches you into new insights. Career goals become clarified and a heightened marketing ability may blossom. Pluto intuition ignites your passion onto a bold new inspirational highway.

The Pluto meridian offers you a business and problem-solving capability. You can figure your way out of troublesome situations with poise. The desire to research your favorite life passions intensifies.

This meridian shows you how to deal with loss and teaches you valuable life lessons. The Pluto meridian has a way of strengthening your inner clarity when you are willing to let go of the past and embrace a new present. This planet guides you toward a deeper understanding of the processes of life.

Your Cosmic Mirror Planet

There is a planet for your Sun sign that acts as a cosmic mirror, or mirroring agent, to help you intuitively maintain a clear perspective about your current and future goals. This is the planet that rules the Sun sign opposite your own Sun sign. Your own cosmic mirror planet will be discussed in the dawn section of your sign chapter. For instance, the cosmic mirror planet of Aries is the planet Venus and is discussed in the dawn section of the Aries chapter. The following table identifies your cosmic mirror planet for you.

Think of your cosmic mirror planet as a special helper or even partner that offers intuitive guidance in clarifying your goals. Life is often a balancing act, and when we are in challenging circumstances, the cosmic mirror planet can be the lighthouse offering the light to see your way out of the darkness.

Sun Sign	Ruling Planet	Opposite Sign	Cosmic Mirror Planet
Aries	Mars	Libra	Venus
Taurus	Venus	Scorpio	Pluto
Gemini	Mercury	Sagittarius	Jupiter
Cancer	Moon	Capricorn	Saturn
Leo	Sun	Aquarius	Uranus
Virgo	Mercury	Pisces	Neptune
Libra	Venus	Aries	Mars
Scorpio	Pluto	Taurus	Venus
Sagittarius	Jupiter	Gemini	Mercury
Capricorn	Saturn	Cancer	Moon
Aquarius	Uranus	Leo	Sun
Pisces	Neptune	Virgo	Mercury

Your Final Departure for the Sign Chapters

If you are new to astrology, you might want to refer back to this chapter—which describes the planets and their meridians—as you read a sign chapter. You will be shown how the planets inspire your Sun sign to dig a little deeper into intuitive awareness. There is no right or wrong way to learn how to trust your intuition. There is no set time table for developing your intuition on a deeper level. It comes with practice and trusting your ability to make use of this very valuable energy. Let it become an ally, a friend, and the path to new growth, and you will discover an evolutionary intuition.

Bon voyage!

Chapter 2

ARIES

Aries (3/21–4/19)

Archetypes: Warrior, Pioneer, Leader
Key Focus: Identity and Assertion
Element: Fire
Planetary Ruler: Mars
Cosmic Mirror Planet: Venus

Welcome to the Aries sign chapter. Your Aries enthusiasm to put your ideas to work finds great intuitive insight when making use of the planetary meridians. Channeling this vital energy so it can shine like a sparkling diamond is possible when you let your intuition guide you. Your identity finds clarity and your mind feels a sense of renewal.

Intuition moves swiftly through your fiery sign. This is similar to your own desire to initiate bold actions on impulse. With the wisdom of intuition embedded in the planetary meridians, you can be successful in your relationships, work, and key life goals.

Your Aries Dashboard Meridian Summary

Don't forget that you are the captain of this ship. You have the freedom to make choices that are to your benefit. What might prove interesting when you are in the middle of a difficult situation is to realize you have these meridians at your disposal. Think of this as a chance to summon or call on the meridian (or more than one) that can come through for you when you need it most.

Another thing to remember is that there are ten meridians constantly available to you. As an Aries, there will be times when you are moving so fast expressing with the creative Sun meridian that you could lose sight of the other meridian energies. We often make use of more than one meridian at a time, riding the waves of these energies simultaneously. For instance, you could be pulling on the sleeve of the Moon meridian in making changes to your home, while the decorating touch plays off the Venus meridian. There is often a blending of meridians that we connect with intuitively.

Your Aries Sun meridian keeps you thinking and feeling young, inspiring your vibrant creative energy. The Moon meridian soothes you with rich emotions that nourish your intuition. When desiring to sharpen your learning skills, you will be playing the strings of the Mercury meridian. When desiring more companionship and wanting to socialize, the Venus meridian comes into focus. If you need greater assertiveness, look to the Mars meridian. As a fiery Aries, you enjoy latching on to the optimism of the Jupiter meridian. The focus of the Saturn meridian assists you in manifesting your most serious plans. The Uranus meridian suddenly surprises you with new opportunities to explore. The Neptune meridian urges you to follow a dream and feel renewed inspiration. The Pluto meridian helps you passionately display your creative power.

I hope you enjoy this tour of the planetary meridians and how they make themselves readily available to you. The self-discovery and evolutionary growth you can experience are endless. Keep exploring and enjoying your life voyage.

Creative Expression:
Sun Meridian Activating Your Aries Intuition

Light: Strengths

The creative vitality of the Sun filters vivaciously through your birth sign, Aries, giving your personality a lively nature. You display a tendency to act on impulse. You entered this world forcefully, with a deep desire to act courageously. People may accuse you of being impatient, while you prefer to think of this as your need for instant gratification. You want the world to greet your future plans warmly and wish this had occurred yesterday rather than down the road.

The Sun sign of Aries gives you a bold spirit, lighting you with a passion about your favorite life interests. How might the Sun influence the sign Aries to make use of your intuition? The infusion of intuition into your consciousness from the Sun gets ignited when you deal with a new challenge, one that might even intimidate you. Why is this true? Because it is then that your self-orientation moves just enough out of the way or recedes far enough into the background to let a ray of intuitive sunshine through. When you rise above your fears and anxieties, an intuitive flow can occur. This can result in having a fiery spirit that manifests a spontaneous laser beam of enthusiasm. Your warrior sign is quick to put intuition to work while everyone else is still thinking about taking the first step. Creative power manifests like a bolt of lightning. However, there is the other side of the coin to consider. There are times when intuitive forces will ask you to slow down, the reason being that Aries actually gets greater results when pausing for a moment to consider the consequences of actions. Also, long-range planning or adopting a little reflection empowers the intended plan. The reward for taking the time to deepen an intuitive awareness is spending less energy to get the same result, maybe even a better one. The harmony that manifests when Aries utilizes clear intuition leads to more balanced relationships, career success, and a clearer sense of identity.

The Sun is linked to the heart or central energy center in your body. When you believe in your creative capacity, your intuition releases with great force. It encourages you to promote your talents and skills with extra confidence. Your willpower will not take a back seat to anyone. The love you feel for others may be a catalyst to launch your intuitive goals. Creativity can grow out of the harmony you create with others.

Shadow: Challenges

Since the Sun is symbolic of our ego and need to show our capabilities to the world, it is easy for you to get too attached to the results of your actions. This causes your intuition to get blocked or to operate at a lower voltage than you need. The result is not as rewarding or pleasurable. People will not be as supportive of your goals if you have to be the center of attention. Also, rejection is a lot more painful when you lose your intuitive clarity. Your life feels out of balance. Your creative aspirations lack energy and follow-through. Your determination is not as strong and burnout is more possible when you become too self-focused and not as in tune with your intuition, which helps pace your thoughts and movements. Having a bad sense of timing is likely to occur more often.

Dawn: Maximizing Your Potential

There is an inner dimension to the Sun that radiates from within its bright meridian, sending clear light into your insights. Solar intuition focuses on your behalf when you relax into the creative process. There are times when you face the great challenge of having the confidence to let go and move forward so you can be guided into the quieter eye of the hurricane. This is the process through which you learn how to flow with the power of your self-expression instead of trying to force it to happen. An evolutionary intuitive synchronicity manifests, as evidenced by the fact that your creative self-confidence produces great success in the world. When you realize you don't need to change your world overnight and can find contentment in little everyday accomplishments, the intuitive beauty of the Sun will shower you with its warmth. Be grateful for what you have and you will be surprised at and more appreciative of what you receive from life.

Creating a Home and Expressing Feelings: Moon Meridian Activating Your Aries Intuition

Light: Strengths

The Moon complements your dramatic Sun sign of Aries with a more subtle touch. This watery planet combines with your fiery Aries energy to produce raw emotion. This is actually how the Moon entices you to tune in to your intuition. When you take a moment to reflect before reacting too quickly to outer influences that the world throws your way, this powerful ally helps you see your way through any challenge that might confront you. Remember, your moods are a barometer acting as messengers to let you know your intuition is knocking on your door.

You were born under a restless sign, so it may be easier for you to feel your intuitive impulses when you're on the move than when you remain still for too long. What works for another sign may not be the same formula for you to activate your intuition. There will be times when taking a leap forward will kick-start your intuitive power into high gear. Even exercise or being in a competition of some sort serves as a catalyst to get your intuition into motion.

How do you attract Moon intuition to be more active in your life? Since the home is a symbol of the Moon, the feng shui of your residence can be important to consider. Your home must feel like it is in sync with your identity. Why? Because your Sun sign, Aries, is a territorial sign requiring a large wingspan. A cluttered living space blocks your intuitive connection. You need to sense that there is a lot of room to spread out in where you reside. The energy in your living space must support your self-image. This is a primordial need that goes back to the beginning of time.

The city in which you reside is just as important to consider if you want to experience the full potential of your intuition. It needs to provide the necessary outlets for your desire to fulfill the goals that best express your identity. The right location will provide the stimulation to get you to act on courageous intuitive impulses. It's possible that the Moon will guide you toward the home, city, or country that is the best fit for your intuition and that will solidify your identity.

Shadow: Challenges

If your dependency needs get out of balance, you will not be in tune with your Moon's intuition. This means you could be leaning too much on others for support or enabling people to weigh you down with their demands. This causes your relationships to not be as fulfilling. An equal give and take in partnerships will make you happier.

Of course, if you act like you never need anyone, it will be difficult for others to want to come close to you. There is such a thing as needing so much alone time that you appear distant and too removed emotionally.

Denying the insights that your moods and feelings are trying to inform you about leads to missed opportunities. The external world does not encourage you to listen to your inner voice. Our minds are easily focused on our outside reality, and that in itself is not a bad thing. But doing this to the exclusion of exploring your inner landscape causes you to lack the depth you need to handle situations that are emotionally demanding, whether this be in the area of relationships, career, or general problem-solving.

Dawn: Maximizing Your Potential

The Moon meridian helps you keep your dependency needs balanced so that your relationships stay harmonious. Your mind and emotions then work together in the right way. The Moon is an intuitive ally that you want to rely on whether in times of happiness or sorrow. You soar to new heights when walking along this magical intuitive circuit. If everyday life distracts you, you might forget that this wonderful energy is available. It could take some determination to keep this Moon meridian alive and vibrant in your life.

The Moon guides you to seek a new home, city, or country. This is how your soul tries to get you in sync with its guidance. The idea is to align you with the best opportunity for creative harmony and love. It may simply take a rearrangement of your current residence or maybe only applying a new decorative touch to your home to create the right feeling of inner happiness. The Aries warrior in you could use a home that recharges the energy you spontaneously pour into your daily routines.

The Moon offers you the watery emotion you need to balance that fiery way you engage the world. She brings you an intuitive capacity to reach out and hold the hand of a lover who offers you a sense of security. The lunar part of your intuition is never out of your reach. An evolutionary intuitive synchronicity is born through bravely walking toward those choices that best represent you. You then find the answers to that quest for inner peace and finding the people, places, and work that strengthen your identity.

Mental Insights:
Mercury Meridian Activating Your Aries Intuition

Light: Strengths

Mercury stimulates your mind intuitively to be intellectually curious about new learning. On the intuitive level, this very fast-paced mental planet is a good match for your speedy Aries style. The winged messenger signals helpful-hint insights about a situation far ahead of your normal mental operating awareness. This planet assists you intuitively in reassessing a plan quickly to give you the best possible positive outcome. Your Aries nature is at times focused so straight ahead that you are not thinking of important details. Mercury may intercept your sense of direction and alter your thinking just a bit. A slight tweak could make all the difference in solving a career dilemma or another key decision.

Your way of communicating with people is likely direct. You prefer to get to the point fast. Mercury helps you figure out the best way to get your point across and create a win-win outcome. The intuitive dimensions of Mercury come through to assist you in creating new communication patterns. Rather than causing conflict, this adaptable energy shows you how to be assertive without offending others.

You coax Mercury to activate your intuition by escaping from your everyday routines. This sharpens your intellect and draws out the magic of this planet and gets it to weave its insights into your conscious awareness. Reading books, studying a new subject, or challenging your mind to try something more adventurous is the way to get this very mentally exhilarating planet to work for you.

Shadow: Challenges

Changing direction is okay! If you get out of step with Mercury's intuitive energy, you could forget this. Be flexible. It does not mean you have to trade in your own strong ideas for beliefs that are not you.

Adaptability gets you out of difficult situations or at least relieves the stress. You don't want to lose sight of the big picture.

There are times when you will need to go slower so you won't miss important details. This is where Mercury really helps you. Patience is a mantra you will need to repeat over and over. If you allow impatience to rule you, then you will likely repeat the same mistakes again and again.

Another side of being out of sync with Mercury is self-doubt. Perfection is a problem. Nobody is perfect. It is okay to make a mistake. You could beat yourself up too much, which is a waste of this valuable energy. Dwelling in negative thinking keeps your mind in tune with Mercury's lower voltage. If stuck in negative thought patterns, you will miss out on opportunities and will be too non-assertive when you need to be more direct.

Dawn: Maximizing Your Potential

Tuning in to Mercury's more subtle frequency levels in this mentally upbeat meridian keeps you functioning at a high level without the anxiety. You are a fast-paced sign. Mercury enjoys moving briskly in step with you. This planet knows you will tune in with your intuition during the most hurried of times! You use this planet's ingenuity to discover new work skills or to explore a subject of interest that stimulates new insights.

Your perceptions about people deepen significantly under this planet's sharp guidance. Strengthening your negotiating skills becomes a passionate desire and empowers you. Communication ability could become developed in such a way as to make your relationships have greater clarity. Your perception about people becomes a powerful asset that even enhances your career success.

Getting Mercury to assist you in being a more positive thinker comes through not being afraid to learn new ways of perceiving yourself. Your identity is harmonized by letting stimulating and refreshing energy circulate through your mind so it removes negative debris. Remember, a shift in perception is a miracle and can be the evolutionary intuitive synchronicity you seek.

Relationship Tendencies:
Venus Meridian Activating Your Aries Intuition

Light: Strengths

Venus comes into your intuitive sphere of influence in more than one way. The first and foremost is that she loves to be involved in all of your people connections. This is Venus at her best, showing off her talent in social situations, whether in romance, friendships, or business communications.

You likely have a tendency to move quickly into relationships because that is your natural way of engaging others. Diplomatic Venus may coax you to follow her intuitive footsteps in staying clear of people not worth your time. She might even ask you not to rush into a new partnership and to take your time in being sure someone is a suitable match. Forming alliances is part of the Venus package. This fair-minded planet wants to ensure you will be treated as an equal. She will whisper intuitive guidance to remind you not to lose your identity by being too overwhelmed by someone of interest.

If you happen to be an Aries lacking assertiveness, this planet will do its best to show you how to find a little more boldness. How does Venus do this? By getting you to believe in your self-worth. In other words, you deserve to share your sensuality, resources, and energy with a person who appreciates you as a valued asset.

Another Venusian theme is abundance and increasing your productivity. As an Aries, you may find yourself tuning in to this planet's enterprising spirit and market your talent in a brave new way. The intuitive business wavelength of Venus stretches far and wide if you will reach out and meet her halfway. If you make the time to take an inventory of your abilities and skills, you could package them into a more profitable lifestyle. Combining your adventurous Aries nature with the business instincts of Venus could take you onto a more abundant highway.

A third Venus theme is aesthetics. There is a creative artistic dimension to Venus that your intuition enjoys intersecting with in this muse-like meridian. This enriches your creative energy. Your inner and outer worlds benefit. You can enjoy expressing Venus intuitive power in taking care of business and as a path to internal harmony. Whatever way you use this, it surely will strengthen your identity.

A fourth theme is finding harmony and peace. For an Aries like yourself, balancing a competitive spirit with easing down into a more relaxing atmosphere confirms when you are tuning in to the intuitive awareness of Venus. Downtime is essential to keep you from burning out.

Shadow: Challenges

What are the indicators that you may have taken a wrong intuitive turn regarding Venus? You could be looking for too much of yourself in someone else. Sacrificing your own needs for the benefit of others may seem like an exercise in humility, but it may be that you are selling your own goals short. If you are regularly compromising to make another person happy, then you may not be listening to the higher frequency of Venusian intuition.

There is a natural self-focus in Aries, so be careful not to always demand to have your own way. It will produce tension. If you reflect a bit, it will lead you to see that there is a way to create a win-win situation with people. Give and take is a far better use of Venus energy.

A lack of self-esteem could put a dent in your bank account in that it keeps you from putting your best foot forward in marketing your ideas as well as weakening your emotional well-being. This is due to not tuning in to the more empowering messages of Venus that are trying to break through and get you to believe more in yourself.

A constant being on the go may require you to learn to blend in more relaxation time. Aries is a fire sign that does not always remember to take a break when needed. Finding the road to inner peace is just as vital as taking action. Peace of mind is essential for your mental and physical health. When you make choices that keep you in a constant state of stress, you are not in alignment with the clear intuition Venus is sending you.

Dawn: Maximizing Your Potential

What is the benefit of flowing with Venus intuition? There are several. For one thing, your relationships find balance and ring with increased harmony in this meridian. Your chances of finding the right partner definitely are in your favor. How would you know if Venus is working for you? There is a feeling of being loved and appreciated. The relationship may not be perfect, but it features a mutual respect. There is an equal exchange of support for each other.

Perhaps the biggest indicator that you are on the right wavelength is that your identity feels secure. You are not needing to be someone you are not to please others. Venus rules Libra, the opposite sign of Aries. This opposing factor allows Venus to serve as a cosmic mirror, or mirroring agent, to reflect back to you how to balance your own goals with those of someone else. Think of Venus as sitting on a scale with your Aries nature. This is a delicate balancing act but one that is there to help you keep your serious present and future plans in clear focus. Venus sends you intuitive messages that keep you aware of how your own actions influence people. Think of Venus as an ally helping you sense if you are being too pushy to get your needs met or are not being assertive enough.

When you embrace the Venus intuitive pathway, your self-esteem reaps the reward. You will have a sixth sense in gaining inner strength. When being true to this planet's positive influence, it will become clear how to create a more abundant life. The inner calm you feel even when embarking on a new courageous goal is a sign that you have arrived at an evolutionary intuitive synchronicity.

Initiating Action:
Mars Meridian Activating Your Aries Intuition

Light: Strengths

Mars is the ruler of Aries, giving this planet extra importance in your life. It represents your get up and go. You may find yourself more often than not connecting intuitively with this fiery planet while you are on the run to start a new plan. This is a pushy type of intuitive energy. You may not even be in the mood to move on an idea and then spontaneously cannot resist the temptation. Your competitive spirit gives you an edge in business or in manifesting a career goal.

The courage to forge ahead is what makes you appear charismatic to others. You attract success through a single-minded belief that you cannot fail. Blazing a new trail becomes a reality when you tap into the intuitive gifts of Mars. The key is to not look back, at least not repeatedly. People will support your goals when they sense your heated enthusiasm.

Patience is an ally but may require a lot of practice in getting good at it. Moving under the umbrella of good timing really delivers results and confirms you are tapping into the higher intuitive frequency of Mars. This allows you to build your energy more productively and gets the world to respond to you instead of you trying to force your ideas onto others. This is how your personal power multiplies.

Anger is a raw emotion. When you don't let your emotions build to the boiling point, it makes it easier to stay on a more even keel in temperament. You actually get positive results on a more regular basis when trusting that being assertive, rather than becoming overly aggressive, is the road to travel.

Shadow: Challenges

How would you know if you are not in the flow with Mars's intuitive messages? There is more than one indicator. Constantly overreacting to situations is one possibility. You may be too impatient in what you expect from yourself or others. There is nothing wrong with being competitive or even aggressive to push for a successful result. It is only when you are always pushing life to deliver what you need in a hurry that you get into trouble.

Lacking assertiveness is another way you miss the boat with Mars. This sounds like a contradiction in terms when considering the forward burst of energy available to you under the push of Aries and your ruling planet, Mars. You are waiting too long to get your goals into motion, causing missed opportunities in this instance. Rather than riding the initiating energy of Mars, you are getting cold feet.

Either using anger to bully people or not expressing the way you really feel causes you to feel off-center. As an Aries Sun sign, there is a natural outpouring of energy constantly wanting to come through you. Mars intuition allows you to light a fire when needed to put your best foot forward to enjoy life. So it does require careful channeling of this very fiery passionate energy to get the best results. If you don't light the spark by pursuing a life interest, you will never know how successful you might have become.

Dawn: Maximizing Your Potential

As an Aries, you have the inside rail over the other eleven signs when it comes to riding the Mars intuition meridian. Why? Because this planet rules Aries, giving you a natural link to this energy. Follow your life passions, because they can be turned into big winners. Just exercise moderation when needed. Don't fear becoming too obsessive in following a dream. You can always tone down your fiery enthusiasm if necessary.

Your self-image flourishes when letting Mars take you toward inspiring goals. Don't be afraid to try a new relationship, career, or a bold start in a new direction. Even a little competition might bring out your best.

With experience, you will learn which battles are worth fighting. Some are best left alone, as they drain you for no good reason. The stronger you become in life, the more people there will be who want to challenge your personal power. The more wisdom you show in choosing the high ground in disputes, the better off you will be.

Finishing what you begin makes people like you. Your initiating impulses are almost without rival. If you lack assertiveness, it only takes a little practice to strengthen this side of you. Your charisma grows immensely when you move forward with self-confidence. Remember not to lose sight of those you love as you take on new challenges or deal with problems. You attract the support you need from others when you give as much as you receive.

It is okay to get angry, as this is a natural expression. But if you use this as a weapon, people will distance themselves from you. If you use your emotional intensity to bring people closer and to create clarity, you have found your gateway into the evolutionary intuitive synchronicity you seek.

Expanding Knowledge:
Jupiter Meridian Activating Your Aries Intuition

Light: Strengths

Little drops of Jupiter intuition sent your way inspire you to seek a broader perspective in planning your future. Seeing the cup as at least half full is the positive energy you need to try a new life path or stimulate your current circumstances. There is not much room on your plate for negativity when you are making use of this planet's meridian energy.

You create your luck through believing in your goals. If you are looking for a competitive edge, then connecting with the full-speed mental optimism of Jupiter may be just what you need. If you are lacking the assertiveness to get a project started, remember that Jupiter gives you the push needed.

There could be times in your life when taking a trip allows you a greater vision in obtaining the clarity you desire. A change of scenery to a different longitude and/or latitude allows your mind to free-associate its way into an intuitive flow to help you see a solution to a problem. It could be that even a short journey will inspire a new insight into a question you have. Restlessness is not so unusual for an Aries like yourself. Being on the go might be a way to see the big picture.

Developing an ability to defend your ideas with conviction is possible under Jupiter guidance. A deep philosophical passion influences you to seek positive solutions to disagreements. Sensing intuitively the right moves to make ahead of time saves you time, energy, and resources. Why might this be true? Because Jupiter is a planet that paves the way to keep one of your Aries feet planted into the future while one rests in the present.

Learning a new subject or developing an innovative skill keeps your mind energized. Being a fiery Aries, you probably don't like your mind to grow dull from not maximizing its potential. There are times when you will find exploring an alternative perspective on a situation helpful through making use of Jupiter intuitive energy.

Shadow: Challenges

What could occur if you don't use Jupiter intuitive energy correctly? When you put a fiery planet together with an action-oriented sign like your own, it is possible to move so fast you forget to look before you leap. There are times when this will get you into trouble. You may wish you had considered the consequences of your actions first rather than later. Your mind races so fast that you miss key details, irritating others and frustrating yourself.

Another theme is expecting life to deliver results without making the needed effort. You could misread Jupiter intuition as taking the path of least resistance to the point of missing an opportunity. The relaxing and leisurely atmosphere of Jupiter is intoxicating. The problem here is that you are holding back at the wrong time.

Your optimism may lack logic. Overconfidence may lead to a failure to prepare. Your competitive spirit loses its strength in this scenario. Your focus gets lost in lofty thoughts that are not grounded. Jupiter expands your mind and does require focus and discipline at times to get the best mileage from this planet.

Dawn: Maximizing Your Potential

When you are flying high with the Jupiter meridian, your life feels very rewarding. There is an intense optimism lighting up your entire spirit. Your actions are met with positive regard from others. You attract good fortune by believing in your goals. The past seems like it has less control over your happiness. It is easier to integrate negative thoughts into more productive perceptions. You feel less inclined to be weighed down by worries.

A burning desire to explore the world from various vantage points occurs. The desire to expand your mental horizons is heartfelt. The teacher and counselor in you might intensify under Jupiter's guidance. Promoting your talents comes naturally.

You win the support from those you love by encouraging them to believe in their own cherished plans for the future. Being a good listener takes practice. Lending your support to others gets them to want to do this on your behalf.

Your impatience can be converted into an inner contentment. Rather than rushing into new relationships or other important experiences, you perceive that the right choice is to slow down. Contemplation is a blessing. You will find that the Aries adrenalin to move quickly is there if a situation calls for it.

Travel to a new location sparks new insights. It allows you to change your reality through an expanded imagination. Your mind hungers for Jupiter's stimulating intuition. It is a ride that takes you to high adventure and to places within you yet to be discovered. This large planet in the sky paints pictures in your psyche that point you toward greater creativity that takes you into a magical evolutionary intuitive synchronicity.

Career and Ambition:
Saturn Meridian Activating Your Aries Intuition

Light: Strengths

When you take the time to tune in to Saturn intuition, you realize your most serious ambition. Career aspirations get fired up! This focusing agent of the universe even points a fiery soul like yourself into clearly defined paths for success. The discipline you require is imbedded in the lining of this planet's meridian aura. Your sign is not known for its ability to finish what it sets out to do. However, with this reliable heavenly wanderer at your side, it is amazing what you can complete. No task or challenge is truly out of your reach.

How do you tune in to Saturn intuition? Often it simply starts to manifest when you make a commitment to begin a serious goal. The instincts you need come forward while you are in motion. Overcoming the resistance to taking that first step is the key. Sometimes it is a fear of failure that holds you back. When you allow yourself the freedom to explore new adventures, you grow by leaps and bounds.

The past is a friend when you learn from it. There is wisdom imbedded in Saturn's meridian that is a constant bank account from which to draw. Patience is not easy for an Aries to naturally show. Saturn is the great teacher that leads you to understand delayed gratification. There is inner strength that is a reward when you learn not to follow your first impulse.

If you lack assertiveness, Saturn intuition helps you to see that there is nothing to fear when asking for what you really need. Your identity is clarified when you take a risk occasionally and leave caution behind. When you see that rejection is not the end of the world or that a failure need not stop you from trying again, your determination to succeed gets that much more empowered.

Even past-life patterns get resolved when you tune in to Saturn intuition. Whether you are too aggressive or not pushy enough in getting your needs met, Saturn helps you to find the middle ground. This could be an issue that has followed you from one incarnation into another. Now is your chance to get it right. Even having a clearer sense of your self-image could be linked to past-life issues. Saturn is the right energy to ride into being clearer about your identity and what paths to follow to keep you centered. Channeling your anger into productive outlets could be another past-life pattern you have come into this life to balance.

Redefining your current reality is another Saturn theme. Tuning in to the messages of Saturn helps you make the choices that solidify your present and future. When you connect clearly with the Saturn intuitive wavelength, you move into career roles that match your skills and talents. Trust your ability to take a bold Aries step toward paths that truly represent your inner convictions to be all you can be.

Shadow: Challenges

When you don't flow clearly with Saturn intuitive energy, there might be a tendency to force issues. An indication could be that you are putting too much pressure on yourself to make something happen. This manifests as being too demanding to get your own way and not putting your best compromising skills to work. The cause of this is feeling you must be in control in a compulsive way. This depletes your energy rather than replenishing it.

Fear results when you lose your clear or strongest connection to Saturn. It is as though your perceptions get hijacked by a lack of self-confidence. You freeze when it comes to acting spontaneously. This leads to missed opportunities and life just isn't as much fun.

Career focus might become too consuming. It's as though you are looking for too much of yourself through your work. Forgetting to keep your success drives in perspective throws your life out of balance. It is fine to have drive and ambition. You just don't want to start thinking you are your job.

If your intuitive intensity with Saturn takes a big dip, then negativity becomes too dominant. You forget to think positive. Isolating yourself or refusing to show your vulnerability makes for a worn-out Aries warrior. When you don't let down your defenses, it is hard to get out of troublesome thought patterns.

Past-life karma is a Saturn symbolism. This does not mean you cannot transcend past-life patterns. You may be repeating a couple of themes, one being acting like everything is fine in your life even when it isn't. This keeps your closest allies at a great emotional distance. Another potential past-life issue is dealing with channeling anger. You are either too aggressive in showing this or are hiding it. Anger in itself is fine. It is only when it is used to manipulate or push your ideas to the extreme that it is a problem. If you hold on to anger for too long, it becomes explosive or even causes you health problems, as this pent-up energy is not being channeled properly.

Resisting change works against you intuitively. When you adapt to a new situation, it sends your intuition into a nicer flow. If you misread Saturn energy, you will hit the brakes. Stopping for too long when it would be better to proceed full steam ahead works against your best interests. You become mentally and emotionally confused.

Dawn: Maximizing Your Potential

The Saturn meridian, with its focused intuition, is a real gift for you. Your conscious mind may not see it immediately, but don't be too disturbed by this. It isn't meant to. Your higher consciousness or soul loves to embrace Saturn's highest intuitive frequencies. The beauty of Saturn is that it allows that Aries fiery spirit inside of you to follow through on your highest aspirations. It offers you a sense of commitment like no other planet can. The more difficult challenges you could fear are warmed by an inner knowing that you can be a success. Being bold enough to take a first step toward fulfilling your most cherished dreams allows your passion to kick in.

Choosing the roles that best express the real creative you finds focus under Saturn's tutoring. When you embrace the intuitive power of Saturn, your determination to succeed has no rival. Learning to use your time wisely in a disciplined manner is possible. Knowing you are on the right path to make your dreams come true becomes a reality.

Past-life patterns can be integrated into empowering tools full of ageless wisdom when you don't fear making use of Saturn's guidance. Anger need not rule you but rather becomes part of your creative power. A lack of assertion is broken through by taking a new risk. It is then that you see you had nothing to lose in the first place. When you are too aggressive, an intuitive insight can come in the nick of time to modify your intensity into a more harmonious expression. The experience you gain in making the right choices comes through for you over and over again to be the lighthouse guiding you to being in the right place at the right time.

Reality-testing makes you stronger, because it is then that you see if your ideals are going to stand up to the test of time. Knowing your boundaries keeps your dependency needs in check. You will sense when to act with strength and when to show you need support from others. It is not weakness to show a little vulnerability. It is when you relinquish the need to be constantly in control that the universe rewards you with an evolutionary intuitive synchronicity.

Future Goals and Inventiveness: Uranus Meridian Activating Your Aries Intuition

Light: Strengths

Uranus is the one planet that can keep pace with your intellect and fast physical movements. This mentally speedy heavenly wanderer has the instant intuitive radar to be in sync with your every move and most exciting ideas! Uranus is the manufacturer of inventive insights that can fire rapidly from your brain. You only need to open up to the electricity that this innovator is sending you.

If you feel a need to reinvent yourself, this planet can ignite you into a new direction. If you get going on an unconventional path, you can count on the accompaniment of Uranus. He likes to keep close to free-thinking individuals. When you are desiring more freedom in your life, the intuitive flash of Uranus is only a breath away.

Belonging to the air element clan (as the ruler of Aquarius), Uranus adds objective awareness to your fiery emotional zeal. When you connect intuitively, this planet gives you that extra dimension to step back with new insights. This can guide you not to overreact to situations in which you might ordinarily do so. Uranus can broaden your vision to gain a great perspective of challenges, more like seeing the whole picture rather than getting lost in the details. Your perception of unfolding events can tap into a sixth sense, allowing you to make the right moves ahead of time.

The unique nature of Uranus offers you a new vista in grasping progressive technologies. When you trust the intuitive messages of Uranus, you can tap into talents that you never before realized were there. It's a chance to discover creative ability.

You can get energized by discovering new trends before everyone else does. This could be a real boost to your career goals or investment possibilities. Taking a creative risk now and then may further your growth.

Establishing new friends and groups may strengthen your identity. With the right choices, you can join forces with others of like spirit, lifting your self-confidence. Your peers stimulate you to think positively.

Shadow: Challenges

Moving forward without a plan occurs too regularly if you ride Uranus the wrong way. Lacking foresight causes you to feel like you are on top of a wild bronco rather than connecting with a smooth intuitive flow. People will become frustrated with your constant need to change direction in midstream.

Aloofness will distance you too much from those you love. Those wanting to care about you start feeling that it isn't worth their time. Not revealing your feelings produces tension in your relationships. A tendency to break off communication with others abruptly can disrupt your life.

If you surrender your individuality to a person or a group identity, you lose touch with yourself. A sense of confusion pervades. You don't want to be so dependent on others that your individuality and unique goals disappear. It isn't any better to become too self-focused, as you irritate others with this behavior and lose sight of any sense of camaraderie. If you demand too much space in your intimate partnerships, your behavior will be seen as escapism. This causes you to distance yourself from the love you seek.

Dawn: Maximizing Your Potential

An electrifying intuition is at your beck and call in the halls of this exciting meridian. You need only summon it. Making contact with this exhilarating planet causes your life to never be the same again. You will be surprised as new doors of opportunity manifest suddenly to walk through. Inventiveness is at your fingertips. Your intuition only needs the freedom to explore new fertile ground.

The past need no longer rule you. Your future goals ignite you into a reinvented reality. Creative sparks burst from within you like never before. A refreshing new atmosphere lifts you out of everyday routines that have dulled your intellect.

Making new friends occurs spontaneously. Finding a peer group that understands you is reassuring and comforting. Supporting the goals of those closest to you causes them to return the favor with reciprocating force.

You discover a new assertiveness to boldly pursue your plans. Knowing when to push for your own needs works best when balanced with assisting others to fulfill their own hopes and dreams. An intuitive sense of seeing just how to stimulate those closest to you to pursue their own future becomes masterful.

Achieving a deeper understanding of your individuality frees you from pretending to be someone you may not be. It is truly liberating. The wonderful thing about change related to Uranus intuition is that you never feel a need to return to behavior patterns that no longer serve a useful purpose. An evolutionary intuitive synchronicity finds birth by tuning in to the perceptions that point the way to your most unique creative power.

Creative Imagination and Idealism:
Neptune Meridian Activating Your Aries Intuition

Light: Strengths

At first glance there seems to be a contradiction in Neptune's reflective intuitive energy trying to link with your desire for immediate action under the radiant warmth of your Aries Sun sign. But with a deeper look, you ride the magical idealism of this mystical ambassador of the galaxy toward new horizons. You may have to retrace your steps now and then to see where you missed the guidance of this mysterious energy. Your inner being grows in ways you never imagined when you connect with the passive push of this gentle giant of the universe. Faith in your identity and creative power find reassurance when fueled with the nourishment in this Neptune meridian.

When you fall in love, it may be Neptune moving your heart and feelings. This watery planet has a way of enticing you to let down your guard even when you think you are not ready. You may encounter a new lover and experience that there is no veil between your minds. You could feel as though you know what each other is going to say before it occurs. Your self-image gets bolstered by the inspiration and love aroused by falling in love.

A spiritual awakening occurs when you connect with Neptune's highest intuitive frequency levels. Your warrior self bravely desires a transformation of your old self so a new identity can emerge. It is as though you have found renewal. Your emotional and physical bodies feel cleansed. Your actions become more aligned with ideals that bring greater clarity and purpose into your life. A desire to feel whole or at one with the universe is a definite Neptune intuitive signal. This is a very sensitive passageway into a new reality that requires a surrender of what you think you may need to the reality of what you really need. Don't feel bad if this takes several attempts. It is okay to make a mistake. It is better to creatively express yourself and let Neptune lift you to a higher plateau where you see clearly.

You may discover that you have healing energy. The more you explore your inner world, the more likely it will be activated. New Age and traditional healers make use of the Neptune meridian. This energy is waiting to come through people willing to be healers.

Aesthetic talent is linked to Neptune. You may find that expressing artistic skills can be used in your profession or as a hobby. You find a refreshed sense of identity and great joy in developing creative skills.

The collective unconscious calls to you to tune in to new symbols that inspire you to grow. Career changes often occur when you align yourself with this intuitive powerhouse of a planet. You can wonder why you are being rewarded at certain times when you are making the same effort you have always put forward. Sometimes it is when you show the collective you are serious about your creative energy that the gifts get delivered. If you want to deepen your exploration of metaphysics or the arts, this Neptune meridian is the superhighway to get there.

Be careful with trying to be too perfect. Neptune will tempt you to keep perfecting your favorite passion. She will also try to let you know when it is time to trust that you are ready to show the world your talent. Have faith that you will be a success in what you know how to do and the doors will open in ways you never imagined.

Finding the right causes is essential to your well-being. Just make sure that they are enhancing your self-image and that your devotion is being fully appreciated. Selfless service is a Neptune theme. Giving your time and energy to help others makes you a better person. When your devotional offerings are making the world a better place, it is fulfilling. Sharing quality time with those you love brings all of you closer and keeps them supportive of your goals.

Escaping from the demands of the world recharges your emotional and mental batteries. Learning to appreciate quiet moments helps you maintain your centeredness. Meditative experiences strengthen your willpower. The Neptune meridian takes you deep within yourself if you will let it. She reveals your innermost spirit and the source of where much of your intuitive power resides. The love you want to find in the world is linked to the spiritual power within you. Making your inner world a strong ally clarifies the path toward wonderful relationships, inner peace, meaningful careers, and complete harmony.

Shadow: Challenges

When you misread Neptune energy, what happens? For starters, you could lack faith in your beliefs and turn your ship around far too early before really giving yourself a chance. It might be that as an Aries you have plenty of start-up energy but it gets diluted by extreme emotional attachment to the outcome.

Romance and passion are a good thing, but you need to keep your expectations in line. You can't be perfect, and neither can your friends or lovers. Knowing your boundaries is essential to your happiness. It gets trickier in your most intimate relationships to maintain emotional clarity. A key message from Neptune is not to rely solely on silence as though you expect others to read your mind. Communicate with the intention of being understood. It's amazing how this often clears away Neptune cobwebs and fog.

An endless search for perfection is frustrating. It keeps you feeling like you are walking in circles or endlessly treading water. Your plans lack focus. You will disappoint others who are waiting for you to finish what you promised to deliver.

Your spirituality deepens with self-honesty. This is easier said than done. A problem in the Neptune meridian is denial. If you hide the truth from yourself, your life purpose becomes unclear, as do your most important people connections. Running away from the truth only makes your problems larger, and they never really disappear. It is counterintuitive for an Aries like yourself to avoid dealing with obstacles facing you.

There are good escapes and bad ones. Constantly avoiding conflict is the wrong way to walk. You lose that beautiful fiery creative spirit within you by fearing to see reality. There is nothing wrong in taking time to pause before making major decisions. Taking a break in the action is wise. It's the procrastination that causes problems. It is the road to nowhere.

Finding a cause or mission that captures your idealism is uplifting. It is when you let a group or leader expect you to surrender your own goals exclusively for the good of the organization that you lose your way. Your identity gets lost. Your life goals get pushed back on the rear burner.

If you grow too self-absorbed by wanting excessive attention, it causes tension to surface in your relationships. This is riding the Neptune highway in the wrong lane or forgetting there are two lanes, one for you and the other for a partner.

Dawn: Maximizing Your Potential

Being an Aries, your tendency to act very assertively is a normal instinct to get your needs met. The Neptune intuition meridian will beckon to you to let go. Try trusting people. See if you can create win-win situations with some degree of compromise. You need not win every argument or disagreement. Relinquishing power brings you harmony if you tend to be too forceful in using it. It attracts greater success your way.

Neptune brings you creative energy in a big way. The challenge is to keep moving forward after launching your first step. If you want to develop your aesthetic talents, this planet points the way to get there. The right-brain power of Neptune has no rival. If you stay determined and very patient, the magic of Neptune comes forward to greet you. You do need to structure your creative efforts in such a way as to allow the mystical forces to work for you.

Finding a soul mate is fulfilling. Riding the Neptune energy leads you to a person with similar beliefs and with stimulating ideals. You will be inspired by the love you feel to accomplish great things. The alchemy of merging your Aries warrior-like adventurous self with a lover strengthens you in a deeper way. The archetypes of courage and leader become enlivened by falling in love with the right person.

A higher self manifests that goes beyond everyday routines and concerns. Feeling like you have found a greater purpose is the nourishment from this Neptune meridian. When you give to others, it brings that much more to you. The collective unconscious becomes part of your waking reality. Tapping into symbols that elevate your faith in yourself is possible. The collective teaches you how to reach your goals without always feeling like you must be an aggressor. You learn to reflect and take more quiet time to become more aware of the processes of life. Your actions will become more decisive and hit the mark on the first attempt. Locating the seat of your soul relaxes your mental intensity. Your intuition then makes a very reliable guide.

When you deal directly with adversary circumstances, you become more grounded. In not denying your faults or personal issues, you allow Neptune to work as a healer. Your willingness to walk toward resolutions brings you into a world of evolutionary intuitive synchronicity where harmony and abundance walk happily with you.

Personal Empowerment and Passion: Pluto Meridian Activating Your Aries Intuition

Light: Strengths

Pluto has something in common with Mars, the ruler of your Aries Sun sign, in that they both are cut from an intensely passionate mold. Pluto has been called the "higher octave" of Mars. Why? Because Mars calls on us to more spontaneously act on impulse, while Pluto is more restrained in action and reflective in nature. When you tune in to the Pluto intuitive meridian, you are more likely to hold back your reaction time. Pluto guides you to view life as a process. Both Mars and Pluto arouse sexual energy. Pluto is indicative of the bonding power that keeps you in a romantic partnership for many years. As an Aries, it is passion that sometimes will link you to the intuitive power that Pluto offers you.

There is no meridian offered by a planet that takes you to a high level of self-mastery like Pluto. Your ability to stay on message in pursuit of a goal is bolstered when making use of Pluto energy. You possess a laser-like mind that cuts through any obstacle in your way to be successful. Finding a centered place within yourself makes you a match for any competitive force facing you. There is a beautiful comfort in self-mastery. You know you can rely on your inner strength to be a reliable ally in handling your life experiences.

In the Pluto meridian, charisma and personal power ride hand in hand for you when showing decisiveness. It is even true that in displaying patience, you make better informed decisions. You are allowing the power of Pluto to build a solid foundation of clarity for you when you take the time to get focused. Your insights find a renewed wisdom.

You magically attract success through really developing your skills. There are instincts to delve deeply into the creative process offered in this meridian. Researching your favorite subjects of interest leads to great levels of satisfaction. By persevering through challenges, you prove to yourself that you can survive any crisis. When you realize this, you want to indulge more in fun experiences. This allows you to eagerly seek a road to harmony because you see that this is how conflict melts away.

Pluto is called the planet of rebirth. What might this mean for you? Rising above negative thought patterns is a renewal in itself. It releases a new you. As an Aries, you thrive on a new challenge now and then.

Starting a new business, pursuing an educational goal, or embarking on a stimulating career plan unleashes new creative power within you. Leaving behind past behaviors that haven't worked on your behalf is part of discovering a new you. A magical metamorphosis occurs when you ride the power of this Pluto meridian.

When you face your fears, the Pluto meridian becomes an agent of transformation. You will attract the abundance you need. When you trust your deeper insights, they reveal the paths that will lead you to your greatest success. You become your own therapist and heal old wounds. When you forgive those who have caused you emotional pain and you are harder on problems than people, you find your way into an inner world where there is true peace.

Shadow: Challenges

What could possibly happen as an Aries if you miss the mark with this Pluto meridian? You might feel like you are taking three steps back for every one you move forward. In reality, you may be doing fine with a plan but your mind is translating your actions erroneously as though you are making a mistake. It is self-doubt that causes this, and sometimes even a fear of success. It sounds like a contradiction, because the very self-empowerment you seek is leaking out to negative thoughts.

Passion can be a beautiful thing, but getting lost in obsessive ideas leads to frustration, pain, and even a loss of your resources. Losing your balance causes you to lose your way. An endless desire to live in the fast lane causes burnout. When you lose your perspective on this meridian highway, it is difficult to be happy with what you have. This does not mean you should not seek a better life or a more abundant one. It is only saying to hold on to the people who keep you grounded and to maintain a firm grip on the inner peace you need to live happily.

If you become too dependent on a person, you could be out of alignment with this particular meridian energy. Your personal power gets severely diluted when you become over-reliant on others. Mutual give and take works better in getting your needs met. Denying your own hopes and wishes to make someone else happy does not serve your own best interest. The harmony you seek is lost in trying to please others to the extreme.

There is another side of relationships that is true as well. If you are an Aries who is too me-focused without paying attention to what your partner needs, your relationship might get out of balance. There is probably going to be friction that could be avoided by developing greater insight into your people skills. When you don't listen with an open mind to what a lover, friend, coworker, or family member needs from you, there is bound to be a great gulf between your minds.

Manipulating someone to get your own way will usually backfire. This takes away from your personal power. Another related behavior that causes problems is passive-aggressiveness. You are really angry, but instead of communicating honestly, you are purposely sabotaging the possibility of working toward harmony or resolution.

This is a meridian that allows you to hide your feelings and intentions better than any other. Secrecy is not bad in itself. You can't trust everyone. However, if you don't trust anyone, there will be problems. The end result could be a lonely life or at least one where you never get any support from others when you might need it the most.

Dawn: Maximizing Your Potential

There are times in your life when you will come to a crossroads. One path keeps you stuck in the same routine while another offers you a sense of rebirth. When you don't take a creative risk, you lose the opportunity for great growth. When you accept a new challenge, it strengthens you spiritually, mentally, and emotionally. The process of rebirth is not necessarily a pleasant experience. When you are surrendering past behaviors or thoughts that have kept you from mental clarity, it is intense, as this is the nature of the Pluto experience. The old saying "No pain, no gain" applies here. But the payoff to being willing to change your reality into an altered transformation in your thought patterns is priceless.

Deep subconscious patterns can be traced to Pluto. This cellular memory stays with you until activated. It is quite empowering to tap into this energy. There are hidden talents your intuition connects with that could be channeled into profitable experiences financially and spiritually. Even old worn-out behaviors that were negatives in the past may be converted or composted into positive expressions. The past need not rule you. The joy in cleaning out these old closets of self-defeating memories is wonderful. It helps pave the way for happier, harmonious days to celebrate life.

Your instincts in improving and sustaining your wealth are heightened through tapping into the Pluto meridian. Knowing when to make the right investments or negotiating for a better salary are linked to Pluto. Following your passion guides you toward the work arena that best shows off your work abilities.

When you don't fear conflict or adversity, you display a boldness that brings you faster fixes to problems. Learning to be patient in responding to challenges is when you experience an evolutionary intuitive synchronicity that produces results that have a transforming quality. The self-mastery you discover by moving forward to pursue new, adventurous goals leads you to renewed insights.

—— *Chapter 3* ——

TAURUS

Taurus (4/20–5/20)

Archetypes: Investor, Artist, Entrepreneur, Nature Lover
Key Focus: Stabilizing, Economizing, Maintaining, Persistence
Element: Earth
Planetary Ruler: Venus
Cosmic Mirror Planet: Pluto

Welcome to your Taurus sign chapter. Your Taurus plans for a reliable future find intuitive inspiration when making use of the planetary meridians. Creating the stable happiness you seek occurs through following your intuitive guidance. Abundance is at your fingertips when tuning in to your intuition.

Intuition moves at a smooth pace through your earthy Sun sign. This reflects your own natural inclination to make decisions with great patience. With the insight stimulated by the planetary meridians, you are able to successfully pursue meaningful relationships, work, and paths to fulfill your dreams.

Your Taurus Dashboard Meridian Summary

Remember, you can summon the meridians as you need them. They are there at your beck and call. There is at least one or more ready to join you for any situation you encounter. As a Taurus, you have ten meridian paths to ride to find the creative fulfillment you hope to express. We are often simultaneously using more than one meridian. For instance, in solving a financial dilemma, you could be tuning in to the Venus meridian to decide which expenditure would make a nice reward. The Pluto meridian would help you see the bottom line and stay pragmatic. There is often a need to play the strings of more than one meridian to meet a challenge.

Your Taurus Sun meridian fills you with confident creative power. The Moon meridian comes into play when you are trying to make decisions regarding your home and family. In sharpening your mental ability, the Mercury meridian comes into focus. Your desire to mix with the public or to form new relationships is stimulated by the Venus meridian. If you need to activate greater energy to pursue your goals, the Mars meridian is a real friend. The Jupiter meridian offers you a broader life philosophy by venturing beyond the borders of familiar territory. The Saturn meridian gives you the focusing power to define your ambition clearly. The Uranus meridian ignites your mind into new, stimulating ideas. The Neptune meridian tempts you to dare to dream big. The Pluto meridian empowers you by asking you not to fear rising above old worn-out thought patterns.

So you see you are never alone in this world. Keep embracing the growth offered by the meridians and you will never feel a need to be too attached to the past but rather will feel more self-assured in the present. The evolutionary growth you will discover is without limitation. Keep moving forward and developing new insights.

Creative Expression:
Sun Meridian Activating Your Taurus Intuition

Light: Strengths

The creative vitality of the Sun moves in a relaxed way through your birth sign, Taurus, influencing you to walk slowly and consistently through life. Your earthy spirit moves as though each step along the way must have solid ground underfoot. How might the Sun energy entice a Taurus like yourself to make use of intuition? Intuitive forces are welcomed if they promise to lead to practical results. Stability is the lifeline of your sign. Creative power builds slowly and releases with a force that can knock any obstacle out of your way. On occasion, the universe will ask you to allow the intuition it sends to get you to think and move with greater spontaneity. Why? So you might roam more freely to point the way to new, abundant turf. Intuition will entice you to drop your resistance to trying alternative ways to happiness and seeking greater challenges. There are times when intuitive forces will encourage your Venus-ruled sign to have greater belief in ideals and not fear fighting for them. The self-fulfillment that might result when you have faith in intuition is a life of balanced inner peace sitting alongside an outer life that is aligned with creative potential.

The Sun sign of Taurus solarizes you with a patient mental nature that aids you in developing sharp work skills. Your follow-through in meeting life challenges has few rivals. There are times when greater flexibility will get you further along the path to harmony in relationships, work, and finding inner peace.

The Sun is associated with the heart or central energy center in your body. Following your most heartfelt inner drives allows your intuition to come forward confidently and forcefully. When you balance give and take in your people connections, life feels more rewarding. Indulging in creative outlets helps integrate your mental, emotional, and psychological natures.

Shadow: Challenges

Stubbornness can be a problem for you when you resist change. Your intuition gets hijacked by not flowing with change or considering different courses of actions. People will be less supportive of your goals if you cannot compromise. A fear of change freezes your best plans for the future into ice cubes that are hard to thaw. Holding on to the past too tenaciously keeps a more productive future out of reach.

Another theme that inhibits your intuitive flow is low self-esteem. This keeps you from manifesting your most abundant ideas. When you don't value your own opinions or goals, they lose creative power and you miss out on opportunities. Your intuition becomes lost in confusion.

Dawn: Maximizing Your Potential

The inner radiance of the Taurus Sun emanates from this meridian, transmitting bold confidence into your mental horizons. Solar intuition is a miraculous thing of beauty when you embrace the intuitive guidance being offered. Some people might perceive you to be playing it too safe while you explain this as saving for a rainy day or even two of them. Your self-expression is bolstered when your self-esteem is operating at a high level. Your ability to persevere through a tough challenge adds to your inner strength. An evolutionary intuitive synchronicity finds birth when you take a creative risk. Through balancing patience with taking action you attract success. Learning to reward those who love you and showing that you appreciate their emotional support solidifies your happiness.

Creating a Home and Expressing Feelings:
Moon Meridian Activating Your Taurus Intuition

Light: Strengths

The Moon provides your very stabilizing Taurus Sun sign with a soothing energy. This is a compatible blend in that this watery planet encourages you not to doubt your intuitive instincts. It may be that when you are not sure which is the better of two choices, the Moon comes through for you, subtlety pointing the way to clarity. It is important to realize that your moods are the Moon's way of communicating intuitively with you. Learning not to overreact to stressful situations but rather to patiently wait for an inner calmness allows your intuition to guide you toward more positive outcomes.

You were born under an astrological sign that likes to proceed a bit cautiously. The Moon may surprise you by pushing you to act more quickly on instinct to make sure you don't miss out on opportunities. In other words, your inner landscape may get a ripple in it, like throwing a stone across a lake. Calmness and peace and comfort zones are fine, but there are times when you need to make a move in a new direction. You may find that you will not be as overcome by emotion and less filled with self-doubt if you act decisively.

There are ways to attract the Moon's intuitive pull your way. What might they be? The home is a Moon connection, so it is important that the place where you live reflects your Taurus values and especially your need for beauty and comfort. The natural surroundings and landscaping need to support your intuition and be in sync with your emotional needs.

The city or community in which you reside must feel like it gives you a sense of abundance. Taurus is a pragmatic sign, so you need to feel that your standard of living is supported by your location. Having opportunities to put your practical know-how to work strengthens your intuition. There is a voice within you, a sixth sense related to the Moon meridian that is trying to guide you to make your home a castle that makes your self-esteem a powerful entity.

Shadow: Challenges

If you lose touch with lunar intuition, there are usually signals telling you this, one being that you find yourself clinging too much to the familiar and feel afraid to take a risk. Caution is okay. After all, you are a Taurus and know that taking chances can get a person into trouble. However, if you never try something new, you miss out on fresh experiences that stimulate you into new insights.

If you happen to notice that you are looking for too much in material things, you may feel like something is lacking in your life. It is natural for a Taurus to take pride in what he or she owns. There is nothing wrong with earning a good living that pays the bills. It is only when you start believing that accumulating more than you need will keep you secure that you get into trouble.

Another signal that you may not have a clear use of your intuition is that you might fall into denying yourself rewards. You could be displaying a poverty consciousness. This only leaves you feeling sad. Depriving yourself of pleasure or items that bring you comfort from a belief of not feeling you deserve a better life actually blocks your intuitive power.

Dawn: Maximizing Your Potential

The Moon meridian offers you a wonderful intuitive flow that guides you to find the inner and outer harmony you seek. Furnishing and decorating your home with items that symbolize your core beliefs is a way of energizing your intuition. Finding a home and location that offer you the abundance you require keeps you feeling fulfilled.

The Moon offers you the emotional strength you need to meet everyday challenges. Having the right supportive lovers, family, and friends in your life helps you maintain the mental and emotional balance you seek. Letting a soul mate know your inner world brings forth more intuitive clarity for you. Getting past your inner anxiety about losing control brings you closer to the inner clarity you desire. Moving past your comfort zones to experiment with new experiences bring you into an evolutionary intuitive synchronicity.

Mental Insights:
Mercury Meridian Activating Your Taurus Intuition
Light: Strengths

Mercury speeds up your thought process to act faster on an intuitive instinct. Even if you tend to prefer a slower pace on the mental level, this breezy planet gets you to learn information in a brisk manner. Your business and work ambition does not skip a beat when riding the upbeat waves of the Mercury meridian.

There are times when Mercury will send you messages to change directions fast. Your natural inclination as a Taurus might be to resist altering a plan even if new options offer greater opportunity. Mercury allows you to see more possibilities that never before seemed possible.

As a Taurus, you may not react well to stress. Finding peace and quiet is more your style. You may have noticed that your best mental energy comes forward when you find a sense of calm. You like to feel in control of situations. The interesting thing about Mercury working for you intuitively is that it may become more powerful in the midst of a crisis or serious challenge. It is then that this mentally invigorating entity comes alive for you in a real way. So don't fear some adversity or upset to your normal routine. It could be that when you are disrupted out of your normal thought waves, the real magic of this curiosity-producing planet will manifest for you.

Shadow: Challenges

Your intellect will grow dull if you don't give it regular exercise. The intuitive clarity offered by Mercury will lack sharpness if you don't challenge yourself to learn new information. Staying too attached to the same surroundings lessens your chances of grasping new growth. Giving yourself various types of stimuli opens up your expression of this wonderful planetary meridian.

Doubting your ability to perform as well as others in the work arena blocks your intuitive ability to learn new skills. There are times when you will need to leave caution behind and ride the wings of this messenger of the gods to exciting creative heights. Hiding your light under a bushel, as the old saying goes, takes away from your best intuitive perceptions.

The biggest impediment to getting full mileage from Mercury is having too many negative tapes playing in your head. Regularly replacing these self-destructive thought patterns with positive messages allows the bridge to Mercury's intuitive beauty to come through for you.

Dawn: Maximizing Your Potential

It is okay to analyze circumstances until you feel comfortable proceeding. It is your Taurus patience that makes a nice blend with mentally fast Mercury. The two play off each other to allow you to maximize your efforts. Mercury likes to dart in several directions at once, so your Taurus nature gives Mercury some needed focus. There are times when you will benefit from allowing Mercury to spontaneously guide you to new goals.

Learning new skills and letting your mind have fun sifting through the information highway awakens your intellect to new insights. Traveling on the mental or physical level provides the added spark to make the Mercury meridian a close ally and take you into an evolutionary intuitive synchronicity. It is amazing how simply exposing your mind to new subjects or a change of scenery stimulates clearer intuition.

Networking with others keeps you abreast of current trends. Why might this be important? It may be just the vehicle to let you see the path toward new creative possibilities. The more you maintain an eagerness to grow mentally, the greater the chance of empowering your Mercury intuition.

Relationship Tendencies: Venus Meridian Activating Your Taurus Intuition

Light: Strengths

Venus and your Taurus Sun sign are a match made in heaven. Why? Because Venus is the ruler of Taurus, giving you a natural affinity to utilize her intuitive gifts. Venus is best to use in cultivating wholesome partnerships and making friends with people who share your value system. This diplomatic giant of the universe even helps you get along with those who may not agree with all of your opinions.

When you need to calm your nerves, this planetary agent of relaxation is willing to be of assistance. She will guide you to stay cool in the middle of a crisis so you can make contact with clearer intuitive reasoning powers. Your decisiveness gains strength when you don't feel so overwhelmed by obstacles in your path. So in soothing your nervous system, whether through eating enjoyable food or escaping to enjoy some entertainment, you empower your intuition.

Don't forget to reward yourself for completing a difficult job. There is magical intuition that comes alive when you do this. Being in the company of those with whom you enjoy spending time is another way for your intuition to come through this planetary meridian. When your chemistry combines with lovers, friends, or family members, the alchemy energy produced stimulates you to be more intuitive.

Shadow: Challenges

How can a match made in heaven between Venus and your Taurus Sun sign possibly go wrong? If you grow too possessive of others in controlling ways, it lessens your intuitive ability. You won't really perceive others clearly if you act in this way. Your intuition loses its strength as it is siphoned off by your relationships being out of balance.

If you allow yourself to be taken advantage of by people who don't value your needs, you fall into a dysfunctional pattern. Relationships either bolster your intuitive power or hinder it. If you sacrifice your own goals to others, you lose your intuitive way in the world. This causes you a lot of emotional disorientation.

Making enough money to survive and to buy extra items for fun is something you deserve. If you lose sight of this, you weaken your intuitive sharpness. It is equally limiting if you try to hide your sorrow in buying things you don't need. Running away from problems by escaping into material things weakens your intuitive gifts.

Dawn: Maximizing Your Potential

The Venus meridian is a rich valley of intuition ready to reward your relationship choices. The key is to make the right ones. If you follow this intuitive highway correctly, you unlock your relationship fulfillment in a heartbeat. It is important that you seek equality in your partnerships. This makes sure that your intuition is operating at a high level. You attract more of what you need when being true to your highest values, which is an important ingredient to getting this meridian to work on your behalf.

Balancing a desire for creature comforts with dealing with problems as they surface is vital to your happiness. Finding a balance between taking the path of least resistance and facing life head-on empowers your intuition. There is a natural desire in your Taurus Sun sign to enjoy peace and quiet. Your intuition guides you smoothly when you find quiet moments to listen carefully.

It is in pushing to explore your talents and showing them to the world that you tap into the essence of your intuition. Believing in your values and highest ideals elevates you into an evolutionary intuitive synchronicity that has an endless payoff with no limitations.

Initiating Action:
Mars Meridian Activating Your Taurus Intuition
Light: Strengths

Don't look back is how to get into the swing of the Mars meridian. This highly energizing, dynamic fireball of a planet sends you forward with tremendous thrust. Your intuition ignites like a rocket. A Taurus like you may be moving slowly toward a goal. If you let your passion express itself, then guess what? You are only a breath or two away from running like a person possessed with positive zeal toward a goal.

The trick with this Mars meridian to get it to work for you rather than against is to patiently plan a strategy. But what if the immediate present calls for you to act. You may need to summon the courage and scrap some of the steps in the plan. In other words trust your gut feeling and go for it. Meeting life demands directly brings out your best. This is when the rubber hits the road in this meridian as the current in it is asking you to be decisive. You can edit what you have done later.

Mars didn't accidently get called the "angry red planet" for nothing. In astrology, Mars points to how we express anger and assertion. When you say what is on your mind, you likely will find the intuitive power of the Mars meridian at your fingertips. When you show compassion and empathy for others even when expressing strong opinions, they are more likely to embrace your ideas more positively. If you show patience even while in a hurry, great insight accompanies your actions.

Shadow: Challenges

Impatience with no insight is the potential downfall of misusing this Mars meridian. So try not to go there too often with this attitude. Your goals will stay out of reach and the future will never get here the way you hoped. You will be running in circles and on the road to nowhere. Ignoring the signposts that say slow down leads to health problems and disappointment. The illusion is that you are moving briskly toward solutions, but in reality you are creating problems. Why? Because you are denying the magic of a wonderful intuition tapping you on the shoulder but not getting your clearest attention.

If you lack assertiveness, it might be because you depend on others to fulfill your identity. This will continue to be a problem until you turn this pattern around. This does run in the opposite direction from how Mars wants to work for you. Rather than letting this energy push you forward assertively, it is getting drowned out in a path of denial. You miss out on life's rewards and abundant gifts when you relinquish too much power to others.

Hastily throwing anger at others without considering the consequences is not in your best interest. You don't create compromise or win-win situations by adopting a strong-arm tactic. People will want to fight you more than join forces if you are constantly perceived as an adversary. Usually this reflects a lack of trusting your intuition about others and being out of touch with your own emotions.

Dawn: Maximizing Your Potential

The Mars meridian picks you up on a rainy day and lifts you into the sunshine faster than in any of the other meridians. It only takes some patience, honest introspection, and a clear view of the future. This is a very direct energy planet influencing you to deal with problems as they surface. However, it is also important to remember that your Taurus patience might be needed to get the best solutions.

Tuning in to your emotions is the pathway to get a fast link to the best this meridian has to offer. Feelings in many ways are the footsteps internally that ignite the intuitive power of the Mars meridian so that you can be a success in the world. The courage and decisiveness you seek are embedded in this meridian.

When you channel your anger and passion constructively, you are knocking on the door of an evolutionary intuitive synchronicity. Developing the mental eagerness to keep enlarging your life philosophy attracts the success you desire. Your relationships flourish the more you realize the impact of your actions on others. Your identity deepens as you figure out how to fulfill your own needs and not lose sight of those you love.

Expanding Knowledge:
Jupiter Meridian Activating Your Taurus Intuition

Light: Strengths

Being overly confident is a wonderful problem to have, don't you think? Happy-go-lucky Jupiter does not believe in waiting for you to feel intuitive but rather is constantly sending you waves of positive energy to move forward forcefully. This fiery spirit attempts to lift your mind above your current perceived obstacles to happiness and point you toward more abundant possibilities.

Luck sometimes occurs by accident. Then again, it may be more determined by the effort you put into making your dreams come true. This enthusiastic planet beams stimulating energy into your thinking to inspire you to trust your intuition. Jupiter symbolizes the essence of faith or believing you can accomplish whatever you plan to make into a reality. There is no looking back when Jupiter pushes you to gaze into the future.

What types of activities might awaken your Jupiter intuition? Travel to places that offer you new learning gets you to think and feel in new ways. Sometimes changing your surroundings even for a short time period gets your mind to seek alternative possibilities for self-growth. Studying and reading attract Jupiter's intuitive magic to assist you in finding ways to increase your earning power. Jupiter and abundance often walk hand in hand.

Building a solid present to enhance your potential for a happier future is part of the Jupiter repertoire. As a Taurus, you desire a life path that you can count on whether the chips are up or down. You prefer reliable people that you perceive as dependable in times of trouble. You would rather work in a job that has long-term potential. When you reach out to Jupiter, the sky really is the limit, as the old saying goes. Keeping your mind bathing in positive energy accelerates your happiness and success potentials.

Shadow: Challenges

How can a planet offering so much hope possibly cause any problems in your life? If you forget to believe in your potential to be a success, your self-confidence takes a dip. It is then that you lose out on Jupiter's intuitive beauty. Self-worth for a Taurus like yourself is a must to feel happiness. If you don't value yourself enough, then you don't get the results you desire. You settle for less in relationships and in your work. This is at cross-purposes with the Jupiter meridian, with its land full of hope and good luck. This planet offers you this instantaneously when you transcend negative thought patterns.

Inertia occurs if you lose your focus on the cherished plans you want to make happen. Rather than riding the inspiring Jupiter waves

of energy, you are stuck in self-doubt. This keeps you from the fulfillment you seek. Your cup is not anywhere near half full. Jupiter tends
to expand a positive thought into endless possibilities. It has the opposite effect and increases a negative obsession if you don't direct
this giant of the sky in a positive direction.

Your health suffers if you dwell on what is making you sad or less
than fulfilled. Finding comfort in food or your favorite passions is a
good thing. Running to escape from problems into excess indulgence
works against you. When you lack the faith to face life directly and
live in denial, it takes away from the gifts Jupiter could deliver to you.

Dawn: Maximizing Your Potential

The Jupiter meridian awakens you to a fresh way of perceiving the
world. Your intuition learns many new ways to keep strengthening in
confidence when aligning with this cosmic force of optimism. Finding a belief system that guides you through times of plenty or lack is
the reward of being true to Jupiter's influence. Make this planet a
constant friend through improving your learning skills. Keep up
with current trends and you will intuitively discover a business or
career idea that will increase your earning power.

When you balance your own goals with those of your favorite
and most influential people, life is more rewarding. You can't please
everyone. Trying to do so proves frustrating. Keep your expectations
reasonable but your positive energy upbeat. You attract the luck and
success you need when being open to opposing viewpoints. It is
when you are willing to travel beyond the familiar borders of your
own everyday thinking that an evolutionary intuitive synchronicity
infiltrates your thought patterns and guides you to great self-growth.

Career and Ambition:
Saturn Meridian Activating Your Taurus Intuition

Light: Strengths

Saturn and your Sun sign, Taurus, have a natural affinity for each other. Why is this? Both are firmly embedded in the earth element, giving you an extra edge to tune in to this planet's intuitive gifts when it comes to marketing your abilities. The serious determination symbolized by Saturn is an equal match for the persistent side of you that won't give up on a plan without a good fight. There is a strategy dimension that aligns your mind with the Saturn meridian that serves you well. The patience that is frequently displayed by you actually deepens in purpose when you make use of the intuitive power in this meridian energy.

When you learn to navigate wisely through obstacles, Saturn will guide you in a clear way to make the right decisions. Your very deliberate movement to proceed forward cautiously gets a strong push from Saturn when you are willing to take a risk. So it is in your best interest to trust your ability to assess a situation and put your best foot forward.

Past-life patterns are part of the Saturn experience. Learning from the past is wise. It fills you with solid knowledge that is used to make your life more fulfilling. In some past incarnations, you were too controlling. In other lives you did not assume enough power. Conquering low self-esteem or not trusting others can be achieved in the present. This life is a chance to find the right equilibrium. Learning to be more flowing or even learning from past mistakes in negotiations provides very valuable insights. Flexibility in your thinking attracts greater success in all areas of your life. Saturn assists you in knowing when to stick to a direction and when to compromise.

Obstacles and challenges strengthen your resolve. Keeping a sense of humor helps you maintain a positive attitude. You can't be a success all of the time. When you show humility in this planetary meridian, you actually have an easier road to making contact with the intuitive gifts of Saturn. Like a tree that bends when facing strong winds, you make adjustments to get the best results.

You can excel in any field you want to master. The key is becoming aware of the resources it will take to make your dream come true. Accepting the possibility of delayed gratification gives you the confidence to proceed with a sense of purpose. You feel less anxiety when you have a well-developed plan. However, your career and business mind becomes more intuitive when you travel outside of your comfort zones and accept a new challenge.

Shadow: Challenges

Rigidity is your biggest nemesis in tapping into Saturn's intuitive airspace. When you are stuck in the mud and resist change, you sink deeper into trouble. Your intuitive flow gets lost to everything from panic to a feeling that life is out of control. The focusing power of the Saturn meridian becomes pointed in directions that limit your imagination.

Denying your emotions is another wrong way to express Saturn energy. People will distance themselves from you. When you become as guarded as the rings that encircle Saturn, life is not much fun for you. It becomes difficult for your closest lovers, family, and friends to connect with you. You feel isolated and very alone but refuse to reach out to someone for help. Your job and relationships lessen in enjoyment.

Karmic patterns are reenacted when you negatively connect with Saturn. Often it is related to fear. There is too much attachment to material things and not enough balance with your highest values. Past-life tendencies need not continue to be a problem. However, if you deny there is a problem, these issues tend to resurface. Your self-esteem may have been too low in certain past incarnations and you are getting a chance to get it right this time around. If you gravitate to not valuing your own needs, it does limit your options. Other past-life themes include being too worried about job success and carrying too much responsibility for others. When you don't delegate or let someone know you need help, you get weighed down by being too responsible.

Letting obstacles stop you from making your most cherished aspirations a reality is another issue. You could give up before you give a plan enough time to be a success. When you focus too much on the whole job it could scare you. Forgetting that everything begins with a first step will keep you from getting started.

Dawn: Maximizing Your Potential

The Saturn meridian offers you many outlets for your work skills. It is the most powerful landscape to get you moving forcefully to put your abilities to work in a very focused manner. The staying power you find when tapping into Saturn's intuitive dimensions is without limits. When you show flexibility in your commitments to people and plans you find great happiness. Accepting change is the best lubricant to flowing with Saturn influences.

You turn liabilities quickly into assets by learning from the past. Being willing to recognize your faults is just as important as knowing your assets. People respond better to you when they perceive you as willing to compromise. Your follow-through and determination to see a plan through to the end is admirable. It strengthens when you tap into the intuition residing in the Saturn meridian. It allows you to see you are never truly alone and connects you to an evolutionary intuitive synchronicity.

Past life patterns empower you rather than take away from your successes. How? When you overcome a compulsive drive to accumulate you relax into your intuitive power. Developing higher beliefs that balance your inner and outer selves allows you to integrate past life karmic patterns harmoniously into your current life. When you become a team player not only focused on your own needs you bring people to support your goals. When you rise above low self-worth the roads to fulfillment are closer to a reality than you might imagine.

Future Goals and Inventiveness:
Uranus Meridian Activating Your Taurus Intuition

Light: Strengths

If your nervous system is excited more than usual, then you could be a Taurus tapping into the electrical grid of the dynamic and unpredictable Uranus intuition. Be ready for a surprise or two and maybe even a wild ride of adventure. Just as Uranus spins in a unique way on its own axis far up in the sky, it influences you to look at the world through replenished eyes. If you are looking for a new door to walk through, this is the right meridian to explore.

Your relationships could begin or even end suddenly. Knowing what you want from others becomes more of an urgent need when you start interacting with Uranian intuition. It is as though you really knew what you needed all of the time. The past does not seem quite as worrisome. This meridian has a way of getting a Taurus like you, who probably holds firmly onto the present as though it is the only reality, to loosen your grasp and look more excitedly toward the future.

Your inventive mind points you into new career directions or to change the way you operate a business. Sensing current trends keeps you one step ahead of the competition and what the public desires. This is a meridian that connects you directly to the pulse of a city or country.

This is definitely the planetary terrain in which to spice up your life. When you live life with an attitude full of openness to alternative thinking, there is no end to the opportunities you create.

Giving yourself the freedom to develop new perceptions is stimulating for your mind. Changing your daily routines once in a while allows your intuition a greater chance to put this interesting planet to work on your behalf.

Shadow: Challenges

If you miss the boat with the Uranus meridian, you feel like your goals are in reverse gear. This is such a future-oriented energy that you wonder why your hopes and dreams are not manifesting. It could be that you are getting talked out of your ideas. Another possibility is that you are changing direction too many times, meaning you lack focus. This does run contrary to the consistent tendency of your normal Taurus inclinations. If you rebel unpredictably too often, your sense of direction might get lost. Also, if you do not concentrate long enough on a goal, it will not come to fruition.

Another negative issue that can surface if you are out of sync with Uranus energy is that your relationships lack balance. You attract very self-centered people who are not aware of your needs. You don't want to try to live out your independence through other people and neglect your own freedom needs. Another possibility is that you could be the one not paying enough attention to what a lover or friend requires to be happy. This creates great tension in your relationships, sparking a lack of cooperation.

Dawn: Maximizing Your Potential

The Uranus meridian moves you forward into an exhilarating reality like no other meridian delivers. If you need your mind stimulated, then tuning in to the intuition offered by exciting Uranus is the path to take.

Gaining new insights into a situation occurs through this meridian. Your inventive mind is in the right wheelhouse with Uranus. Your career can be reinvented in ways you never imagined. This is the planet that relocates your mind, body, and spirit suddenly into an evolutionary intuitive synchronicity. Making new friends who share your view of the world may occur. Being exposed to ideas that open you to new perceptions is very valuable. This is a meridian that changes your life to such a degree that you never want to go back to the way it was before.

Creative Imagination and Idealism:
Neptune Meridian Activating Your Taurus Intuition

Light: Strengths

Neptune, the cosmic inspirer, takes you dreamily along a path that fills you with a new intuitive vision. Your idealism gets rejuvenated in this meridian. If you need emotional healing, then you have come to the right place. This is an atmosphere where dreams of a better today and tomorrow do find birth.

A romantic love nature becomes enlivened when tuning in to the Neptune influence. An existing relationship finds new vows that bond you closer together. The distance between your hearts disappears. Falling in love all over again is possible.

Neptune takes you in search of a soul mate. The desire to find someone with similar values is stimulated through this planetary meridian. You sense a magic in the air guiding you toward a person. Your belief that you can find the right partner is intensified.

Taurus is known for having a pragmatic mind. You are more concerned about material welfare than some of the other astrological signs are, which is fine. Neptune shows you how to integrate a spiritual longing and to rise above a fear of lack or loss. It is the intuitive power sent by this planet that fills you with the faith to transcend a focus on what you don't have.

Your creative instincts get a lift through this meridian, which contains a great deal of aesthetic knowledge. Your psyche aligns itself with the creative power of Neptune. You only need to surrender your resistance to be taken into this energy and go with the dynamic flow.

Neptune grabs your conscious mind by the hand and walks it through the fields of the collective unconscious. You are introduced to a new cause or learning material that strengthens your self-confidence and helps elevate your talents. This is a watery meridian dripping with symbols that quench your mind's thirst for new perceptions. You only need to display a willingness to be shown the way to greater intuitive clarity.

Shadow: Challenges

Perfection is a challenge. It could surface if you don't manage your intuitive energy in this meridian. It leaks out if you don't know when to stop trying to make something too perfect. Frustration is the result. The stability your Taurus Sun sign relishes is destabilized when you don't get a strong handle on perfection drives.

Denial manifests in various ways if you misread Neptune intuitive energy. You may refuse to acknowledge that you are in a dysfunctional relationship. Sweeping problems under a rug only prolongs the agony. Denying the insights you have about a person in order to maintain a partnership does not serve you well. Your fulfillment is far below what you deserve.

If you expect too much unrealistically from yourself or others, it won't make you happy either. The beauty of Neptune energy lifts you to seek a better life. It is when you are confused into thinking there is a perfect person waiting for you that you stay disappointed. Divine discontent in search of the right career or job keeps you from patiently furthering your skills and enjoying what you have accomplished. You could find yourself moving too quickly from one job to another and not developing a long-term strategy for success.

Material things can be an illusion in that you could look for too much happiness in them. Your higher values get so diluted that you operate in the world in a very uncertain way. The inner compass you require to keep you on course loses its reliability.

Dawn: Maximizing Your Potential

The Neptune meridian has a vibration that has subtle ringtones of intuition that are not always easy to contact. But if you quiet your mind, you can tune in to their essence. Is it worth the trouble? Yes. There are treasures here that are hard to put a price tag on, even for a Taurus like yourself who likes to know the value of things well ahead of time. If you are wanting more inner peace, then this is a meridian worth investigating. If you desire more creativity, you certainly don't want to overlook this intuitive paradise.

Finding a renewed sense of purpose is easier to cultivate through Neptune. This ancient god of the oceans has a way of whispering to those places in your mind that need reawakening. Neptune lifts your consciousness to pursue more inspiring goals. You don't need to change the world but perhaps could use a refueling of emotion toward a future filled with self-growth.

The search for a soul mate is ignited by this planetary meridian. Your wanting to share your life with someone who is able to read your unspoken language is nurtured by the Neptune influence. Finding a greater life purpose is part of the package when you walk toward the offerings of this gentle yet powerful intuitive teacher of the sky. When you are open to the magic of Neptune and allow this energy to shapeshift your thinking into a greater intuitive awareness, an evolutionary intuitive synchronicity can occur.

Personal Empowerment and Passion: Pluto Meridian Activating Your Taurus Intuition

Light: Strengths

The planet Pluto and your Sun sign, Taurus, have a lot in common. One big thing is that both have excellent money instincts. This comes in handy in the business world and gives you a natural doorway into Pluto intuition. Your passion to market your skills comes very much alive in this meridian. Another theme you share with Pluto is staying power, meaning you can fight to the end to finish what you set out to accomplish. Some may accuse you of being stubborn, and at times rightfully so, but you see this behavior as rugged determination.

Tuning in to Pluto guides you to greater patience, which points you toward self-mastery. Being willing to go beneath the surface of things deepens your resolve to understand yourself on the deepest of levels. Investigating life's mysteries ignites new insights. Facing your fears prepares you for whatever challenges life sends your way.

As a general rule, Taurus is not known for showing emotions easily. When connecting with Pluto energy, you may choose to share your hidden feelings with people you trust. Why do this? Because it empowers you. Also, it allows others to come closer when you reveal your inner world.

When you align with Pluto intuition, your ability to create a feeling of abundance in your life is greater. Whether in the eyes of the world you are sized up as rich or poor, your own self-confidence soars to a higher level. This sustains you whether in times of plenty or of lack. Even if you need to start over after a loss, your survival instincts will carry you into a new start when you connect with Pluto's embracing arms. The positive memories from the past can propel you forward to make a better present. You sense a great rebirth.

Forgiving others serves as a healing force for old wounds. When you let go of negative memories, your creative power magnifies. This is part of the magic of Pluto. Rising above your anger and resentments allows an inner transformation that puts you in the driver seat to create a more positive life. There is no limit to how far you can go when you make peace with the past. This is how you attract the success you seek.

Shadow: Challenges

What keeps you from experiencing the true essence of Pluto intuition? One thing is a fear of your emotions. It is your feelings that open the door to Pluto. If you are in the habit of not expressing how you feel to others, then you don't connect with the full power of this meridian. If you try to overpower others through manipulation in order to get your own way, it keeps you from the beauty of this meridian energy. It is emotional insecurity that blocks you from enjoying the fulfillment found in this terrain.

If you surrender too much of your power, your life lacks balance, and this is another way you miss the boat with Pluto. It is in the equal sharing of power with people that you align yourself with the intuitive beauty found in this meridian. When you don't claim your power, you attract people into your life who desire to control you. This prevents you from realizing your own dreams. You will only be living out the goals of others and neglecting your own.

Power struggles only get in the way of receiving the best Pluto has to offer you. There is nothing wrong with negotiating in business. However, if you are constantly fighting with others, you will become drained and waste a lot of time and resources in the process.

Passion is a good thing, but if you become obsessed with your desires, your life gets out of balance. Too much attachment to material things lets you down if you lose them. Having a solid higher-belief value system keeps you on course to greater fulfillment. Self-honesty is the road to the clarity you seek.

Running away from conflict takes away from your personal power. In dealing with situations in a more direct manner, you find greater self-reassurance. Your creative intensity finds more outlets to show the world what you can do.

Dawn: Maximizing Your Potential

The Pluto meridian is a passionate place that stimulates your Taurus determination to display your abilities. The intuition in this landscape is rich with the motivating energy that can excite you into exploring new skills. The researcher and entrepreneur in you flourishes when you tap into Pluto intuition. There is an innate drive to dive beneath the surface of things that springs forth from this meridian energy.

Pluto rules Scorpio, the opposite sign of Taurus. Pluto is the cosmic mirror, or mirroring agent, for your sign. How might this work? This opposing factor allows Pluto to beam back to you a strategy for keeping your power balanced with others. Visualize Pluto on the opposite end of a seesaw from your Taurus energy trying to guide you in keeping your own agenda empowered while you do your best to be supportive of others. Pluto is enhancing your ability to push for your own agenda in life while at the same time keeping the goals of those you care about in sight.

Psychological strength is enhanced when you connect with Pluto intuition. There are levels of self-mastery you attain in channeling your creative potential that produce an evolutionary intuitive synchronicity. Remember, if you are in need of a rebirth or need the perseverance to push through obstacles, this meridian is always there for you, just waiting for you to use it.

Chapter 4

GEMINI

Gemini (5/21–6/21)

Archetypes: Teacher, Reporter, Networker, Writer

Key Focus: Communication

Element: Air

Planetary Ruler: Mercury

Cosmic Mirror Planet: Jupiter

Welcome to your Gemini sign chapter. Your curious Gemini mind will find an endless amount of intuitive exhilaration when exploring the planetary meridians. Allowing your ideas the freedom to roam spontaneously accelerates your intuitive growth. This allows your insights into challenges facing you to find intuitive strength.

Intuition moves excitedly through your airy sign. This matches your eagerness to find new knowledge and endless ways to entertain your restless mind. With the power of intuition found in the planetary meridians, you discover stimulating and energizing relationships, work, and goals.

Your Gemini Dashboard Meridian Summary

It is good to remember that you have the freedom to choose how you want to use the meridians. They respond very much to what you are currently focusing on or the goals you are wanting to reach. Usually more than one meridian at a time will combine to help you solve or respond to a situation. As a Gemini Sun sign, this is probably not surprising for you to hear. You enjoy moving on more than one front at a time anyway.

There is often a magical blending of meridian energy working with you at any given moment in time. When trying to exert your willpower to accomplish a goal, you are pulling on the intuition of your Gemini Sun meridian. If you are trying to make decisions about your home or where in the world is best to live, the Moon meridian is very much involved. Your desire to communicate and stimulate your learning ability reaches out to the Mercury meridian. Your need for romance and finding a peer group is leaning on the Venus meridian. Getting your adrenaline to move fast on a goal is responding to the Mars meridian. The Jupiter meridian asks you to broaden your life philosophy and fill your mind with positive thoughts. The Saturn meridian encourages you to not fear having ambition and to follow through on commitments. The Uranus meridian wakes up your inventiveness and sudden need to express independence. The Neptune meridian enlarges your need to dream and have faith in your ideals. The Pluto meridian points the way to rebirth and passionate feelings.

This tour is meant to help you see that there are many paths to self-growth. The meridians are constantly at play for you. Just knock on their doors and they will gladly help you on the road to self-discovery.

Creative Expression:
Sun Meridian Activating Your Gemini Intuition

Light: Strengths

The creative flares of the Sun filter in a lively manner, even doing somersaults, as they dance through your birth sign, Gemini, coloring you with an adaptable personality. Your intuition depends heavily on the accuracy of your mental perceptions. In many ways they work hand in hand to guide you in navigating your way through the world. Your willingness to change directions quickly makes you a fun person to get to know in the eyes of many.

The Sun sign of Gemini solarizes you with a curious spirit, one that approaches the world with wide open eyes at the thought of learning new information. You don't mind having a full plate of activity but don't appreciate being pinned down to one choice. After all, you are a sign that prefers to move in multiple directions, reflecting the fast-paced mind you possess. What do you detest the most? Boredom? It dulls your intellect and stifles your intuition. So you need to keep learning and growing. You are more likely to follow through on a plan if it promises enough excitement or different mental scenery along the way.

Communication is one of your strengths. You enjoy influencing others through ideas. Your intuition comes alive when you are selling a proposal or trying to convince others of the merit found in your words. You are not happy if people doubt your logic. Some may see you as lacking focus, while you see this as your own unique way of perceiving the world.

You have to be heard or you feel devalued. If you find others truly listening, it stimulates you intuitively. You have the talent to think your way out of any situation. When you are centered and patient, your intuition comes across forcefully, as though nothing better get in its way. You excel as a teacher or advisor. Friends, family, and lovers appreciate your input into their own plans for the future. You win admiration through sharing the knowledge you possess. People win your loyalty through supporting your goals for success.

Shadow: Challenges

You get so excited by the intuition in this meridian that you lose your focus. Your creative energy evaporates in midair, usually because of mental exhaustion. This may be due to extreme worry about the outcome of situations. Sometimes this is caused by fretting too much over details, which results in you losing sight of the big picture.

Another theme that causes problems is not trusting your intuition. You are too stuck in your mind. This keeps you from connecting with your intuition. If you refuse to let your intuition act as a guide, your life is not as flowing. There is nothing wrong with using that wonderful Gemini intellect. It is only when you allow yourself to be separated from a river of intuition that your mind is actually having to work overtime. You lose creative power in the process.

Dawn: Maximizing Your Potential

The Sun meridian offers you a vast land of rich intuitive energy. Your mind gets fanned into more than one direction at a time without losing your balance. After all, your Gemini Sun sign gives you that opportunity to perceive life from a deep and wide vantage point. You need plenty of mental stimulation to keep your goals activated. When you are experiencing a minimum amount of worry or mental anxiety, the intuitive world is at your fingertips.

It is your willingness to explore life openly with a mind that views new experiences with eagerness that brings an evolutionary intuitive synchronicity your way. When you combine your intellect with the combustion engine of intuition found in this Sun meridian, you can climb the steps of your highest aspirations to success.

There are instances when the universe will ask you to intuitively change course and pursue deeper knowledge that takes your curiosity right into self-mastery. The self-realization that manifests when a Gemini Sun sign like yourself learns not to fear using emotional energy is a life filled with a clearer mental balance and less psychological burnout.

Creating a Home and Expressing Feelings: Moon Meridian Activating Your Gemini Intuition

Light: Strengths

The Moon joins forces with your breezy Gemini Sun sign to enable you to feel your way toward the right choices that will bring you a sense of security. The Moon is a watery energy with intuitive power that helps you sense the right direction to move toward even in the midst of a crisis. Pay attention to your moods, as they are the lighthouses in the distance trying to alert you as to how you are feeling about situations.

You experience more nervousness than many of the other astrological signs do. You just happen to have been born under the influence of a sign that is hypersensitive to external stimuli, meaning you tend to react quickly to what you perceive is occurring. This lunar meridian gives you an extra edge in slowing down your reaction time and processing life experiences quickly. You are not someone who enjoys moving too slow mentally or physically. There is a payoff if you will let the Moon guide you to intuitively get a handle on decisions before leaping too fast.

You pull the Moon influence to you when trying to decide where to live. The residence you pick probably needs to be in a location offering plenty of opportunities for growth. You are a restless soul in that you need a geographical longitude and latitude filled with potential to have friends from many walks of life. There needs to be learning options that keep your Gemini mind plenty stimulated. You need an atmosphere in a house or city that gives you plenty of elbow room to stretch out and convince you that there is unlimited wide-open space to maximize your brain power.

Shadow: Challenges

If your mind and emotions are running in opposite directions, that is an indication that your intuition is not operating at full strength. You could be worrying too much about the past. If you are trying to forget situations that have occurred without really dealing with them, it depletes your intuitive energy. Denying your true feelings keeps you at arm's length from the intuitive clarity offered by the Moon meridian.

Emotional confusion results from indecision. You may feel pulled in too many directions by other people and not able to steer straight ahead at your own goals. If you are constantly giving in to the demands of others without satisfying your own dreams, your intuitive clarity suffers the consequences.

Staying in locations or jobs that don't offer you enough growth potential will limit your ability to market your talents. If you don't look to greener pastures, you will one day regret not giving yourself the chance to prove that you could excel if only you were in the right place at the right time.

Dawn: Maximizing Your Potential

The Moon meridian fills you with emotional strength that balances your Gemini mind. This creates a nice fusion of dynamic energy that lights up your perceptions with extra zeal. You get extra mileage out of your ideas when you let the Moon be an equal partner in your decisions.

When you remain true to your feelings, your perceptions deepen. In dealing with the past, the present and future are less treacherous. Facing your problems rather than hiding from them brings the Moon meridian's intuitive force into play for you. Revealing your inner world to those closest to you takes you right into the center of your intuitive world.

Trust your instincts. They point the way to the locations in the world that are best for you to set up house and allow your goals to fly more freely. You like to keep your options open and fluid. You are at your best when adapting to new experiences without fear, as this leads to an evolutionary intuitive synchronicity.

Mental Insights:
Mercury Meridian Activating Your Gemini Intuition
Light: Strengths

Mercury feels right at home in its connection to your Gemini Sun sign. Why might that be? Because Mercury is the ruler of Gemini, giving it a special intuitive access into your consciousness. This is great news for you! The side of you that enjoys sharing information with others and hungrily stays abreast of news sound bites gets energized in this fast-paced meridian. The world of ideas in your head is readily excited in putting the quick-footed, mentally alert Mercury to work on your behalf.

Communication is something you likely enjoy. Without exchanging ideas, you feel lost on a deserted island. Words are your way of influencing others to believe in you. Your intuitive grasp of new concepts gets a great super-charged lift in this Mercury terrain. This is the landscape that produces great speakers and people with convincing ways of selling concepts. When you trust your ability to forge ahead into new information frontiers, doors of opportunity reveal themselves to you.

Changing lanes to take advantage of sudden new life directions is aided by Mercury. You are at your best when showing the world that you can multitask with the best of them. Your love of diversifying keeps your mind sharp. People are attracted to your way of helping them make greater sense of their own lives. Your way of presenting difficult subjects in simple terms shines when you make use of Mercury intuition.

The Mercury meridian helps you anticipate when to make changes in the nick of time. It's knowing when to pursue a goal at full speed and when to slow down into a focusing mode that gives you a competitive edge in the job market.

Shadow: Challenges

Mercury intuition loosens some of its impact if you start second-guessing your abilities. Why might this happen? If you wait for the perfect moment to arrive before pursuing a dream, that day may never come. Life just does not work that way. When you fear making mistakes, you lose the momentum you need to achieve your goals.

You become too adaptable, changing your mind too quickly. Losing your sense of direction is the result. Being willing to change to meet the demands of the present is a good thing, but lacking the discipline and concentration needed to finish what you start is not going to get you the desired results. People will feel they can't depend on you when they really need your support. They will be less willing to be your cheerleader.

Your left brain runs too much interference blocking your intuition from optimum performance. Your fondness for scrutinizing details becomes an obsession. Rather than trusting your intuitive instincts, you are doubting their potential to guide you to greater harmony.

Dawn: Maximizing Your Potential

The Mercury meridian delivers intuitive ideas faster than you blink your eyes, and that's pretty quick. You only need to let this energy work for you. When you use your ability to decipher fact from fiction with that detective-like mind you possess, there is nothing you can't figure out. When you show flexibility, you are at your best and life is ready to bring you its rewards.

Your communication is electrified by the exciting stimulation you receive from this planet. When you patiently point your mind at what you want to accomplish, the intuitive outpouring intensifies from this lively mental meridian, making an evolutionary intuitive insight a reality for you.

Trust your perceptions, but at the same time be open to new ideas. When you allow new learning to influence you, life is much more enjoyable for your curious mind. Leave self-doubt behind and show the world your ideas with convincing force. When you have faith in your knowledge, people want to believe in you.

Relationship Tendencies:
Venus Meridian Activating Your Gemini Intuition

Light: Strengths

This is the meridian that allows you to show the communication ability you possess with a wide range of people. Your brain enjoys exchanging information with people from a wide variety of backgrounds. Venus is the planetary energy that pushes you outward into full public view. If you tend to be a quiet person, then Venus will entice you to speak up for yourself. If you are a more talkative type, you will walk the path of the Venus meridian toward others excitedly.

Venus can inspire you to develop a career strategy. This is a planet whispering ways to earn money into your ear. Turning a favorite pastime into a marketable business is another one of her methods to get you to think abundantly.

There will be occasions when Venus will blow her intuition in your direction, signaling it is time to take a break. If your nervous energy goes into a frenzy, the calming sensation of this relaxing meridian might be just what you need. You only need to be willing to breathe deeply and slow down to make contact with this soothing planetary spirit. You may find yourself in the middle of a stressful decision between two appealing choices. If you can't make up your mind, Venus may influence you to relax and move forward.

Perhaps the most outstanding feature the Venus meridian will offer you is the opportunity to seek a soul mate. She infiltrates your intuition with romantic ideas and images. When you tune in to Venus, you find a partner who shares many of your values and dreams.

Shadow: Challenges

What could possibly go wrong for you in such a miraculous meridian? You may become too overwhelmed when facing too many choices. Venus urges you to weigh your options carefully. This could result in causing you great indecision. If you don't calm yourself down or utilize your favorite downtime methods, you could become exhausted. Fatigue and even health problems are caused by extreme worry.

Another theme that might surface is denying your own needs in a relationship. You could be doing this to maintain a dysfunctional partnership. You are getting the short end of the bargain, much to your detriment. If you are the person doing too much of the taking without enough giving in return, it will cause friction. Balance in either scenario is lacking to the point that the relationship may end due to a lack of equality.

Dawn: Maximizing Your Potential

The Venus meridian gives your mental curiosity about people plenty of room to explore. The stimulation you enjoy creatively when exchanging ideas with others gets a lift from Venus energy. If your emotions grow confused over difficult life challenges, you are never far from getting a boost from your friends in this people-oriented and quite gregarious meridian.

There is no time to deprive yourself from an abundant life if Venus has anything to say about it. This heavenly body wants you to reward yourself when working hard. You are supposed to receive the message to value your self-esteem as if it were a priceless gem.

In relating to others, this fair-minded, diplomatic planet will send you waves of intuitive energy to preserve your sense of equality. This is the goddess of give and take hoping you will keep the scales even in your partnerships when it comes to getting your needs met.

When you fight for your values, an evolutionary intuitive synchronicity gets launched. Honoring your beliefs keeps you pointed toward fulfillment and harmony. You will never feel or be alone in the world when tuning in to this meridian's intuitive gifts.

Initiating Action:
Mars Meridian Activating Your Gemini Intuition

Light: Strengths

The Mars meridian and your Gemini Sun sign have something in common. What might that be? Both of you are fast moving. Mars gets you to act on impulse. Gemini is quick to put ideas into motion. So you could say Mars + Gemini = putting ideas to work rapidly. The idea is to take advantage of an opportunity.

When you tap into Mars intuition, some people will accuse you of being too impatient. You probably explain this as your desire to see what a creative risk might produce even if it does appear to others as a bit reckless. If you are needing courage, then you have entered the door of a fiery meridian that pushes you to act first and ask questions later.

How might you get Mars involved in your life? The spirit of competition is one way. If you believe in your goals, a blast of Mars energy blows you over the finish line. Mars says to let go of your hesitation and take charge. What have you to lose anyway? You can always begin again if needed. Be assertive. The Mars meridian encourages you to make your thoughts known. There can be wisdom offered by Mars that comes in the form of sensing which battles are worth the fight and which are better avoided.

Shadow: Challenges

If you misread the Mars messages, your nervous energy escalates in a hurry. Your mind feels like it is in a pressure cooker. It is as if you are running in circles. The focus you need is difficult to master in this instance. Impatience causes you to miss important details and proves frustrating.

Expressing anger merely to blow off steam causes a lot of tension in the human relations department. This might be due to not really saying what is on your mind. Angry outbursts could be a symptom of your refusal to recognize and deal with issues that you have with people. The assertiveness normally provided by the Mars meridian is getting distorted by confused emotions.

If you don't believe in your goals, you won't push forward to complete them. The courage to act with conviction is operating far lower than required to fulfilling a plan. A little fear is okay, but you don't want to freeze before realizing the new reality you want to create.

Dawn: Maximizing Your Potential

The Mars meridian accelerates your Gemini mind to think boldly like no other meridian can do. This is the landscape where courage is plentiful. When you grab hold and don't let go, Mars will carry you forward forcefully. "Walk your talk" could be your mantra when tuning in to Mars intuition.

Making quick decisions with great accuracy occurs when tuning in to Mars. Courageously pursuing a new dream sparks an evolutionary intuitive synchronicity. Moving fast with poise without impulsively rushing shows you have mastered the essence of the Mars meridian.

Expanding Knowledge:
Jupiter Meridian Activating Your Gemini Intuition
Light: Strengths

The Jupiter meridian offers you a vast panorama of new ways to excite your learning processes. This very large planet has a tendency to get you to enlarge your hopes for a better future. There is a constant flow of optimism running throughout this expansive terrain. You only need to believe in your ideas to allow them to come to fruition.

Your Gemini mind cannot help but smile when you embrace Jupiter. Your intuitive instincts gravitate to a higher plateau of faith. Your energy levels get easily stimulated by this fiery planet brimming over with positive energy.

The teacher and the student in you are highly energized in this meridian. Your communication skills find greater power and multiply quickly. Your desire to acquire knowledge to improve your opportunities is enhanced.

When you travel to other locations, whether they be far away or near, it gives Jupiter intuition a chance to seep deeply into the core of your thinking. It is as though your problems and worries have receded into the background. The planet filled with forward momentum is allowing you to disengage from the past, even if only for a short interval of time, to give you a much-needed break from stress. The idea is to increase your belief in abundance.

Luck will come your way when you trust in your goals. This meridian will be your partner when it sees you bravely believing in your ideas. A new relationship, career, or simply a wonderful feeling that life is good can occur. Keeping a gratitude journal so you can keep track of what has gone right in your life helps erase negative thought patterns and, better yet, allows Jupiter to keep a watchful eye over you from the confines of its upbeat meridian home.

Shadow: Challenges

How can such a wonderful meridian get you into trouble? One possibility is thinking you can't lose even though the odds are stacked against you. This is similar to fool's gold in believing you have discovered the real treasure but it is only an illusion. Blind faith results if you don't do some reality testing.

Dogmatism and narrow thinking are potential problems. You could become so excited by new ideas that you refuse to tolerate someone else's point of view. Rather than agreeing to disagree, you hold on to your own version of the truth at all costs. This will not make people like you.

Putting too many goals on your plate at the same time causes you to lose your focus. You grow disappointed in not finishing what you set out to do. If you promise others too much, they will grow frustrated with you if you don't follow through.

Going where you think the grass is greener too impatiently will find you leaving good relationships and jobs too quickly before giving them a fair chance. You might be depriving yourself of great situations. This may have more to do with running away from commitments.

Dawn: Maximizing Your Potential

The Jupiter meridian fills a Gemini mind like yours with an endless amount of enthusiasm for self-growth. The urge to expand your learning and earning potential has no better place to get you motivated than in this lively meridian. You don't need to long for the past when you ride the Jupiter highway. Your travels to other geographical locations and to new, stimulating experiences closer to home are inspired by jovial Jupiter.

When you open your mind to differences of opinion, you increase your knowledge. In not fearing to take on a new subject of interest or to learn new skills, you pave the way for more opportunities. Empowering your mind with positive thoughts magically produces an evolutionary intuitive synchronicity.

Jupiter rules Sagittarius, the opposite sign of Gemini. Jupiter is the cosmic mirror, or mirroring agent, for your sign. What might this mean? Jupiter mirrors back to you a widening perspective as to how to take your analytical mind to a higher level. Rather than getting snagged by the details of a situation, Jupiter lifts you to a greater altitude to see where each step along the way is really taking you. Jupiter broadens your outlook into a wonderful display of possibilities for fulfillment. Good fortune comes through confidently following in the tracks of your highest belief system.

Career and Ambition:
Saturn Meridian Activating Your Gemini Intuition

Light: Strengths

The Saturn meridian offers you an intense way to get focused. Your Gemini mind, which enjoys darting to and fro in search of information, joins forces with this get-down-to-business planet to make a dream come true. When you take on a serious project, Saturn intuition comes through to help you keep your mind well organized. Structure comes under the domain of this celestial wanderer.

This meridian produces determination like no other. You can summon the mental strength to outlast a stubborn obstacle. If you stay committed to a plan, the power of the Saturn meridian assists you in seeing it through to completion.

Building a business or career is Saturn speak. Finding the patience to slowly put together a job strategy step by step is how to make use of Saturn. You intuitively discover more efficient ways to manage your time with an assist from reliable Saturn. You pull Saturn intuition into your work by making a solid stand for the profession you want to master.

If you overcome a fear of failure, you are well ahead of many in utilizing Saturn intuition to its highest potential. Don't judge yourself by the success of others. Be true to your own career plans to get the best results.

Past-life patterns are linked to this planetary meridian. It is possible that your thinking was too rigid at times in past incarnations. You are getting a new chance to create a more flexible reality. Keep your mind open to new ideas. It is the key to reversing a tendency to refuse to change. Another past-life theme is connected to being too negative in thinking. Adopting a positive outlook frees you from much of the residue of this pattern. It might take some practice, but when you flow with Saturn's persistent patience, you overcome these old patterns and turn them into creative power.

There is great wisdom that comes through when you align yourself with Saturn intuition. You learn from past mistakes and see them as learning material. Being harder on problems than on people is wise. Your relationships are more fulfilling when you choose not to be too controlling. Asking others to do the same for you is a fair bargain. Your lovers, friends, and family are apt to stay with you for many years when you communicate honestly. Trust is a powerful bond that maintains your people connections throughout the good and bad times.

Shadow: Challenges

If you are out of step with Saturn intuition, the result might be bad timing. You could find yourself forcing the outcome of situations rather than waiting for the right time to push the idea. This is due to a lack of faith that things will work out in your favor with patience. Your impulse to move too fast could use some restraint.

Fear of failure holds back your creative drive. Opportunities slip by. Too much worry about being prepared or doing something perfect causes you to freeze in your shoes. That first step remains elusive.

If you resist redefining your goals realistically, you will be stuck in a limiting present. The result will be jobs that have limited growth potential and relationships that don't make you happy. When you don't alter your perceptions to see other possibilities, the insights you need are not available.

Certain karmic patterns keep you trapped if you deny they exist. Rigid thinking and a negative outlook are two that limit your hopes and dreams. Repeating the same limiting behaviors leftover from previous lifetimes hijacks a successful present if you don't consciously attempt to make changes.

Dawn: Maximizing Your Potential

The Saturn meridian has an aura of ambition that rubs off on you. All you must do is stay focused on your most serious dreams. The structure and planning you need are part of the Saturn meridian. This is an intuitive meridian that requires your concentration and intention toward what you are trying to accomplish. This is the key to bringing this meridian energy your way. You may not be able to control the result, but you can go far in giving your goals a chance to manifest.

Lighten up. The harder you hold on to life with worry, the less it cooperates. Believe in yourself. When you make a commitment to a career or relationship, let the energy flow. You will enjoy the ride much more.

Your relationships will have better possibilities to succeed if you allow plenty of breathing room for communication. If you trust each other, only good things develop. When you give a romance a chance to keep growing through mutual support, you find harmony. Whether the relationship just started or already has many years behind it, if there is equality, there will likely be happiness. Give your attention to another person consistently and he or she is more apt to be at your side for many years to come.

You can't change a negative pattern overnight that has been with you for several years and possibly over many incarnations. This is the gift of Saturn intuition in that you will receive the right messages if you show a determination to transform negative mental trends. When you concentrate on life's abundance and show greater faith in positive energy, you can reverse past-life patterns and walk right into an evolutionary intuitive synchronicity.

Future Goals and Inventiveness:
Uranus Meridian Activating Your Gemini Intuition

Light: Strengths

You are reading the right meridian if you want to move at light speed into the future. Your Gemini mind gets very excited when you connect with the mentally quick Uranus. The planet that rules your sign is Mercury, which shares much of the mental love of learning new information featured by Uranus. This gives you a natural path into the world of this inventive meridian world laced with all kinds of surprises. Life is never the same once you enter the home of Uranus. In many ways, you will never want to look back.

Have you ever felt like reinventing yourself? Uranus guides you there like no other planet. This is the meridian of a new today or tomorrow. You do need to fasten your seatbelt when riding the roller-coaster-like presence of Uranus. There are times when this unique heavenly body will actually steady your gaze but suddenly whisk you off in a new direction to shake up your old routines. The idea is to allow you to perceive life from outside of the box.

Freedom. It's a seven-letter word that is taken very seriously in this meridian. Your thinking is liberated when you grab the hand of this free-spirited entity. The fresh air breathed into your psyche tends to invigorate your mind with refreshing energy. Breaking away from limiting circumstances is par for the course in this territory. Cutting the shackles to a limiting relationship, job, or even the location in which you reside can be a heartfelt urge, the reason being to ignite your goals to speed up their coming into fruition.

Developing new friends and important contacts is a definite Uranus theme. These associations prove vital to keeping you abreast of new opportunities and are great ways to exchange ideas with others. The networking you enjoy expands your circle of friends.

Your interest in new technologies and making use of them for communication peaks in this meridian. Uranus is the planet that is directly linked to the computer world and information age. It is possible that your job or having a business will feature a strong use of innovations.

Your goals and instincts about the future rely heavily on tapping into this exciting meridian. Staying grounded is wise, so you have a strong base from which to move forward. This is the land of experimentation. Trying out various ways to stimulate your creative expression might unlock new doors of self-discovery.

Shadow: Challenges

The Uranus intuitive power is wonderful when you are in harmony with it. But what if you are not? You might be moving so fast in your head that you lose your sense of direction. You already have a high-strung nervous system just being born under the Sun sign Gemini.

Uranus multiplies the intensity ten times if you don't understand the energy trying to manifest through you. If you don't have meditative ways or physical activity to slow down your brain, you won't have the insights available to think your way through situations.

Refusing to embrace your freedom will be a problem. What is likely to occur is attracting people to you with extreme freedom needs of their own and not really paying attention to your goals. You will have a tendency to remain in limiting relationships or jobs when you don't reach out for the freedom you require. In other words, you are selling your chances for new growth very short.

Another theme that manifests is living so much in your intellect that you can't express feelings. This distances you from the people you are trying to be close to. Hiding behind your mental nature may become a pattern to keep others from seeing the real you.

It is possible that you could be the person asking for too much independence or always getting your own way. Losing the spirit of compromise and equality will cause problems in connecting with people. It is as though your desire for freedom has reached such extreme proportions that you are too aloof.

Dawn: Maximizing Your Potential

The Uranus meridian is the land of new ideas. If you ever want to reinvigorate your mind, this is the terrain for you. Freedom is the hallmark here. Feeling a sense of liberation and a new lease on life are the rewards for tapping into Uranus intuition. Your Gemini attraction for learning won't miss a beat in this meridian. Education furthers your opportunities for abundance and fulfillment.

The desire to make new friends or business contacts is stimulated. The momentum for starting a business gets a boost through tapping into Uranus intuition. Inventiveness finds you discovering new ways to market your skills.

Your perceptions become more long-range, helping you envision the future in such a way that an evolutionary intuitive synchronicity finds birth. This terrain satisfies your hunger to feed your mind knowledge, whether learned through reading books or surfing the Internet. Travel to other locations keeps you mentally sharp and in touch with current trends. Uranus energy has a capacity to free you from limiting thoughts and launch you into a brave new world of adventure.

Creative Imagination and Idealism: Neptune Meridian Activating Your Gemini Intuition
Light: Strengths

The Neptune meridian energizes your mind by showing you how to work smarter rather than harder. How? By getting you to trust your intuitive instincts and to tune in to your mind and body to know when it is time to relax. Pacing yourself teaches you how to get the best mileage out of your thinking and actions.

In this arena, there is tremendous idealism like no other. Your mind enjoys diving into an ocean of intuition to find new insights. The power of the magical force embedded in this terrain recharges you. You sense the eye of the hurricane in knowing how to stay calm in the middle of a stressful crisis. Tuning in to Neptune frequencies comes with practice. Having faith in your ideals attracts Neptune to be your ally.

The intellectual side of you finds greater intuitive paths to creative heights. If you desire to show your writing or artistic abilities, then this is the right meridian to visit regularly. If you want to become a healer or master a metaphysical subject, Neptune makes the ride into these fields of interest easier.

Your dreams while sleeping may suddenly send you informative messages like never before. Your connection to a larger collective world unfolds in interesting ways. A grasp of information beyond your conscious mind might happen more spontaneously.

If you stay grounded, Neptune is easier to utilize. It does take a bit of being rooted to the earth with a regular routine or grounding ritual to channel the empowering energy of the Neptune meridian harmoniously.

Your closeness with others and romantic relationships deepen when tapping into Neptune. Feeling like there is little separation from a lover gives you a soul-mate feeling. Neptune has a way of instilling a search for a simpatico partner.

An inner connection to a higher power relieves you of feeling insecure. When you walk forward with confidence in your highest beliefs, Neptune's gentle guidance is never far away. Neptune asks you not to fear the inward journey. It helps strengthen your resolve to deal with life in your outward quests for fulfillment and self-growth.

Shadow: Challenges

The magical land of Neptune is difficult at times to tap into clearly. You may think you are perceiving situations accurately with your sharp Gemini mind, but in reality you are only in the presence of an illusion. You so badly want a desire or goal to be true that you could be denying what is really happening. The right-brain flooding that occurs when you are in the middle of emotional situations can be intense.

In romantic relationships, Neptune energy clouds your judgment. You see more wonderful qualities in a person than he or she possesses. You want so much for a relationship to be functioning positively that you might be denying what is really occurring. If you don't do some honest thinking, this will lead you into trouble. Keeping your expectations reasonable of yourself and others is a challenge in this meridian.

Escapism is always a concern with Neptune for any astrological sign. A Gemini like yourself can try to drown negativity by over-indulging in obsessions that are not necessarily good for your mind, body, or spirit. If you run from problems, you are only prolonging their hold on you.

You have a strong mind. Is this not true? If you don't balance an over-anxious mind with some right-brain relaxation, you lose a lot of energy. The Sun sign Gemini in particular has a natural inclination to use the analytical left brain more than the other signs. Worrying excessively over details can happen if you don't occasionally distract yourself from overthinking about situations.

Dawn: Maximizing Your Potential

The Neptune meridian helps you develop your intuition in a big way. This energy bypasses your conscious mind to make access into the intuitive world easier. Trust it. The Neptune meridian knows how to raise your awareness to mental and spiritual levels that the other meridians only dream about. It does take reality testing and staying grounded to get the best mileage out of Neptune intuition.

The romantic in you loves this meridian. Your search for a soul mate is guided by this gentle oasis. Finding that magical someone who inspires you and touches your heartstrings is straight out of the Neptune meridian playbook.

Living out your highest ideals and spiritual values lifts your Gemini mind into an evolutionary intuitive insight. When you pursue your most inspiring dreams, there is no need for escapism. In dealing with life challenges directly, you empower yourself with the majestic presence of Neptune intuition cutting right through the veil of an apparent obstacle.

Personal Empowerment and Passion: Pluto Meridian Activating Your Gemini Intuition

Light: Strengths

The Pluto meridian intensifies your mental depth. The intuition featured by this very passionate territory fits in well with your Gemini mind. Why? Because the energy in this Pluto world challenges your willingness to look beneath the surface of things. The intuition offered by Pluto allows you to sense if people are telling you a straight story or withholding important facts. Sound familiar? If yes, then you are already making good use of this meridian highway. Pluto has a way of getting you to be a bit of a detective and not be afraid to investigate situations carefully.

Pluto instills passion in your mental quests. Mastering a subject or a skill of interest is strongly pushed by the intuitive flow of this powerful meridian. The laser-like beam of focus provided gets you to find the inner determination to conquer any field you truly want to learn.

Your ability to communicate difficult concepts in everyday, understandable language becomes a talent. Breaking down complicated material into a step-by-step learning process helps you to assimilate information.

You motivate others to believe in your ideas through charismatic explanations of how you can accomplish them. Researching your favorite interests might be enjoyable and even allow you to market your insights. Business sense comes through trial and error. When you learn from previous mistakes, you tend not to repeat them. If you make this meridian your friend, you instinctively know which challenges are worth your time and stress levels. You will know which goals are the ones to fight for no matter how difficult the road is to success.

Learning patience makes your life easier. Tapping into the goldmine of impulse control offered by Pluto shows your wisdom. You use this meridian to find the best time to make a dream a reality. Negotiating with a carefully conceived plan can occur.

Changing negative thought patterns into positive energy heals old wounds. This is a path to personal empowerment. Letting go of the past frees you to experience a rebirth. Pointing your mind toward the future with a new attitude of self-exploration transforms your thinking into replenished happiness.

Shadow: Challenges

If you are on a disconnect trip with Pluto intuition, you lose out on a clear channeling of your emotional intensity. It gets bottled up in various ways, one being anger at yourself. Eventually this could turn into blaming others for your problems. Your closest relationships suffer the consequences. Rather than being empowered, you are leaking out your best energy into unfruitful expressions.

If you rely too much on others, your own sense of self-worth takes a dip. Without a mutual dependency, you lean too heavily on people. This throws your relationships off balance. You find yourself trying to live out your own abilities and talents through others. A loss of self-confidence results.

Becoming too power-oriented will distance you from people you would like to come closer to you. There could be a tendency not to trust to the point that you alienate people. If you try to dominate the thinking of others, they will pull away.

Staying in jobs and relationships that limit your opportunities is another way you could be out of sync with this meridian. If you surrender to what is impossible, unhappiness is the end product.

Dawn: Maximizing Your Potential

The Pluto meridian is here to fill you with passion. You will be delighted to have such a feeling. You are tempted to challenge yourself in big ways to pursue empowering goals. Sometimes it only takes that first move toward a positive perception of life for Pluto to come forward forcefully to blow its intuitive power your way. It is as though this emotionally intense celestial wanderer fills your psyche with its energy.

Seek mutually fulfilling relationships and all will go well. The intuitive fabric of this meridian will guide you to find happiness in partnerships. Building alliances with others that have a solid foundation of trust and sharing ensures long-lasting commitments.

Rising above past negative memories takes you into an evolutionary intuitive synchronicity. It is not in burying yesterday's experiences that you blossom. It is in facing what the past revealed about you that is important. This is the key to creating the present and future you seek.

───── *Chapter 5* ─────

CANCER

Cancer (6/22–7/22)

Archetypes: Mother, Preserver, Healer
Key Focus: Nurturing and Establishing a Sense of Security
Element: Water
Planetary Ruler: Moon
Cosmic Mirror Planet: Saturn

Welcome to your Cancer sign chapter. Your Cancer emotional intensity is focused more productively when tuning in to the gifts offered by the planetary meridians. Your determination to be a success at whatever you attempt to achieve rises to the occasion when following the guidance of your intuition.

Intuition moves cautiously and carefully through your watery sign. It gives you a chance to reflect so you can more clearly direct this valuable energy. With the intuitive power presented to you by the planetary meridians, you can walk with confidence in forming new relationships, finding meaningful work, and tuning in to harmonious goals.

Your Cancer Dashboard Meridian Summary

The choices influenced by the meridians are your path to greater insight. It is important to remember that you have a lot of wiggle room to steer your intuition toward inspiring goals in whatever ways you choose. It is exciting to tune in to the planetary meridians required to complete a project. Usually more than one is involved in our key decisions.

The ten meridians are always ready to be of service. You enjoy the guidance of whatever meridian is needed to proceed ahead with confidence. Your Cancer Sun meridian encourages you to show your abilities with great strength, as this is where you must shine. The Moon meridian is your intuitive barometer making sure the coast is clear to show your deepest feelings. The Mercury meridian will come to your aid in a flash to stimulate vibrant ideas and new perceptions. The Venus meridian is never at a loss to help you find love and companionship as well as abundance. The Mars meridian will launch you forward to display a competitive edge. The Jupiter meridian is always willing to uplift your self-confidence and bring some luck your way. The Saturn meridian delivers focus and ambition like no other planet. The Uranus meridian is the champion of freedom and is able to show you how to break free to a brighter future. The Neptune meridian guides you into an in-depth spiritual quest and breathes idealism into your intuition. The Pluto meridian will make sure you tune in to the passion channel and find personal empowerment.

This is a tour that perhaps will get you to see how intuitive helpers are always nearby. There are evolutionary insights waiting for you to discover. Keep pursuing your dreams and enjoy the journey.

Creative Expression:
Sun Meridian Activating Your Cancer Intuition

Light: Strengths

The creative vitality of the Sun filters bountifully through your birth sign, Cancer, coloring your personality with a strong feeling nature. Your emotions are strong players in your creative expression. You react strongly to getting attention for your talents and take the opinions of others very personally. The people who show they can be your trusted friends in the best or worst of times win your heartfelt admiration. There is a loyalty that reaches out to your lovers and friends that support your goals.

The Sun sign of Cancer solarizes you with deep moods that are pathways to your intuition. Tuning in to your inner world is what nourishes your creative power. The outer world tests how secure your footing is within yourself. Your home must be a place of peace and have the imprint in its presence that allows you to feel a sense of harmony. Your residence helps launch your intuitive strength.

You find great joy in family, pets, and plants. Each in its own way gives your life meaning. Privacy is what sustains your soul and intuitive sanctuary. You will have your secrets that must be kept even from those you love. Why? There is a sacred pact between you and your inner being. Call it your inner spirit, connection to a higher power, or perhaps the collective unconscious. Part of you does not belong to the everyday world, with all of its responsibilities and distractions. Your intuition is a gift that works differently than for the other signs. It requires you to find that quiet time where you get replenished. When you are balanced mentally and emotionally, your intuition instinctively finds creative outlets.

You excel in whatever profession or pastime you choose to explore. It is your inner resolve not to give up that makes you a natural competitor. Your rugged determination might not be that visible to the outside world. But you have an ambition that feeds off of your intuitive knowing which direction to move toward to manifest your best chances for success.

Preserving your health goes far in making you an intuitive force. You get energized in witnessing the building of new projects, whether it be a business, home, or family. When you balance your needs for closeness and distance with people, you find happiness. You get stimulated when you feel your abilities are needed and valued.

Shadow: Challenges

How might this meridian not work so well on your behalf? If your moods get out of control, your intuition does not function as smoothly. You are blessed with rich emotions. They feed your intuitive power. If you are in relationships that drain your energy, you get confused in a hurry. Your dependency needs have to stay in check. If someone depends on you too heavily on a regular basis, it takes its toll on your mind, body, and spirit. If you become too reliant on someone to the extreme, it has the same end result. You lose your sense of direction.

A need for privacy comes naturally to you. If you become a recluse, you may miss out on opportunities. Fearing closeness could be due to not trusting very easily. If you never take a risk on a relationship, you may miss out on a great partner. It is not that you must be in a long-term partnership. But if you truly desire one and don't give yourself a chance, you could be selling yourself short.

Fearing being alone keeps you out of touch with your emotions and intuition. Having to always be in the company of others could be a way to hide from personal issues. In not dealing with past issues, you block a fulfilling present from manifesting. When you face internal conflicts, you empower your intuition.

Dawn: Maximizing Your Potential

The Sun meridian gives you plenty of room to expand your intuitive prowess. Establishing stable relationships and a secure home base gives your intuitive instincts the leverage they require to run smoothly. Growing comfortable with solitude recharges your mental and emotional batteries. Your inner world is a vast network of connections to the collective unconscious, a world of inspiring symbols just waiting for you to connect with them. There is an unlimited potential for you to find creative pleasure.

You own a great deal of healing energy. You can offer this in the form of nurturing those you love and care about. Taking care of your own emotional welfare preserves your intuitive strength. Don't be afraid to reward yourself. It helps stimulate your self-esteem, and this is yet another method to invigorate your intuition.

Move forward with a spirit of facing adversity. Why? Because this sparks an important evolutionary intuitive synchronicity. It is in dealing with life challenges directly that the deepest intuition comes forward for you spontaneously. As a matter of fact, it manifests in waves, one powerful current after another! Your self-confidence grows in a big way with each little success. Taking that first step toward a goal melts away your fears and lets your inner voice guide you.

Creating a Home and Expressing Feelings: Moon Meridian Activating Your Cancer Intuition

Light: Strengths

The Moon meridian plays a very special role in activating your intuition. What might that be? The Moon is the planetary ruler of your Cancer Sun sign, putting it right in the middle of your intuitive inclinations. This gives you easier access to an intuitive flow that the other signs could envy. Be sure to learn to be aware of your moods. They are clues to your inner motivations for actions. The Moon meridian offers you a wonderful barometer to sense the feelings of others. This helps you in all of your human relations.

You learn to anticipate the impact of your actions by tapping into lunar energy. Also, if someone is angry with you, this meridian teaches you how not to overreact too quickly. You may even get good at not escalating arguments by intuitively knowing how to calm others in the heat of the moment. This same process assists you in being assertive with great awareness to get what you need from others in a negotiation.

Emotions are often intensely felt by a Cancer person like yourself. This is a wonderful terrain to tune in to methods to calm yourself down, whether it is a nice meditation, spending time with a pet, or being out in nature or talking to a friend.

At home, you need to feel secure and have a feeling that you are insulated from the world and its stresses. Your home has to be a refuge that is calming and allows you to be centered. You require a community or geographical location that is supportive of your need for a life purpose and that allows you to establish an intimate connection with a special someone. The more at home you feel, the more you extend out and make friends.

Shadow: Challenges

How could your experience of the Moon meridian not be flowing the way you like? If your emotions are not grounded, you will feel like you are walking on the Moon. You could have trouble completing an important goal. The underlying reason might be due to feeling insecure or mentally off-center.

Your dependency needs must be balanced. If you are too dependent on others for emotional support, they will feel drained and distance themselves from you. Letting people always take from you without giving in return depletes your energy. Your relationships will not be as fulfilling without true equality.

If your home is in a state of chaos, it will make you a nervous wreck. If your residence does not feel harmonious, it is aggravating for a Sun sign Cancer like you to live this way. Without peace in your home, it is challenging to get that downtime you seek. Your mental and emotional bodies stay tired and lose their creative vitality.

Dawn: Maximizing Your Potential

The Moon meridian is a fertile valley in which to refuel your intuitive power. It guides you in times of harmony or discord. Your instincts are naturally attuned to this planetary ruler of your Cancer Sun sign. Together they can dance closely in perfect rhythm, showing you how to get the most out of your actions. Your creativity and ambition find new spark when nourished under the watchful eye of the Moon.

When you feel internally secure with the world around you, your intuition has a way of leading you to fulfilling experiences. Placing your home in a longitude and latitude that energizes your spirit makes an evolutionary intuitive synchronicity occur.

Keep your dependency needs reasonable and your relationships will be bathed in happiness. Be true to your ideals and values and they will point you toward abundance. If you don't deny what you are feeling, the world will anxiously respond to your need to knock on new doors of opportunity.

Mental Insights:
Mercury Meridian Activating Your Cancer Intuition

Light: Strengths

The winged-messenger meridian of Mercury helps you pinpoint just how you want to aim your intuition accurately to get the results you desire. This clever planet features a two-sided personality. One is Mercury's adaptable nature, which helps you adjust to changes in the blink of an eye. The trick for you as a water sign is to tune in to this airy and breezy planet's messages. You lasso this slippery heavenly wanderer's movements when you are emotionally calm and collected. It is that much easier to ride this brilliant planet's guidance when you are feeling centered and somewhat in control of your life.

There is a second key theme about Mercury, which is staying organized to ensure your actions stay on target. Your Sun sign is known for wanting to initiate actions when you sense it is time to jump on an opportunity. You do like being well prepared before leaping. This meridian assists you in making sure your footing is solid as you proceed ahead to complete a goal.

Your hope to master particular skills or to integrate new possibilities into a business is enhanced by Mercury energy. When you are willing to learn other job functions and to empower yourself through knowledge, this planet will run to help you.

You like having the information you share appreciated. You attract friends through a willingness to help them problem-solve. It is your generosity that makes people loyal when you need them the most.

Shadow: Challenges

If you use Mercury as a defense mechanism to hide your emotions, it causes trouble with people trying to get to know you. This is a very mental meridian ruled by a highly intellectual planet. Rather than communicating honestly, you could be hiding behind a cloak. This causes you to steer conversations away from intimate exchanges of information. People wanting to come closer will sense you are on your own island.

If you obsess over situations that you cannot change, your mental and emotional energy will get depleted. You lose momentum to complete key goals. If you expect too much perfection, it is a signal that you are not tuning in clearly to this meridian. If you don't learn techniques to turn off the worry button, you lose out on a lot of joy.

Dawn: Maximizing Your Potential

The Mercury meridian fills your mind with a wondrous quest for new learning. This planet has an intuitive presence that will entice your brain synapses to move beyond the borders of your comfort zones. How might Mercury accomplish this? By opening the eyes of your deepest and most soul-searching perceptions to see ways you can market your knowledge. Broadening your communication skills and not being afraid of learning new skills prepares you for the future. The wings of this high-flying planet carry you over obstacles in your path. It only takes a small amount of willingness to let go of negative thinking, and before you know it, you are in the midst of a magical evolutionary intuitive synchronicity. Learning that life is more harmonious when you let go of your worries is a great step in tuning in to greater creative power. This is an amazing meridian, full of surprises, if you stay curious and eager to expand your mental horizons.

Relationship Tendencies:
Venus Meridian Activating Your Cancer Intuition

Light: Strengths

Your Sun sign, Cancer, and the planet Venus have a great deal in common. What might this be? As a watery Cancer, establishing a comfortable atmosphere in your home is likely highly desired. The Venus meridian is an intuitive place for tuning in to multiple ways to create peace and beauty in your everyday life, especially in your residence. Knowing you have a living space that reflects your values and even what you prefer in the aesthetic world is stimulated by this meridian.

Venus is a big relationship planet. She influences how you want to bond with a lover and other key people in your life. Your intuition joins forces with this socially adept celestial heavenly body to seek and maintain valuable partnerships. Your romantic and non-romantic alliances get highly charged by this people-oriented meridian. Whether you are an introvert or extrovert, Venus will push you to step out and mingle with others.

You probably like your space in relationships. Trust comes with time. As a Cancer, you don't like to be rushed into romance. You like to really get to know someone before intimacy seems right. Lovers who show patience and who are good listeners are more apt to win your heart. You like people to really show they appreciate any emotional support you give them.

Venus energy strengthens your self-esteem. If you are in balanced relationships, you will find the intuitive road to utilizing Venus easier to follow. Sharing your resources with those you love and care about keeps them close. Remember to reward yourself at regular intervals, as it raises feelings of self-worth.

Shadow: Challenges

If you are trying too hard to make people like you, there is a good chance that you are not tuning in to the Venus meridian clearly. There is interference for more than one reason. Usually it is insecurity or low self-esteem. If you don't believe you are worthy of a fulfilling relationship, then you will not create one. Your desire for equality is not being defined in a way that is getting the best results.

Becoming a hermit, like a crab in a shell, due to a fear of closeness makes for a lonely existence. There is nothing wrong with a need for privacy. This is an innate need for a Sun sign Cancer like yourself. But hiding from the world keeps you from finding a soul mate. This could be due to an underlying fear of rejection.

Settling for jobs and relationships that limit your potential for greater abundance is not wise. Keeping yourself from branching out into new directions cuts you off from new enterprising activities.

Dawn: Maximizing Your Potential

The Venus meridian is readily available to make your relationships harmonious. You only need to follow the guidance of this socially curious planet. How do you put this into action? Seek balanced relationships. The scales of giving and receiving need to be equal. The soul mate you seek is easier to find if your inner world is bathed in a solid self-esteem. You have a wider circle of friends when connecting with Venus intuition. She will ask you to stay tolerant of differing belief systems. It is not sameness with a lover or friend that necessarily makes you feel fulfilled, but rather it is someone stimulating you to believe in your values and let your actions be passionate expressions of the real you.

A life with abundance is nourished by this meridian. There is no greater landscape than the one Venus occupies to intuitively grasp peace of mind. If you hold on to your highest ideals with one hand and reach out toward paths that challenge you to release your creative power with the other hand, an evolutionary intuitive synchronicity finds birth.

Initiating Action:
Mars Meridian Activating Your Cancer Intuition

Light: Strengths

This fiery meridian ruled by the angry red planet Mars mixes with your watery Cancer Sun sign to produce passion. This is you spontaneously wanting to display your talents for the world to see. It is a sudden burst of assertiveness to introduce yourself to new friends. Mars pushes you to act courageously in pursuit of finishing a task. Your adrenaline gets pumped when tuning in to Mars energy.

Anger is an emotion. Your moods are a dead giveaway if you are emotionally upset with someone. When you say what is on your mind, it releases your anxiety and keeps it to a minimum.

You are healthier mentally, physically, and spiritually when dealing directly with people and problems. Your timing gets better with practice if you need to confront someone about a disagreement. If you are too angry, you might need to take a pause to collect yourself before communicating about a dispute. You will win more negotiations through thinking before you act on too fast an impulse.

Mars will get you to focus on your own hopes and wishes. If you have been denying your own needs, this is the meridian with the remedy to fix this. If you are too self-absorbed, you will need to do a better job of listening to what you can do to be supportive of others.

Shadow: Challenges

What happens if you are not connecting with Mars in an intuitive way? Your get-up-and-go could stop in its tracks. This might be due to a fear of either starting a project or getting stuck in midstream due to being very anxious about how to finish. Emotional upset or confusion about a sense of direction makes it difficult for you to put Mars into high gear. You could be too sensitive to criticism and too easily talked out of a plan. This leads to frustration. Being assertive is stuck in reverse.

Using anger to get your own way will alienate people. Rather than communicating honestly, you are resorting to a bullying type of behavior to get what you want. This will cause the people closest to you to pull away.

If you hold too much anger within, it can eat away at your feeling the peace you seek. Your identity gets fogged. There is a possibility that you could suddenly explode due to stuffing your anger.

Dawn: Maximizing Your Potential

The Mars meridian is a high-energy place. If you need to get your momentum lit, then this is the planet you need to align your mind and body with. Your spirit will come along for the ride. If you show courage and a feisty belief in a plan, Mars will come aboard, guiding you to act forcefully.

In mythology, Mars was the god of war. There are times when you will need to show your competitive side. Being assertive rather than extremely aggressive will take you further in your relationships. This is a passionate meridian that awakens a drive to begin a project and take on a new career. Directing Mars with patience keeps you from having to start an activity over and over again. When you learn to pace yourself, you get better mileage out of this fast-moving dare-devil meridian.

Facing emotional wounds from the past illuminates a magical evolutionary intuitive synchronicity. There is healing power in this warrior-like atmosphere. You only need to use your intuition to deal insightfully and bravely with past issues to release your creative prowess.

Expanding Knowledge:
Jupiter Meridian Activating Your Cancer Intuition

Light: Strengths

Jupiter will expand your confidence in your intuition. This good-natured meridian reflects the optimism generated by this very large cosmic entity. If you show your belief in your goals, Jupiter luck may manifest right in front of your eyes. The universe opens doors of opportunity if you walk with positive shoes.

The teacher, advisor, promoter, and student within you get stimulated through this meridian. Learning a new job or taking on a fun hobby keeps your mind invigorated. Travel and simply being on the move motivates your creativity. The endorphins in your brain like to remind you to stay awake, because you never know when the good fortune delivered by this adventurous planet will pay you a visit.

As a Cancer Sun sign, you could have a tendency to stay with what you know. Routines do keep you organized and on schedule. However, don't forget to mix in variety, as it is the spice of life. Jupiter energy is always present and trying to remind you that there is no time for boredom. This fiery planet tempts you with a dose of restlessness so that you might leave the confines of being too comfortable. Jupiter pushes you not to fear wearing your explorer hat.

In Jupiter's world, happiness is a state of mind. You can combine work and play. Keep a sense of humor, because it is good for your health and keeps life in perspective. If you find it difficult to finish a project, try distracting yourself with a pleasurable activity. It is the Jupiter way of saying insight comes when you stop worrying or forcing something to happen.

Ride this meridian to a new future. Adopt the rituals and belief system that will strengthen you. Be true to your highest ideals and this meridian lavished with hope will always be there when you need it.

Shadow: Challenges

How might you not be tuning in to Jupiter intuition? It manifests as a lack of self-confidence. Negative thinking becomes too dominant. Not having faith in your ability takes the air out of your Jupiter connection. You could be allowing people to negate your plans before they even begin.

Another way you could be out of step with Jupiter is expecting results to come too easily. Your effort is weak due to expecting life to deliver good things without you really trying. This is taking the relaxed symbolism that Jupiter represents to an extreme.

Promising too much to people could get you into trouble. This may be due to trying too hard to please others. You want someone to like you so you exaggerate what you can do for them. This will cause people to become disappointed and not trust you.

Dawn: Maximizing Your Potential

The Jupiter meridian launches your mind into thinking more positively, no matter the circumstances. If you are looking to fill your tank with optimism, you have come to the right meridian for a fill-up. Inspiration is in the natural makeup of Jupiter energy. Your energy gets an enthusiasm tune-up and at the same time you rid yourself of negative thoughts.

Selling an idea gets stimulated in this terrain. You only need to do your best preparation and then let your intuition link to Jupiter faith. People will connect with your energetic thinking.

Keep your expectations reasonable. Patience is wise. Sometimes good goals get started under Jupiter guidance and the payoff comes later. Appreciating what you do have and at the same time not losing your momentum for a brighter future keeps your dreams alive.

When you venture out and try a new experience, it could ignite an evolutionary intuitive synchronicity. Be open to the innovative ideas that you come across. This may be the path you seek to create greater opportunities.

Career and Ambition:
Saturn Meridian Activating Your Cancer Intuition

Light: Strengths

If you are a Sun sign Cancer person who has a very focused intuition, you can thank the Saturn meridian for helping you master this skill. There is no better planet to utilize when it comes to a steady, persistent determination than Saturn. You may be seen by others as very dependable. Managing your time is a natural ability when you make friends with this meridian energy. People could be impressed with your awareness to meet a deadline even if you are feeling stressed-out. It is the urgency in which you sense a job must be done that drives you to finish it. Saturn fills you with a sense of responsibility that makes you a solid manager, leader, and supervisor.

A career that offers you a sense of security is attractive. It must capture the need you have for an emotional connection. A job that makes you feel needed and allows you to serve the public could appeal to you. You are sensitive about your reputation in the work world, as you likely have high standards when it comes to excellence. This is a meridian that assists you in planning a business or career strategy. Saturn guides you to sharpen your negotiation skills and to learn how to sell your work experience to a potential employer. Beginning a new job or moving into a new job direction can be scary and exciting at the same time. Stay disciplined and be patient as Saturn weaves an intuitive force into you to ensure your success.

Past-life patterns are linked to the Saturn meridian. This means that you could be needing to overcome trends from previous incarnations or learn how to make peace with them. It may be possible to balance your dependency needs. What might this mean? In some past lifetimes, perhaps you were not self-reliant enough. You are now getting an opportunity to act more responsibly and define a clearer path to be independent. It may be that you were too reliant on yourself in other lives. This lifetime is providing you with a chance to be more inclusive of others. You could be getting better at considering the ideas of people before making an important decision that affects you all. The key message here is awareness. You become empowered by allowing your intuition to align with Saturn energy to shed some light into areas where in the past there has been darkness.

There is wisdom embedded in this meridian when you learn from past experiences. You reach great milestones, whether it is work accomplishments, having a family, or finding fulfillment through a solid commitment to accepting life's ups and downs. You will know you are in sync with this earthy meridian when you feel an inner contentment that is reflected in the unity you establish in your home and all of the life roles you choose.

Shadow: Challenges

Glaciers move extremely slow in the Arctic. When you feel stuck by not tuning in correctly to the Saturn meridian, you feel like you have lost all of your momentum. This might be due to extreme disappointments, whether in relationships or a career. It may have nothing to do with an external problem. Lacking the determination to move through a tough time period gives you a sense of isolation. If you refuse to let anyone know you need help, it is a rough ride. If you are listening to the wrong people, it negates your positive spirit, weighing you down.

Settling for less than you can be is selling yourself short. Staying in relationships with a lack of clear definition is disorienting. Jobs that cause you not to feel valued deplete your energy. Living in a location with no growth potential limits your chances for success.

If you keep repeating the same negative thought patterns, you will not be happy. This is the meridian that has a lot to do with wisdom and learning from the past. In other words, your history is supposed to empower you. If this is not occurring, then you are out of alignment with this success-oriented meridian.

Rigidity is the biggest karmic nemesis in this meridian. It sends you spinning in the wrong direction. Resisting change leads to trouble. Becoming too controlling in relationships causes problems as well. It is a lack of flexibility that keeps you from the happiness you seek and is likely a carry-over theme from past lifetimes still needing to be resolved.

Dawn: Maximizing Your Potential

The Saturn meridian is a world offering you a chance to celebrate great milestones. The steady determination influenced by this very determined energy keeps your intuition focused and on target with great results. Your commitments to people and goals show you completely inspired by ambition and energized by the successes experienced.

It is your willingness to adapt to the changing reality of your circumstances that stimulates an evolutionary intuitive synchronicity. Intuitively sensing the need to integrate new growth into your mental framework produces miraculous changes. It strengthens your current relationships and infuses new energy into your creativity. Saturn's meridian will embrace your desire to impress the world with a newly invigorated you that has transcended old worn-out patterns.

Saturn rules Capricorn, the opposite sign of Cancer. Saturn is the cosmic mirror, or mirroring agent, for your Sun sign. What does this mean? Saturn mirrors back to you a wave of focused energy to empower your emotional intensity. It helps you identify the means to declare your self-reliance and balance your dependency needs. This sets boundaries that help you maintain a clear glimpse of your own identity. This reality-oriented planet will open your eyes to see you cannot control other people's decisions. When you relax into your intuitive awareness, this meridian will hold on to you in such a way that you never fear reaching your highest goals.

Future Goals and Inventiveness:
Uranus Meridian Activating Your Cancer Intuition

Light: Strengths

If you want to spread your wings wide to exert your independence, then you are likely tuning in to the freedom-oriented Uranus meridian. Suddenly feeling pulled into a bold new direction is not so unusual when the thrust of this very powerful, futuristic-thinking energy grabs a hold of your mind. As a Cancer Sun sign, your first impulse may not be to trust quick change immediately. Then again, if you are looking for greater excitement, you could greet this planetary influence with open arms.

Your perceptions become inventive. People may see you have reinvented yourself into a new career. Starting new friendships is possible. An existing relationship finds new ways to get invigorated through a joint venture. It could be a hobby of mutual interest or taking a trip together that adds vitality to your togetherness.

Moving to a new residence or adding something special to your home gets motivated by this meridian. Your intuition may tell you it is time to move to a geographical location that offers you greater opportunities in the work and relationship areas. Your mind, body, and soul reach an agreement that it is time to move on.

Yesterday's reality may not be meeting your needs of today. This is the primary message of Uranus. It is possible to hold on to what you now have and at the same time blend in a new energy to give you that revitalized life you currently desire. Unique insights can be discovered that are exciting. This is the meridian providing a wake-up call that there is no time like today to put your goals into high gear. Uranus sends you the inspiration to dare to ask for what you truly need in order to be happy and fulfilled.

Shadow: Challenges

If you are not tuning in clearly to the Uranus meridian, there is the potential to cut your bridges to the past without enough forethought. You could be leaving a relationship too recklessly. This may be for more than one reason. A fear of intimacy could be the reason for breaking off a relationship. You are more comfortable on the intellectual level but squeamish about sharing feelings. Running away from closeness makes it difficult to maintain a long-term commitment.

Even on the job front there might be problems. Perhaps you are always rebelling against authority and must work on your own terms with little compromise. Restlessness may keep you from being able to stay with one job for the long haul. A fear of commitment can be the main reason you have trouble finishing what you start.

Being in the habit of not standing up for your own goals is another theme that surfaces in this meridian if it is not functioning properly. Giving in too easily to the demands of others keeps you from realizing your highest potential. Attracting self-serving individuals is probable if you don't live out your own freedom requirements.

Dawn: Maximizing Your Potential

The Uranus meridian accentuates the desire for independence required to reach your unique goals. You will have little time for boredom when this planet influences your thinking. Life is never quite the same if you let Uranus guide you to a new future. This exciting celestial wanderer delights in watching you march to the beat of your own drum, even if it does not always make everyone else happy in your life. There are occasions when you must do your own thing to manifest the road to fulfillment. Don't you agree?

This meridian is filled with the air element due to the presence of Uranus. As a water sign, Cancer, this is an interesting alchemy of energies. Your emotions get dried out and more reflective when run through Uranus filters. You become more objective and not so quick to react to the opinions of others. This adds patience to your life resumé. Your intuition learns how to not get stressed-out by the challenges of today. In the back of your mind are the long-range goals that allow you to remain calm in knowing you are working toward them.

Balancing your own needs with the expectations of others takes practice, but you can get good at this. You can learn how to negotiate in such a way to create win-win agreements.

There is no need to fear closeness with others. If you have the right people in your life, they should be able to adjust to your need for space and you can do the same for them. Spending some time alone recharges your mind, body, and spirit. It gives you time to reconnect with your insights

A change of scenery is stimulating. When you step out of your comfort zone, the magic of an evolutionary intuitive synchronicity occurs much to your surprise. The gifts of Uranus come swiftly and when you least expect them.

Creative Imagination and Idealism: Neptune Meridian Activating Your Cancer Intuition

Light: Strengths

Your watery Cancer Sun sign lives in the same world as watery Neptune. In mythology, this planet was known as Poseidon, god of the oceans. The Neptune meridian invites you into a misty atmosphere lined with a great promise of deepening your spirituality and renewing your idealism. This romantic, poetic-like planet plays on your intuition in subtle ways. You may not even realize how much you are developing your intuition. Your ability to connect with the meaning of symbols grows by leaps and bounds under the tutoring gaze of Neptune.

Faith in your highest beliefs intensifies. Your compassion for others may be expressed in your work. Tuning in to people's feelings is enhanced by this magical meridian. You sense what someone may be thinking before it is said to you.

A deeper need to find a soul mate occurs. Your current relationships could come closer to your heart than ever before. Neptune has a way of encouraging you to make more time for those you love.

Your talent in the aesthetic world might magnify and be a wonderful discovery. A sixth sense to channel your intuition into art, music, photography, and even metaphysical subjects enlarges in this meridian. You can show an above-average ability in helping people to better comprehend their problems and point the way to solutions. The healer in you makes itself known to you in a big way. When you explore this terrain, you find a clearer life purpose.

A desire to find a cause is stimulated by Neptune energy. Serving something bigger than you can be a calling. Your soul senses it has found its way home. Meditation, yoga, and alternative forms of thinking fill you with a new perspective. Trusting your intuition may come as a pleasant surprise.

Shadow: Challenges

There are illusions in this meridian that you must avoid. Seeking perfection that does not exist could prove very frustrating. If you expect too much from yourself or others, emotional confusion becomes too prevalent. Forgetting to reality-test your idealism causes you to lose time, resources, and energy.

Denial in itself is not a bad thing. You can't face your problems all at once. But if you stay in relationships that are not fulfilling, it could be because you are refusing to take an honest assessment of the situation. Trying to pretend you are content will keep you from establishing a happier partnership with someone who truly treats you as an equal.

Watch out for causes that ask you to give completely of yourself without expecting anything in return. This stops you from exploring your own talents. If you are not receiving as much as you are giving on a regular basis, it is a symptom that you are out of step with this meridian.

Exaggerating your abilities is another potential problem area. You may not be as prepared to take on a big project as you think. Your imagination is way out in front of the reality. You might be promising more than you can deliver.

Dawn: Maximizing Your Potential

The Neptune meridian takes you to far-reaching places within yourself, illuminating a new source of inspiration. Ideals and romantic feelings you never thought possible are revealed. Creative insight manifests with great faith. Your conscious and subconscious minds can become good friends and more clearly in alignment. Your ability to tap into the collective unconscious may intensify, sparking an evolutionary intuitive synchronicity.

Through becoming more comfortable with intimacy, a love relationship finds new meaning. A profession that expresses your creativity offers you great fulfillment. This is a dynamic intuitive meridian that spreads throughout your entire being. Giving yourself permission not to be too perfect sets you free. Balancing reality testing with your most heartfelt goals for the future ensures a safer landing into an exhilarating future.

Personal Empowerment and Passion:
Pluto Meridian Activating Your Cancer Intuition

Light: Strengths

The Pluto meridian guides you to find personal empowerment through trusting your ability to create success. The energy circulating throughout this passionate atmosphere stimulates you to seek new job skills. Pluto is a business-oriented planet. You may uncover talents that can be marketed to the public.

When you tap into the lifeline of the Pluto meridian, there is a wealth of information available to you. Your survival instincts become enlivened. If you need to find the inner fortitude to outlive a crisis, then you are knocking on the right door. Keeping your wits about you no matter the challenge is possible with this trusted planet at your side. Pluto will show you better than any other planet how to get through a loss and process the experience.

Your emotional nature discovers rebirth. There is healing energy in the aura of this meridian that takes away your painful memories. It is like a metamorphosis has taken place. Inner clarity comes through, integrating the past and present into a fulfilling sense of unity and awareness.

Your home and city of residence must provide you with a secure feeling. You value your privacy, which probably comes as no surprise to you. Your alone time revitalizes your mind, body, and spirit, allowing you to fully engage the world.

You prefer relationships you can rely on. Closeness excites and scares you at the same time. This meridian presents you with a dynamic inner conflict when it comes to intimate relationships. Finding that middle ground where you can overcome your fears and truly bond with a partner brings you great happiness. Learning to forgive could be a key to solidifying your commitments. Casting aside manipulating behaviors and jealousy tendencies is part of the path to self-mastery. Your intuition elevates when you let go and follow your creative power to wherever it leads you.

Shadow: Challenges

When you fail to tune in to the Pluto meridian with clarity, there are power struggles. You could be forcing issues rather than looking for compromises with others. Or you might become the victim of someone taking advantage of your generosity. Manipulative people will be attracted to you if you do not assert your own empowerment.

Passion is a wonderful part of your self-expression. If you become too obsessed with a relationship or a career, you lose your identity. Emotional confusion results. The extremes in this meridian get you into trouble if you lose your impulse control. Compulsive spending may get you into financial difficulty. Too much of a good thing could use moderation.

If you refuse to communicate openly, your emotional intensity builds to the boiling point. Your relationships will not be as fulfilling. Even your creativity loses some of its zest if you hold your honest feelings back too much. Your intuition lacks some of its luster, as it is weighed down by repressed anger.

Dawn: Maximizing Your Potential

The Pluto meridian brings out your deepest investigative instincts into people, places, and things. This intuitive tendency to delve beneath the surface serves you well in your work. Pluto encourages you to never do a job halfway. Your determination to passionately finish a project is pushed to the limit if you grab the hand of this meridian.

As a Cancer Sun sign, you have a strong emotional nature. Your moods are a link to the most intricate parts of your intuition. When you are internally centered and yet driven at the same time, there is no challenge you cannot handle. When you are not fearful of exploring your feelings, this opens the gateway to an evolutionary intuitive synchronicity. Embracing intimacy releases your creative power. Self-mastery is never far away when you channel your emotions into productive expression. The love you seek is closer than your mind sometimes notices but comes to meet you when you are not afraid to trust.

——— *Chapter 6* ———

LEO

Leo (7/23–8/22)

Archetypes: Promoter, Entrepreneur, Performer
Key Focus: Self-Expression and Fulfilling Ego Needs
Element: Fire
Planetary Ruler: Sun
Cosmic Mirror Planet: Uranus

Welcome to your Leo sign chapter. Your Leo creative power discovers new intuitive ways to put your talents to work when you tune in to the planetary meridian energies. When you let your intuition guide you, greater abundance and harmony comes into your life.

Intuition moves boldly through your fiery sign without any hesitation to express itself. This goes well with your innate desire as a Leo to show the world your abilities. When you make use of the many gifts within the planetary meridians, you find greater joy in your relationships, work, and hope for a brighter future.

Your Leo Dashboard Meridian Summary

It is important to remember this is your own life journey and you have the freedom to choose whichever meridians will be needed to get your needed results. These magical forces are always at work trying to guide you to fulfilling paths. Think of each day as an opportunity to call on the meridian you need to realize your goals.

As a Leo, you can enjoy the way the ten meridians influence you to use their creative energies. They will weave in and out of your intuition usually with more than one interacting with you at a time, especially when you are in the middle of a key decision.

Your Leo Sun meridian is ready instantly to fill you with creative fire. The Moon meridian points you to find a sense of security and a solid home base. The Mercury meridian teaches you to never fear learning new ways to perceive the world. The Venus meridian is your gateway to developing harmonious relationships and finding peace. The Mars meridian instills an assertive spirit, leading you to act with boldness. The Jupiter meridian expands your opportunities for success and encourages you to be an optimist. The Saturn meridian encourages you to be committed to your serious goals and to develop discipline. The Uranus meridian awakens you to new future goals and encourages you to break free from limitations. The Neptune meridian offers you faith and renewed dreams. The Pluto meridian stimulates your passion and leads you to embrace your personal power.

Enjoy your tour through your planetary meridians. Each is there to link with your intuition to help you realize your full potential. Keep being open to new growth and you will be happy with your life journey.

Creative Expression:
Sun Meridian Activating Your Leo Intuition

Light: Strengths

The creative force of the Sun colors your astrological sign, Leo, with great confidence. This fills you with an animated display of personality. Living life in the moment is more your style. You like to make things happen fast. You can roar like a lion when showing the world your talent. Your intuition catches fire when fanned by the excitement of forming new relationships and finding new work possibilities.

Your Leo Sun sign solarizes you with a dramatic spirit. The Sun has a special significance in this meridian for you because it is the ruler of your sign, Leo. You are lit with a strong desire to see results manifest quickly when you put a plan into action. How might the Sun meridian influence you to make use of your intuition? One possibility is promoting your talents or that of someone else in a convincing manner. People believe in your charismatic words and body language. It is as though your aura exudes an expression that shows you know a plan can't fail with you as the driving force behind it.

Your intuition feeds off of enthusiasm. Without it, you are lost. The Sun pushes you to maintain a steady course until you complete a goal. There is a fixed energy running throughout this meridian that influences you to hold on to your ideas until someone shows you a better way.

You love attention. Receiving applause for a job well done keeps you wanting to try that much harder to get others to notice you. Finding the right romantic partner is likely a welcomed challenge. You tend to be a social person and thrive on interactions with people. Social exchanges warm your heart, because intuitively you know that your creative power needs the stimulation.

Staying open to new ideas keeps your mind alert and fresh. Your perceptions are at their best when welcoming the opinions of others, even if they don't always agree with your own. Paying attention to the needs of those you love keeps them in your life and tightens your bond with them.

Shadow: Challenges

How can you misread the intuitive pathways in this meridian? Stubbornness. It could dominate your thinking to the point of causing distance in any of your relationships. When you defend your ideas to an extreme degree, you can't expect people to be happy with you. Losing sight of flexibility is the key culprit here.

Desiring attention compulsively is another indicator that you are out of touch with the best this meridian has to offer. Wanting recognition is a good thing, but demanding it constantly wears thin.

What if you happen to be the type of Sun sign Leo who is afraid to receive attention or to be rewarded adequately? It could be a matter of low self-esteem. Denying your own goals to remain in limiting relationships or job situations could be another problem. This runs contrary to that natural pulse in this meridian trying to elevate you to be assertive and to know you deserve to be valued.

Dawn: Maximizing Your Potential

The Sun meridian is the perfect place for you to put your skills on full display. The heated passion of the Sun is a good match for your fiery sign, Leo. Some people may accuse you of always wanting to be the center of attention. You probably explain this as simply wanting to be sociable and to make your ideas visible.

Your lovers, friends, business associates, and family will appreciate your being a cheerleader for their goals. It is part of your psyche to encourage others to pursue their dreams, whether they want to hear this or not. You are at your best when you allow people to think for themselves in the same way you like to do so.

Creative power manifests spontaneously from your heart when you tap into this meridian. Your intuition gets motivated quickly when you focus vivaciously on a goal. Your inner strength multiplies as you maintain a clear sense of purpose. When you exhibit flexibility and adaptability, an evolutionary intuitive synchronicity is born. Flowing with change leads to new growth potential. Being willing to be a team player as well as a leader wins you many admirers.

Creating a Home and Expressing Feelings: Moon Meridian Activating Your Leo Intuition

Light: Strengths

The Moon complements your Leo Sun sign with intuition that guides your impulse to move fast with a reflective tone that helps you make wise decisions. This does not mean you must stop for a prolonged amount of time. On the contrary, you can move spontaneously but with enough restraint to know when to perhaps exercise patience. Moods are the Moon's way of helping you sense what is the right choice and when to hold off on a decision until a later date.

This is a water-ruled meridian and you are a fire sign. This is a combination that produces plenty of fiery feelings. You are more creative when really finding the passion to inspire your best effort. This is a landscape that comes through for you when you need to find the inner clarity to show your greatest talent. The Moon sends you intuitive insight but may require you to wait and contemplate your next step. Then this lunar majestic entity might just as immediately transmit messages that say "go for it now." It is a radar system that helps you detect interference and know how to fly around any obstructions.

You need a home base that helps you maintain your creative power and at the same time gives you the reassurance that you can retreat from a stressful world. You like your residence to reflect your pride in what you have accomplished in life. It must be a place that gives you plenty of space to relax and find pleasure. The city or geographical location you select needs to match your desire to be able to act out your self-expression. Your goals must have an opportunity to fully reach their highest potential. You are a restless soul. You require a community with enough outlets for your ambition and the roles you want to act out.

Shadow: Challenges

How do you know if you are not in tune with the Moon meridian? It probably goes something like this. You are angry and may not know why. It could be that you are denying the reality of a situation or your feelings are blocked. Your moods could be ruling your logic. Rather than slowing down to determine what is wrong, you are reacting without talking this through. There is another possibility in that you could be too flooded with emotions. Your mind and feelings are in conflict about how to deal with a situation.

If you are afraid to feel anything, your communication with those closest to you is not very clear. You might do fine on the business end of things but not so well in your intimate relationships. This meridian works best when you validate your emotions. You lose creative power when not better engaged with the Moon energy.

Balancing your dependency needs is important. Trying to take care of too many people and in the process neglecting your own welfare will deplete your energy. People may perceive you as a very strong Leo and capable of doing just about anything. Know your limits and when to say no.

Dawn: Maximizing Your Potential

The Moon meridian is a place to rest your mind and get recharged. The Moon will encourage you to make your residence an escape from the world but at the same time will also stimulate you to welcome your friends into your home. It serves you in multiple ways. The Moon meridian guides you intuitively to find the right home and location to nurture your creative growth.

Your emotions, as delivered by the Moon, and your self-expression, as introduced by your Leo Sun sign influence, work in unison to lead you to a very fulfilling life. You perform very successfully in the world when you have a solid home life and roles that showcase your sense of pride. Your self-confidence increases when sustained by a clear inner connection to your intuitive strength.

Balancing self-reliance with showing your closest people connections that you need them is a wise policy. Your lovers and friends are key allies. They are needed to encourage you, whether you are feeling up or down. You need to know that people feel they can count on you. When someone trusts you, it makes you want to be their friend or partner.

This meridian is a big player in your life. You move into an evolutionary intuitive synchronicity when letting your guard down and not fearing exploring the immense inner world just waiting for you to enjoy its many splendid gifts. This lays the foundation for you to develop a long-lasting romance, a deeper spirituality, and enlivened goals and to deepen your awareness of how much magic is always around you.

Mental Insights:
Mercury Meridian Activating Your Leo Intuition

Light: Strengths

The Mercury meridian activates your intuition quickly to perceive the world around you. Being a Leo, you like people to get to the point fast, don't you? Direct communication is likely what you prefer. Your mind reacts with more feeling when someone says what is really on their mind. Honesty is likely highly valued by you, but there are times when your ego may get more bruised than you had counted on. When you don't trust someone, you are apt not to reveal your most important thoughts. You have a natural instinct not to show all of your cards at once until you get to know a person. This can be a positive when it comes to negotiating in the business world or when getting what you need in a relationship.

Fire sign individuals like yourself have a tendency to move briskly. This meridian provides you with intuitive energy to prioritize your goals so that you can move swiftly and maintain a sense of direction. If you want to learn to be more detail-oriented and to create a reliable routine, then you are in the correct meridian airspace. Mercury's job is to help your mind stay organized even if you are in situations that cause chaos. If your work is bombarding you with multiple tasks, Mercury is there to aid you in filing everything to where it belongs and to get it done before a deadline.

Listening does not come easy to a Leo. Mercury teaches you how to slow down your reaction time in response to what someone is saying. This allows you to truly digest what is being said rather than feeling you must interrupt the flow of the conversation. Your lovers, friends, and people you interact with on the business level will appreciate this quality about you.

You can become adept at communicating your ideas. Advertising your skills becomes a natural talent. Teaching, writing, and being an advisor are abilities you could put on display. Talking with self-confidence often assures you of the results you hope to accomplish.

Shadow: Challenges

You lose your clarity in this meridian really quickly if you become careless with details. Impatience is the reason this occurs. You will end up either doing an inadequate job on a project or having to do it all over again. Being in too big a rush to get to the finish line is like moving one step forward and three steps back.

Not being a good listener will cause people to be unhappy with you. Seeing circumstances only from your own perspective causes power struggles. Stubbornly holding on to your own way of doing things will cause great tension in your relationships. Refusing to alter a plan, even if it is not working, will limit your options.

Negativity derails your best preparations by undermining your self-confidence. Feeling like you are treading water rather than moving forward is painful for a Leo. You are too fiery to enjoy sitting still for long periods of time. You get very down if you allow yourself to be talked out of good ideas on a regular basis.

Dawn: Maximizing Your Potential

The Mercury meridian accelerates your mental processes and excites your willingness to learn new skills. Why is this true? Mercury is the champion of intellectual curiosity. Don't ever think you can't figure out a solution to a problem as long as you have clever Mercury fully loaded in your holster. This stimulating planet keeps your Leo persistence on its toes.

This meridian deepens your perceptions about people. Mercury is a catalyst to inspire you to work on clear communication. Gravitating to books or people who expose you to new ways of thinking awakens an evolutionary intuitive synchronicity.

Your creative self-expression finds new life when traveling into the Mercury universe. This meridian will invigorate your mind. Travel on the mental and physical levels brings new information to your mind and perhaps is the simplest way to keep the Mercury meridian as an active component in your life.

Relationship Tendencies:
Venus Meridian Activating Your Leo Intuition

Light: Strengths

People who need people respond well to the Venus meridian. Being born under the sign Leo should indicate there is a warm place in your heart for the relationship-oriented Venus. Why? Your sign often needs the enthusiasm and attention of other people to light your creative power. When you open your world up to a wide range of ideas, it opens you to more possibilities for new opportunities. Allowing for the input of alternative ideas keeps you from getting stuck in limiting situations.

Your self-esteem is crucial to your happiness. When it is high, life is exhilarating. Your goals are more likely to be filled with self-confidence. The world seems to follow your lead when you are feeling self-assured. The abundance you desire is easier to find. Job possibilities and promotions are more probable if you believe in your abilities.

You thrive on relationships that are passionate. Romance stimulates your creative drive. The attention and affection of a lover empower your drive to be a success. Love and ambition play off each other in this way. Showing you are supportive of the goals of those you care about warms their hearts. It is the surest way to ensure longevity in your relationships.

Peace of mind is as valuable as the air you breathe. Being in partnerships based on equality is good for your sense of well-being.

Stress is less likely if you balance work and leisure. Time away from a job relaxes your mind and promotes good health. Resting your mind replenishes your emotional strength. Regular exercise ensures that your mind, body, and spirit will be in proper alignment.

Shadow: Challenges

Demanding too much attention from others is a good indication that you are not flowing with the Venus meridian. You are sailing against the wind. Equal give and take is the only way to get this meridian energy moving with you. Giving away an excessive amount of your time and resources to please others is no better than doing all of the receiving. There is an underlying feeling of insecurity causing this lack of balance in relating to others.

Making no time for a break from stress wears you down. If you are a type-A personality, then you do need plenty of outlets for your restlessness. There is nothing wrong with intense ambition, but it can lead to burnout. If you don't learn to slow down, sooner or later you will pay a price. You will lose important people and your health.

A sluggish motivation for success goes against the natural Leo drive to push through obstacles. Without a carefully conceived plan to reach a goal, it won't come to fruition. This may be due to a self-esteem problem, or perhaps you never got over a previous setback. If you stay in denial, the problems won't get any easier to resolve.

Dawn: Maximizing Your Potential

In some ways, the Venus meridian is your fountain of youth. It keeps you young at heart no matter your age. Why is this true? Being in love with a person or creative goals lights your fiery passion for life. It is this falling in love over and over again with your sources of inspiration that makes you feel very much alive and well. This is the key to your enterprising spirit.

Venus is your inner guide to maintaining a strong self-esteem. This planet will attempt to point you at people and experiences that empower your self-worth. The idea is to help you make good choices in partnerships and even to make sensible business decisions. Money is another Venus theme. Your earning power increases when you tune in to the intuitive messages of this fair-minded celestial wanderer. Finding a job or profession that reflects your values ignites an evolutionary intuitive synchronicity.

Since you are a Leo individual, you need challenges to test your inner strength. Without them, you grow bored. Maintaining a balanced scale when it comes to ambition and comfort is vital to your happiness. Walking with a watchful eye for the doors that open to chances to fulfill a creative risk excites you. Using your other eye to hold on to your most cherished people gives you a sense of wholeness.

Initiating Action:
Mars Meridian Activating Your Leo Intuition

Light: Strengths

If you are looking to be adventurous, this is the right meridian to explore. Mars will push you to the limits of risk taking. The side of a Leo like yourself who sees that investing in a new opportunity is worth the effort gets a shot of adrenaline in this very high-energy territory. Moving forward at full speed is easy to do in this fiery atmosphere. Boldness is the mantra of Mars. You can feel in your bones the passionate intensity to enter a new romantic relationship or make a move on a new job. Caution is not going to be your first and foremost impulse when grabbing the intuitive winds of this fiery red planet. Courage comes in a heartbeat when you align your mind with the brazen DNA of Mars.

Being assertive to get what you need falls in the domain of this meridian. Giving yourself permission to dare to ask for self-fulfillment and to claim your own territorial rights is a Mars hallmark. Fighting for those you love is another theme. Protecting the welfare of others comes when you intuitively connect with Mars. Sometimes it is when you are even in the middle of a stressful competitive challenge that you can summon Mars to be your hero.

Directing your anger forcefully but with insight can be learned. It serves your purposes better when you point this energy into productive outlets. Dealing directly with past or current problems liberates you to create a successful resolution to obstacles. A happier future results when you don't procrastinate for too long in problem solving.

You show great charisma and attract the support you need for goals. People will be attracted to your show of confidence and sense that you will complete what you set out to accomplish. You intuitively impress others with a face that says you can do it.

Shadow: Challenges

Impatience rears its head in this meridian faster than the speed of light. Being a Leo, you probably don't like for a plan to develop too slowly. There are times when you will have wished you had proceeded with more caution, though, especially if it costs you time and money. Giving your lovers and closest friends or business connections a chance to keep pace with you is wise. If you are not patient enough in listening to the ideas of others, it will cause problems.

You like to do things on your own terms more often than not. There is not necessarily anything wrong with this. It is when you constantly refuse to budge on a negotiation that people will fight with you. Rather than compromise to avoid an argument, you might be in the habit of demanding your own way. This will not win you admiration or support.

It is possible that there will be time periods in which you don't feel motivated. This creates a lot of inner restlessness and even confusion. It may be that in not dealing with your hurt feelings, you are mentally stuck. It can happen. If you refuse to analyze what is the cause of your predicament, you remain at a standstill. In not talking to anyone out of pride, you cannot get the help to get you jump-started into a more fulfilling direction. Your assertiveness is asleep. You may become unpredictably moody and have sudden angry outbursts.

Dawn: Maximizing Your Potential

The Mars meridian helps you blaze a creative trail into a future filled with inspiration. It makes you come alive and emboldened like no other meridian. The fire in your Leo energy becomes even brighter when you dip into this passionate landscape. There is no time for fear or caution. Wearing your assertive shoes comes naturally under the gaze of Mars.

Learning to express your anger with insight helps you stay clear of long-drawn-out power struggles. You can polish this energy with patient wisdom. This lets you see that it is better to channel the power of this meridian into positive aspirations. Your goals seem more attainable when you are not wasting your time being distracted by things you cannot change or control.

When you can let go of the past momentarily and fully merge with putting your highest ideals into motion, an evolutionary intuitive synchronicity suddenly takes place. You find yourself in the middle of a new reality, one that seemed out of your reach only yesterday. New relationships manifest that better represent who you are in the here and now. Existing partnerships deepen in their sharing. The fulfillment you so badly are trying to find is realized. All of your problems may not be gone, but somehow they don't seem as insurmountable. The Mars meridian stimulates you to courageously connect with a deeper part of your inner world and at the same time launches you fearlessly into pursuing your future.

Expanding Knowledge:
Jupiter Meridian Activating Your Leo Intuition

Light: Strengths

Your mind and heart delight when entering Jupiter's wide-open frontier filled with an optimistic spirit. There is no time to feel sad in this meridian. The upbeat Leo in you wants to ride the horse of Jupiter into greener pastures as fast as possible. Expanding your gaze into greater possibilities is fanned into an inspired wonderland when you tune in to Jupiter. Just get moving, whether you travel by land or mind. Jupiter responds to your needs faster when you act like you are expecting positive outcomes for your hopes and wishes.

In Jupiter's meridian, anything is possible. Your doubts don't really exist; as a matter of fact, they evaporate into thin air. You experience greater luck if you are willing to make the effort. You do need to make a move toward a goal and not dig up the seed before it has had time to grow. Keep watering your plan with positive energy and you will turn misfortune into good fortune and a mere possibility into a fulfilled dream.

The student and philosopher in you deepens. Sharing your knowledge with others is rewarding. Teaching someone what you know is a marketable talent. Selling ideas increases your cash flow. Keeping an open mind attracts new learning. People from other locales may intrigue you. Filling your mind from eclectic sources better prepares you to adapt to changing situations. Maintaining a sense of humor keeps your problems in perspective in that you may not be able to solve them in one day. A broad perspective keeps your life stimulating.

Shadow: Challenges

Hasty judgments cause you to walk into situations that take away from your time and money. You might enter into relationships that later you know you should have avoided. Blind optimism can be a problem. If you don't use reality testing now and then, you will regret some of your choices for sure.

If you become too opinionated and extremely attached to your own ideas, you alienate people. Your truth may become worshiped as the only truth. Fighting passionately without any compromise in sight is not a wise policy.

People will grow frustrated with you if you don't follow through on promises. You can exhibit overconfidence to impress others. Not delivering on what you say you will do causes others not to trust you.

A loss of hope is counterproductive. You are too vivacious a soul to enjoy being still for very long. You must feel that your goals are still alive or you become despondent. Concentrating more on what is wrong in your life than on what is right keeps you stuck.

Dawn: Maximizing Your Potential

The Jupiter meridian gives you one chance after another to pursue inspiring ideas. Good fortune will come when you stay on a positive track of thought. Jupiter will multiply your opportunities for success if you put two ingredients into the formula. One is believing in what you want to manifest and the other is making a sincere effort to give your goal the proper sendoff. There is no finer meridian in which to make a dream come true than in this one.

Jupiter rules legal matters as well as morals. You will find your mind fighting for justice and principles when influenced by this high-minded planet. Adopting an expansive life philosophy attracts a wide variety of interesting people. Keep your goals balanced with a sober reality to get the best results.

Your intuition enjoys connecting you with a romantic partner and friends who share many of your philosophical beliefs. It is in the exchange of ideas with others that you magically experience an evolutionary intuitive synchronicity.

This is the meridian that encourages you to venture beyond familiar borders, whether of your mind or where you reside. Interacting with the impact of foreign sources of information provides you with a rich amount of knowledge to deal with whatever you encounter.

Agreeing to disagree prevents you from developing dogmatic thinking. It is the freedom you give yourself and others to experiment with new life directions that keeps you moving into self-growth. Drinking from diverse rivers of information ensures that your mind will not grow bored. Abundance will be right at your side if you stay realistic in your expectations and positive regarding the future.

Career and Ambition:
Saturn Meridian Activating Your Leo Intuition

Light: Strengths

Put on your ambition hat because you are in the Saturn meridian, where time is a valued commodity. This great cosmic timekeeper helps you maintain your focus on your most serious plans. Saturn does not want to hear any excuses as to why you don't feel ready to get started on your career moves. This ancient heavenly wanderer helped guide the Egyptians to build the pyramids, so ensuring that you take a first step toward starting a business or improving job skills is well within its scope of possibilities. The key to walking intuitively in step with the Saturn beat is to let go of your fear. Failure only means you have to begin again. Determination comes standard in this perseverance-oriented meridian.

Redefining your current circumstances from time to time may be required to better adjust to the demands of the present. Flexibility does not come easily as a general rule for a Leo. There is a maintaining chip built into your mind. Altering a course of action could be just what is needed to gain new insights. Change shakes up your thinking and allows you to perceive a better way to solve a problem.

Your relationships solidify through the Saturn influence, meaning the commitment deepens. The key to happiness in any partnership is being willing to let others be themselves. If you relax your grip on being in control, people tend to trust you more and enjoy being in your presence. You are much more content when your friends and lovers let you make your own decisions. It offends you if your ideas are not valued. The right soul mate is not afraid to challenge you but at the same time will let you feel free to express your ideas.

You are a good leader. Assuming responsibility comes naturally. People see you as someone able to manage anything from a business to a home. It is important for you not to try to take on more than you can handle. Learning how to delegate keeps your life in balance.

Past-life patterns become empowering as you tune in to their messages. The Saturn meridian will reveal this information to you as needed. It only takes a willingness to want to integrate this energy into the present. A catalyst for opening your mind to these treasures from past incarnations is expressing your creativity. When you intuitively channel your creative power, it awakens your past-life tendencies. Perhaps you were too attached to what you created in past lives. This lifetime is giving you a chance to be freer in the creative process. Another theme connected to past lives is you may have been too focused on proving yourself to others and lost touch with your inner world. This lifetime is another opportunity to be true to your intuition and align it with what you are attempting to accomplish externally.

Shadow: Challenges

Repeating the same worn-out behaviors is a signal that you are not flowing with the Saturn meridian. Your intuition is being drowned out by your inflexibility and fears. Saturn is the great teacher in learning from past experience. If you are frozen in negativity, you are not going to sense how to break on through to the other side where your happiness resides. It is a lonely and cold feeling being cut off from your intuition.

You could be letting others have too much control over you. This is the result of not valuing your own decisions. Your self-reliance meter is not running accurately. There is another side of this pattern. You may be the person who is too controlling. Either behavior does not make for fulfillment. The sharing of responsibility is missing. Enabling someone to rely on you to the extreme is not good for you or them.

You might be settling for less of a job than you are capable of doing. Running away from a challenge might be holding you back. Fear of failure is a tough dilemma. Listening to the wrong criticism may be why you are dormant.

Commitments could scare you. A lack of trust keeps you from developing longer-term relationships. You may never feel ready to settle down with someone. There is nothing wrong with wanting to live alone or with other family members or even just with pets or plants. But if you are really longing for a soul mate, then this is a problem worth exploring. If you never take a chance, you will never find that right person.

Karmic patterns continue to interfere with the current incarnation if you don't deal with them. Denying they exist only makes them stronger. Whether you are too controlling or not independent enough is not the main issue. Awareness is the key to transcending the past. The next step is turning a negative into a positive. Refusing to change keeps you repeating behaviors that don't help you find the success in relationships or in your work. Your inner world stays not as illuminated as it could be.

Dawn: Maximizing Your Potential

The Saturn meridian offers you plenty of opportunities to put your serious ambition to work. Professional goals come alive here. Patience and delayed gratification are Saturn tools for success. This does not mean you can't shoot a full throttle when you are focused on getting your work done by a deadline. Showing the world your abilities is encouraged by this meridian energy.

Tuning in to Saturn comes more easily with experience. If at first you don't succeed, just try again. That is a key message in this terrain. Determination is engraved in the walls of this meridian and can rub off on you.

When you let your intuition guide you rather than try to control life too tightly, it leaves room for an evolutionary intuitive synchronicity. It is in knowing when to choose flexibility rather than rigidity that your creativity will find its greatest outcomes. The message here is to enjoy the processes of life rather than only concentrating on the results. Saturn will teach you how to value the bottom line. But don't forget to enjoy the whole journey.

Your relationships find clearer definition when you tune in to Saturn energy clearly. If you don't fear closeness, people want to be part of your life for the long haul. Trust is essential to your happiness. It might take a while to warm up to a commitment. Be patient. Time is the key with Saturn, the great Kronos in mythology, the god of time. You are probably a lot stronger than you realize when it comes to revealing your deepest feelings. It is what keeps a bond with someone unbreakable.

Pride is a Leo trait. You must locate the roles you want to act out that let you take center stage. Saturn tries to show you how to make your best effort toward mastering the skills you desire. This meridian will keep you on target with your business instincts. Remember to be grateful for what you do have, because this is just as important as the milestones you hope to attain.

Future Goals and Inventiveness:
Uranus Meridian Activating Your Leo Intuition

Light: Strengths

The way to reinvent yourself is by walking through this meridian. It will change your life in such a way that you may never want to look back. Just be careful not to burn any bridges you will need later. This is an exciting highway. It alerts you to new insights. Freedom is a big word in the language spoken in this world. If you seek to be liberated from circumstances that are holding you back, this is the planet that delivers.

Inventiveness is in the air throughout this meridian. You enjoy discovering new ways to operate a business or to develop stimulating job skills. Boredom does not fit in the Uranus domain. Your intuition pushes forward powerfully under the guidance of this futuristic giant. You still enjoy the present and learn from the past. It is almost impossible not to be curious about your chances for a new future when you engage this planetary energy.

Making new acquaintances suddenly occurs. A new romance may appear by surprise. The urge to network and communicate to a wide circle of people is influenced by Uranus. Your desire to be more sociable is likely, even though as a Leo you may already be this way. The impact of exchanging ideas with peers gets you to see your life in new ways. You may look at the world through a new set of eyes. You could sense intuitively how to market your abilities in ways you previously thought not possible.

You may break through obstacles, whether they be in your mind or exist externally. Your willpower is replenished and your mental strength reset. The intuitive instinct to relocate if necessary to find greater opportunity could occur. Acting spontaneously may shock those around you and at the same time elevate your self-understanding to new heights.

Shadow: Challenges

How might not being in tune with the Uranus meridian be shown? You could be rebelling but with no purpose. You are being different just to be uncooperative but without a real sense of direction. The result can be a loss of friends or a job. You are not getting productive results for disruptive behavior. You could be breaking away from commitments too soon. If you don't give a relationship or a work situation a fair chance, you will never know if it was a good thing or not.

There could be a strong resistance to breaking free of confining circumstances. Being in relationships where you are sacrificing your freedom and goals to make someone else happy is not fulfilling. You need a chance to experience your own independence but are not making that choice. Your dependency needs are not clearly defined. You could even be staying in a job that is not challenging enough and is shortchanging your talent.

You can become too aloof and not show any feelings. This is a very mental meridian. If you hide behind your intellect, it will keep those wanting to know your inner world at a great distance. You will always be perceived as a stranger in terms of showing your feelings.

Dawn: Maximizing Your Potential

The Uranus meridian lifts your spirits to a higher plateau. You will like the view. The world below doesn't seem as insurmountable when you connect intuitively with this mental liberator. You will require more room to spread your creative wings. Life brings surprises to launch new insights. There is no time for dull moments. The future roads may have a few winding turns but that is only to exhilarate your imagination.

Uranus rules the sign Aquarius, the opposite sign of Leo. Uranus is the cosmic mirror, or mirroring agent, for your sign. What does this mean? Uranus mirrors back to you a more objective view of how to express your fiery emotional attachment to your beliefs. Uranus tries to enlarge your vision to see the impact your actions could have on others, so you are not too quick to act on impulse. The idea is to help you move forcefully, like Leo the lion, but with foresight. Uranus and your Leo Sun sign moving as partners creates a new reality and yet maintains the stability you require.

Exerting your independence breaks the shackles of confining situations. The mental-foresight binoculars Uranus gives you to see into the future knock on the door of an evolutionary intuitive synchronicity. You may never see the world the same, so be careful what you request. This is a meridian that shows you the way to be able to enjoy the people in your life as well as have a career. Uranus will reward you if you take the chance and fly with this exciting planet. New doors to walk through that offer plenty of opportunities to express yourself are waiting for you to explore. Let Uranus introduce you to these new paths and you will never regret it.

Creative Imagination and Idealism:
Neptune Meridian Activating Your Leo Intuition

Light: Strengths

If you are looking for some style and substance to put into your life, the Neptune meridian may be just what you need. This elusive energy is hard to harness by your conscious mind, but your intuition knows how to run gleefully with it. You may need to slow down at times to tune in to the subtle messages of Neptune. Your creative strength and Leo willpower get inspired by invisible forces to push through obstacles in your path. Don't let a little emotional confusion disturb you along the way. That comes part and parcel with the Neptune drama.

Whether or not you are a natural romantic, Neptune opens your heart to great love. This may be shown as more compassion for your fellow human beings or toward one wonderful soul-mate connection you feel you can't live without. This champion of falling in love may take you into high-minded career goals. It may be a cause that captures your imagination. You can tap into a world bigger than the one you currently live in. This could be the collective unconscious full of an infinite number of symbols lifting you to intense creative expression.

You can have a regular job during the day and be an aspiring artist, musician, writer, or a New Age practitioner in the evening. One work arena may not be enough to satisfy your hunger to show your ability. This meridian intensifies your inner connection with your ideals. There is no telling how this may play out in the external world in the roles you choose to play.

Your emotional wounds can be healed. Your words and actions may make others feel less burdened by their own troubles. The meaning of spirituality could be redefined by what it means to you. You might find yourself attempting to put your highest beliefs into your everyday life. Finding ways to stay grounded helps balance your intuitive growth.

A greater faith in your talent leads you to great success. The relationships you enter can have a shared value system. You will look for friends, lovers, and business connections who believe in you. Why? Because this makes getting up every day and facing whatever comes your way that much easier and meaningful. You may appear less worried to others, because you have an invisible ally through a growing awareness of the Neptune meridian.

Shadow: Challenges

As wonderful as life is when you grow in your understanding of Neptune energy, there is the possibility of taking a wrong turn. What are the indicators that you are not interpreting the messages correctly?

You might be in a relationship with someone you idealize but you are not being treated as an equal. Your mind is only seeing what it wants to see as you live in denial. The end result is that you are in a partnership that is not truly meeting your needs.

Another theme that surfaces is an obsession with perfection. You won't find a perfect person or job. Unrealistic expectations lead to unhappiness. You are searching for the impossible. Your goals for yourself may be set so high, it makes you miserable.

Running away from responsibility can be caused by avoiding adversity. Your fears are taking over. Problems tend to multiply and appear bigger than they are in reality. Escapism is substituted for having faith in yourself. This makes the willpower of a strong Leo wither away.

You can look for too much happiness in the external world and not pay enough attention to developing your inner strength. The illusions the world offers might fool you into thinking they will make you happy without an inner clarity.

Be careful with causes. You could give so much of yourself away that there is little time to know yourself. Your identity becomes so intertwined with a group or movement that you lose touch with your own sense of self. Emotional confusion, disillusionment, and exhaustion could occur.

Dawn: Maximizing Your Potential

The Neptune meridian shows you how to master your connection with intuition in ways that no other meridian will do. Neptune artfully circumvents your conscious mind. Rather than trying to convince your intellect to let this magical energy through, Neptune slips on by in disguise as just another thought process. The result is a new form of creative perception that only your soul or higher mind knows how to serve up.

This meridian will fill your Leo heart with feelings of love, whether it be for a person or something more collective, like a group or movement. Neptune is fueled with emotional power to intoxicate your right brain with a deeper experience of your inner world. You may choose to channel the energy into your profession and relationships and to deepen your connection to spirituality. There is always freedom of choice. This meridian atmosphere is fluid in that it contains the essence of symbols that enter your dreams while you sleep. Neptune is a messenger of the collective unconscious. It stimulates your mind to discover an evolutionary intuitive synchronicity miraculously while you thought you were only conducting business as usual.

Your faith gets renewed by interacting with this meridian. You could feel like you have had a déjà vu experience while traveling through this terrain. It may simply be Neptune tapping you on the shoulder and reminding you that yes, you have been here before and please come back, for this is the land where dreams really do come true.

Personal Empowerment and Passion: Pluto Meridian Activating Your Leo Intuition

Light: Strengths

Your enterprising business spirit won't feel like a stranger in this meridian. Pluto reinforces your shrewdness about sensing a good deal or investment in a flash. Your Leo nature that enjoys taking a risk now and then tunes in to the motivating push of Pluto from within its negotiating cove. When you are in a crisis or must deal with a stressful challenge, your survival instincts will flock to this meridian for help. Pluto points you toward work that gives you a feeling of personal satisfaction.

Your desire to find love and pleasure is intensified by Pluto. You are attracted to passionate lovers and dramatic people in general. You are not comfortable with those who withhold their true motivations for wanting to know you. Trust is the cornerstone of your closest partnerships. Knowing whom to let into your heart and whom to share your possessions with is aided by this meridian. This terrain offers you a sensor to sniff out those not worthy of your time.

Staying empowered without having to feel you must always be in control comes with practice. Self-mastery is an essential component to feeling free. Pluto has a special significance regarding handling yourself with confidence. When clearly in tune with this meridian, your aura projects an energy that attracts the right individuals to join you in creating harmony. The ups and downs will be there in any relationships. It is the equal sharing of power that you require to fulfill the destiny that Pluto promises.

You feel a rebirth taking place when you find new insights and shed old worn-out thought patterns that no longer serve a useful purpose. This meridian deepens your emotions. You may need privacy occasionally to process your life experiences. This allows you to maintain clear communication with those you love and balances your mind, body, and soul. You can deal with any problem or challenge in your path when you are internally strong.

Shadow: Challenges

When you are not getting empowered in the right way in this meridian, it will reveal itself to you in various ways. One is you will be trying too hard to impress others with your abilities. You will look for attention in a compulsive way, which can cause problems in your relationships. It might be that you lack self-esteem, so you are demanding that people pay attention to you too much of the time. Usually it is a lack of trust in yourself or others that is the underlying cause for the behavior.

People expect some drama from a Leo person, but they are not really hoping for extreme mood swings. Unresolved anger issues cause you to become explosive. Honest communication would take the lid off of this intense repressed emotion. If you don't channel this energy productively, it will come out in ways you or others don't like.

Personal power is a wonderful thing to discover, but power struggles are another story entirely. Pushing exclusively for your own way of doing things will bring on a fight. Refusing to compromise is not going to win any friends or the support you need.

If you don't pursue your own goals or needs, there is the potential to attract people into your life who are power hungry. This results in you receiving very little and giving away your best resources. These individuals are more than happy to use you in whatever way you allow, leaving you very unhappy.

Dawn: Maximizing Your Potential

The Pluto meridian activates as soon as you point your attention at your most passionate desires. Emotional intensity comes alive through the doors of this intuitive powerhouse. Rebirth is a promise when you are willing to let go of behaviors that interfere with your self-growth. The rewards are great if you make choices that empower your life journey.

Pluto is often at the heart of business success. The in-depth research mode gets turned on when you want to study a subject deeply. Your instincts for knowing how to make a business profitable find great help in this meridian. The determination not to let your goals fail gets a big boost here.

Facing your challenges with courage is the road to an evolutionary intuitive synchronicity. The interesting thing about this meridian for a Leo is that a conflict or loss will often produce dramatic internal changes. When you don't run from your past, your present is full of clarity.

This is a meridian that takes you into a feeling of self-mastery. It is then that you establish harmony in relationships and accomplish the work that you hope to achieve. The beauty of the Pluto meridian is that once you develop a new insight, it is virtually impossible to act later on like it did not occur. This is the meridian that reveals your true purpose like no other.

—— *Chapter 7* ——

VIRGO

Virgo (8/23–9/22)

Archetypes: Analyst, Perfectionist, Hard Worker
Key Focus: Attention to Details, Developing Skills,
Health Consciousness
Element: Earth
Planetary Ruler: Mercury
Cosmic Mirror Planet: Neptune

Welcome to your Virgo sign chapter. Your Virgo desire to concentrate carefully to make your actions perform efficiently finds even greater intuitive clarity when utilizing the planetary meridians. You get the productive results you hope to achieve when allowing your intuition to guide you. Self-doubt gives way to self-confidence when tuning in to these planetary helpers.

Intuition moves meticulously through your earth sign. This aligns wonderfully with your tendency toward being well organized and having a fine eye for detail. With the intuitive encouragement provided by the planetary meridians, you will find harmony in your relationships, work, and life pursuits for fulfillment.

Your Virgo Dashboard Meridian Summary

You are free at any time to connect with one of your planetary meridians. There is always the chance that you will connect with two or more simultaneously depending on the situations you are experiencing. Your intuition is a magical energy that will lead you in ways your conscious mind only thinks about.

Your Virgo Sun meridian will shine rays upon you that encourage creative self-confidence. The Moon meridian will guide you to tune in to your feelings and the needs of your home. The Mercury meridian offers intuitive perceptions and excites you to stay curious about life. The Venus meridian takes you into the world of relationships to find suitable partnerships and helps you find inner peace. The Mars meridian will give you the initiating energy to begin a new adventure. The Jupiter meridian inspires positive thinking and an openness to exploring new learning. The Saturn meridian helps you stay committed to your most serious ambitions and to stay grounded. The Uranus meridian electrifies your mind with thoughts about the future and guides you to think for yourself. The Neptune meridian awakens your dreams and fills you with idealism. The Pluto meridian points the way to empowerment and letting your intuition take you to a passionate rebirth.

This tour is meant to introduce you to the many ways you can express your intuition. The possibilities to connect with your inner clarity and to find the most fulfilling paths are endless. Keep moving forward and don't look back.

Creative Expression:
Sun Meridian Activating Your Virgo Intuition

Light: Strengths

The creative vitality of the Sun filters ferociously through your birth sign, Virgo, coloring your personality with an analytical tendency. You have a natural meticulous concern about details. This serves you well in work and getting a job done with great accuracy. Your intuition can make good use of this energy in being successful at any task you choose to accomplish. Your self-confidence builds with each successful small step taken along the way.

The Sun sign of Virgo solarizes you with a conscientious spirit lighting you with a deep quest to perform at a high level. You expect the same from others. Your intuition spots imperfection faster than most people. It is a trademark of Virgo to move methodically and attempt to stay very organized. Routine keeps you focused and confident. People soon realize you are the right person to get a job performed for them accurately and with a sincere commitment to getting it done right.

Giving yourself permission to make a mistake frees you with creative power. Realizing that there is no perfect person or career alleviates putting unnecessary pressure on yourself. You can train your mind to think positively and to get good at ignoring inconsequential details. Your intuition will eventually guide you to know how to set the right priorities for yourself.

Communication is something you can get quite good at using. There is a wonderful instinct as a Virgo in knowing how to get ideas across to others clearly. This comes in handy in maintaining close connections with people. You have a built-in radar to serve the public and get them to like you. The skills you choose to learn ensure that you will have the ego strength to show the world your abilities. The abundance you seek multiplies through self-confidence. You attract good fortune and positive results through not doubting your perceptions.

Shadow: Challenges

What happens if you don't connect clearly with this Sun meridian? Your self-confidence loses its shine. This is not supposed to happen. Rather than getting the full power of this very bright Sun meridian, you are living in the dark. Why does this occur? It could be that a setback destroyed your self-confidence. Or it may be that you don't feel like you have the right stuff it takes to be a success. Self-talk that is negative in flavor prevents you from finding the joy you could experience.

The Sun meridian is symbolically connected to the heart. The love you want to find is evasive if you are looking for too much perfection in someone. Criticism is a theme that can be a problem. If you criticize a partner extensively, this creates a great distance between your minds and hearts. Likewise, you can only withstand so many critical remarks from others before you pull back. Either of these scenarios causes a communication breakdown.

Negative thinking is really the nemesis. The Sun cannot break through the clouds of self-doubt if you stubbornly resist letting the sunshine through by thinking more positively.

Dawn: Maximizing Your Potential

The Sun meridian boosts your self-confidence in a big way. You only need to proceed toward a goal and let this radiance light up your momentum. There is no need to doubt your potential for success. If you are worried about perfection, you can always edit what you have done later. If there are those around you critiquing your every move, get good at tuning out their voices. Your inner intuitive voice is the one you need to follow.

Trusting your first impulse may be just what you need to do. Planning ahead is a good thing, but the perfect moment to act may never come. It is when you let go and walk with your intuition that an evolutionary intuitive synchronicity occurs. The magic of aligning yourself with this very powerful meridian lifts you to new creative heights.

Your relationships become more enjoyable when you communicate openly. Holding back your hasty judgments of a person may prove wise. Leaving plenty of room for a romance to get messy is part of life. Working harder on problems than on changing people will keep you happy.

Creating a Home and Expressing Feelings: Moon Meridian Activating Your Virgo Intuition

Light: Strengths

The Moon meridian works with your very productive get-down-to-business Virgo Sun sign to get you to tune in to your feelings. Virgo is a very mental sign wearing a pragmatic hat. The Moon will link with you intuitively to point the way to be comfortable with expressing emotions. Your communication gains more passion when you allow the Moon equal time with your Virgo energy.

Primordial instincts are part of the Moon meridian package. These innate tendencies sense which professional skills will suit you in the long run. In some ways, when you find the self-confidence to show your talents to the public, your intuition kicks in quickly. It is your commitment to excellence that draws the Moon to be an intuitive helper in dong a job that much better.

Home is a major Moon symbol. Your desire for a sense of order at your residence is likely important to you. Even doing your job from home might be possible and be something you enjoy. Having a partner who is equally conscientious in managing a home is valued by you. The city in which you live must provide plenty of job opportunities in order for you to be happy with a geographical location. You probably prefer a community with a lot of resources to utilize.

Shadow: Challenges

If you are not in tune with the Moon meridian, your negative thinking will be showing. This keeps you from intuitively pursuing the paths that lead to success and harmony. Your inner lunar landscape is supposed to be rich in terms of deep, clear emotional energy that preserves your mental Virgo strength. This is not occurring in this case. You experience emotional confusion that has a tendency to drain your energy.

Rather than being able to rely on your instinctual nature to decipher the correct choices, you may have a need for perfection that makes it nearly impossible to be satisfied with options. You could fluctuate so much between two options that you can't make up your mind. Focus is difficult in this situation.

Your emotional expression could get blocked. It may be a lack of trust that makes it hard to communicate feelings. Or you may be waiting for the perfect moment that never comes and keep finding yourself staying on the mental level exclusively. People may perceive you as someone who is difficult to get to know in an intimate way.

Being satisfied with a goal becomes frustrating. You keep thinking there must be a better job or relationship waiting for you elsewhere. This is due to feelings of insecurity or simply setting your standards way too high.

Dawn: Maximizing Your Potential

The Moon meridian is a vast intuitive powerhouse in which to explore choices that will enhance your work and relationship goals. As a Virgo, you have a strong mind through which to analyze the world around you. The Moon helps you to intuitively clarify your choices by guiding you as to what feels right. Establishing a strong inner sense of security helps keep your mind and body balanced.

Locating the right home with the healing energy you require comes under the Moon's domain. This watery planet aids you in finding just the right geographical place to create harmony and abundance. It is important to you as a Virgo to experience being free from stress in the city and neighborhood in which you reside.

When you trust your inner voice to stop worrying about making your life too perfect, an evolutionary intuitive synchronicity takes place for you. Your mind tends to be at work even when asleep more than in many of the other astrological signs. It is as though you are ready to meet future demands with mental readiness. It is finding the calmness inside of you that keeps the everyday stress not so bothersome. The Moon meridian is always available to you. It might be when you are sitting restfully at home or when you gain a sudden new insight in the midst of daily activities that your Moon energy will reassure you to relinquish your worries. This meridian shows you how to have an active mind without losing energy from thinking excessively about the details.

Mental Insights:
Mercury Meridian Activating Your Virgo Intuition
Light: Strengths

Mercury is the ruling planet for your sign, Virgo, so this gives this gifted, mentally adept planet a special significance for you. The Mercury meridian instills excitement into your intuition. It sends energy into your nervous system with such force that it spills over into the furthest reaches of your entire awareness. The desire to learn and try more than one experience at a time is activated by this planet. Your attention to detail is refined even further in this meridian. Staying organized is done in a heartbeat when making use of your Mercurial expertise.

People perceive you as skillful in whatever profession you decide to master. Your communication ability is heightened when tuning in to the highest frequency levels of Mercury. When this planet hears your beckoning call to figure your way out of a problem, the response time to be of help is fast. You have an innate connection to this celestial giant of mental resourcefulness.

You adapt to change more quickly when you don't let yourself get overwhelmed by new circumstances. If you take the time to discover which techniques work the best for you to calm your mind, they really come through when needed the most. Staying centered allows the intuitive magic to guide you through adverse encounters. Poise will come with practice.

The more you challenge your mind through reading and give it stimulation in trying new learning material, the stronger your focus becomes. You will find greater staying power for difficult projects by believing in your ability to be successful one step at a time. Physical exercise is a good balancer to prevent mental anxiety. Taking regular breaks from stressful tasks is another good thing for you to do. It allows you to relax into your intuitive power.

Shadow: Challenges

The Mercury meridian will not work as well if you live in self-doubt. This shuts down the very fast, accurate perceptions available to you. There is nothing wrong with having a bad day now and then. Nobody thinks positive all of the time. But it is a problem if you focus extensively on negative outlooks, because it is sure not to give you the desired results you would prefer.

If you stay in the same routines, it cuts you off from the intuitive flow of creative energy in this meridian. Repeating the same schedule too often will dull your mind. There is a tendency to not think outside of the box and only trust what you already know. You then lack the stimulation that new experiences provide. This causes you to become so trapped in details that you can't see the forest for the trees.

There is another theme that runs against the grain of this meridian, and that is refusing to be organized. It could cause you not to complete important goals. It is easy to get scattered if you don't utilize the structure-oriented talent of this meridian.

Dawn: Maximizing Your Potential

The Mercury meridian allows you plenty of avenues for your intuition to enter new learning experiences. Diversity is the name of the Mercury meridian game. Keeping your options open ensures that you will have multiple ways to achieve success in your work pursuits. Mercury keeps you well organized while you multitask.

Mastering a skill you fall in love with wins you admiration as well as financial rewards. Taking the initiative to start a business puts your finger on a lot of inspiration in this terrain. Your attention to detail will come in handy as you take on more difficult challenges.

Learning to become a good listener will help you become a better communicator. Your willingness to find the middle ground with others promises greater harmony in all of your relationships. Working toward solutions rather than finding fault with others is the wiser highway to travel.

When your mind is bathing in positive thoughts, you are in better company. If you abstain from self-criticism and drop old negative thought patterns, an evolutionary intuitive synchronicity fills the vacuum.

Relationship Tendencies:
Venus Meridian Activating Your Virgo Intuition

Light: Strengths

Being a Virgo, you likely prefer partnerships with pragmatic individuals. The Venus meridian is the lens to look through to find such people. You don't like to have your time wasted. Your intuition is geared toward those who are willing to work with you to get results. This could be true in romance and even in work situations. This meridian is the universe's way of helping you create harmonious people connections. Your search for a soul mate is launched by the romantic push of this very love-oriented atmosphere.

Finding a sense of peace and comfort is aided by connecting with the energy of this shining star planet. Venus separates herself from the other planets by making your social instincts a top priority like none of the others can really do with such grace. If you want to share more love and affection with the world, this is the place to come. The mental and emotional balance you desire finds a true home in the friendly Venus confines.

Self-esteem is more than a concept in the eyes of Venus. It is an entity that is as tangible as the surface of this planet in the sky. You thrive on greater abundance when you value your own needs. Your relationships increase in happiness and pleasure when you choose people who believe in equality. Your career is never lacking in making you feel like a valuable asset to a community or group when you choose work that lives up to your values.

Shadow: Challenges

Where you could go wrong in this meridian is in not selecting partners who value you as much as themselves. This is a direct contradiction to the Venus song of fairness. If you lack assertiveness, you will continue to not get what you need from others. If you do not become a good negotiator, you won't establish a decent give and take with others. Picking supportive companions may be a challenge for you.

If you find yourself sabotaging your chances for a peaceful life, this is another indication that you are not flowing with this meridian. You may not be willing to accept life in a slower lane. Having a competitive spirit is fine. It is only if you don't know when to enjoy some downtime, like a vacation, that you prevent yourself from peace of mind. Too much criticism of others causes tension you don't need. Picking friends and lovers who are in the habit of overcriticizing you is another way you won't be happy.

Staying in a job that does not really challenge your ability is not in your best interest. You could be lacking the confidence to go after a position that better meets your qualifications. Keeping yourself in limiting circumstances prevents you from finding out what you can really accomplish.

Dawn: Maximizing Your Potential

The Venus meridian mixes with your Virgo energy to help you create successful partnerships and to find the right fit professionally for your skill set. Your intuition links with the guidance of Venus to find the inner peace and balance you need. Knowing you deserve an abundant life is a good sign that you are in sync with this meridian.

Your self-worth climbs high when you are in rewarding relationships and careers. Being around people who support your goals is a sign that you are tuned in to the Venus meridian. After all, the Venus world is here to ensure that you seek harmony in all of your endeavors.

When you live your life based on your values, an evolutionary intuitive synchronicity is nearer than you can imagine. Attracting good fortune and abundance becomes your reality when you are determined to act with fairness and to put your best foot forward to make choices that reflect clear decisiveness.

Initiating Action:
Mars Meridian Activating Your Virgo Intuition

Light: Strengths

Your adrenaline gets pumped up in a hurry in this Mars meridian. If you feel anxious to put a plan to work, your intuition locks on to Mars and moves into a very fast lane. An ample amount of courage is in the fabric of this fiery meridian just waiting to be asked to dance with you. If your initiative has been sluggish, never fear when you step into the domain of the warrior planet.

Humility is a Virgo trait. There will be times when not being too pushy about your own ideas is the right thing to do. If you are regularly neglecting your own plans to serve someone else, Mars is there to remind you to think of yourself as well. Giving yourself permission to put your own goals first is one way to reclaim the energy that is rightfully yours. This meridian influences you to stand up for your own rights.

An ability to channel your angry and intense feelings constructively is possible when properly connecting with Mars. Your intuition guides you to get good at directing Mars energy in the appropriate directions. This same expression leads you to be more decisive. You show less anxiety in making choices.

Mars is an inspiring planet to get you to learn new skills. This meridian lifts you past a reluctance to try a new job. Perhaps you have been too patient in waiting for the perfect time to make a move. Mars says the best time to make a move is now.

Shadow: Challenges

If your intuition is not capturing the Mars meridian clearly, it could be due to a few different reasons. One is you are taking care of everyone else's needs but denying your own. It is a good thing to be a helper in looking after people who rely on you. Where you get into trouble is in not focusing on your own goals. This might be due to too much criticism from others. Fear of making a mistake hampers your creative style as well. You hold back your self-expression. If you don't rectify this situation, it keeps you from enjoying your own fulfillment.

You may be afraid to show anger. There are occasions when you might need to speak forcefully, especially if someone is attempting to usurp all of your power. If you lack assertiveness in negotiations, you will not get what you need or at least miss out on a fair deal.

What if you are using anger regularly as a way to intimidate people? This really takes away from your own happiness, as it is really working against yourself. The individuals wanting to get close to you will pull away. You are not using your intuitive understanding of Mars in a constructive way that will bring harmony with others.

Impatience is always a possibility in this meridian. You may be expecting too much of yourself or someone else too fast. Frustration is the result.

Dawn: Maximizing Your Potential

The Mars meridian is your portal to a revived sense of momentum. This is a jet propulsion–like atmosphere ready to escort you into a new frontier. Your goals catch fire when your intuition joins forces with this fireball planet.

Releasing your pent-up feelings is healing. It only takes the courage to be direct about what you have been holding inside. This is the door to an evolutionary intuitive synchronicity. The Mars meridian instills great confidence to explore new relationships and professional ambitions.

Connecting intuitively with this meridian renews your identity. People will perceive a new you. Being assertive without being overly aggressive gets you positive results. Don't ever underestimate the potential of Mars to incite your mind to seek a brave new world.

Expanding Knowledge:
Jupiter Meridian Activating Your Virgo Intuition

Light: Strengths

When in need of extra inspiration, "just call on me" is the Jupiter meridian motto. This is an intricate network of constantly moving energy ready to increase your self-confidence. When your intuition links to Jupiter, life never looked brighter. Your troubles melt away under the optimistic guidance of this benevolent planetary influence. Good luck is an ancient Jupiter symbolism of a troubadour with songs of hope and the inherent goodness of universal forces. Even in modern times this same melody plays tunes of good fortune in your life if you connect with this meridian.

Expanding your knowledge about a subject of interest is stimulated in this large learning center. Think of this locality as a great reference library that encourages your mind and intuition to embrace new challenges. You are motivated to take your business and job skills in exciting directions.

People will be attracted to your positive belief in your ability. This is your best way to advertise your talents. If you act on intuitive hunches, they pay off. Abundance will follow your ascent toward putting your highest values into your work. Teaching and training others your skills based on what you have learned wins you admiration.

Short or long journeys tend to have a positive effect on your mind. Your nervous energy, which sometimes gets the best of a Virgo, is easier to direct into productive outcomes when you feel like you are taking efficient actions. Your restlessness is easier to manage when you stay busy participating in your favorite pastimes. Jupiter teaches you that your intuition is easier to activate into creative thinking when you escape from your normal everyday way of functioning.

Shadow: Challenges

How could such a wonderful meridian go wrong for you? Rather than riding the intuitive bliss of this energy into fulfilling paths, you might take the pleasure principle too far. You could lose your discipline regarding diet and health. Not paying attention to your body brings on sluggishness. This will prove frustrating when you don't have the mental or physical stamina to finish what you start. Your work may be impacted, as staying on a schedule might be difficult. You may be denying the real reasons for this behavior. It might be that you are depressed or not able to break free from negative thought patterns.

There can be a tendency to expect life to be rewarding without making any effort. This runs against your usual Virgo thinking, which is nothing good occurs without trying hard. Maximizing your time and energy is probably the way your mind normally works. A light-hearted face might be masking a hidden fear of failure.

If you put up your best defense against new learning, it limits your options. Your mind becomes convinced that experimenting with a new idea is not in your best interest. This causes you to miss out on new chances for success.

If you look for too much from others without realistic expectations, it creates relationship problems. The perfection theme of Virgo may cause you to be too critical of others. This is due to a judgmental way of perceiving situations. You trigger a lot of nervous anxiety if you don't find techniques for turning off the perfection button.

Dawn: Maximizing Your Potential

The Jupiter meridian injects you with a fine brand of positive intuition. In the Jupiter world, there is no room for negativity. The largest planet in the solar system prefers that you have an expansive vision that refuses to doubt the power of inspirational thinking. Roaming an endless frontier where your mind explores the wonders that life has to offer is Jupiter's hope for you.

When you exhibit intentions for your future by showing an openness to new perceptions, an evolutionary intuitive synchronicity comes into existence. When you open your mind and heart to gaining new knowledge, doors of opportunity open. This brings greater abundance and attracts good luck. You will notice people sending you support for your goals. Your true belief in your path sways others to follow your lead. Welcome to the Jupiter hotel, ready in an instant to serve your imagination and able to bring room service to elevate your most sincere dreams.

Career and Ambition:
Saturn Meridian Activating Your Virgo Intuition

Light: Strengths

A Virgo like you is likely to feel right at home in this Saturn meridian. Why? Your sign and this planet have an innate belief that nothing worth doing gets done without putting out your best effort. Saturn instills a strong career drive. This is the area of life that will attract responsibility to you quickly. Your management ability is showcased on this stage. The milestones you hope to achieve are linked to your ability to tune in to Saturn energy.

Serious goals get plenty of focusing power when you walk into Saturn's home. Long-range plans that require patience and determination are nurtured here like in no other meridian. Delayed gratification is no problem when Saturn whets your appetite with the rewards that come from waiting.

Learning from past experiences is wisdom gained through walking the Saturn talk. You turn painful memories into healed wounds. This strengthens your mind, body, and spirit to handle whatever comes your way in the here and now. You will be better prepared to commit your whole being to a relationship, family, or career.

Karmic challenges and past-life patterns are connected to Saturn. This celestial wanderer reminds you of your past incarnation history. But do you have to repeat behaviors that did not serve you well? The answer is no. Perhaps you were too negatively addicted, with your mind not concentrating enough on the positive. This is your big chance to take small, consistent steps in a new direction. It might take a lot of practice and persistence, but it is worth the time. There is the possibility you were so into the work ethic that relaxing was not important to you. In this life you are being shown ways to stop and smell the roses. Another theme is being too concerned about perfection. This time around, the wheel of life is trying to spin you into creating a boundary line where you can keep an eye on expecting the impossible from yourself and others. The main message here is that you have new ground to break that is fertile with insights to keep you free of going back to the same behaviors that did not make you happy.

Self-reliance is a big part of this earthy land of Saturn. Seeing yourself as dependable means a lot to you here. Finding romantic partners, friends, and business associates you can count on is stimulated by this meridian. Your desire to create long-lasting relationships is met when your intuition walks in the rock-solid shoes of Saturn.

Shadow: Challenges

What might be an indication that you are not in the flow with this meridian? You become too serious about even the little things. Trying to be too in control will become aggravating for you and those living with you. If you don't let others make their own decisions, resentment will be shown. Likewise if you happen to be on the receiving end of someone trying to dictate your every move or discounting your decisions—this does not lead to fulfillment.

All work and no play is a potential problem in this meridian. You can misread Saturn energy as signaling to keep going until you burn out. This is not good for your health and even detracts from your job performance in the long run. If you don't learn to enjoy rest and relaxation, you are not going to have the balance you require.

Inflexibility causes you not to adjust well to change. It does not help you in the area of relationships either. If you refuse to accept your differences or the unique needs of your most significant people, it does not create mutual understanding. It creates great distance between you and others.

Repeating old, worn-out behavior patterns means you are not learning from past experiences. You won't find perfect people or careers. Learning to accept that life has its ups and downs is more liberating than demanding that it fit into rigid guidelines. If you are continually stuck in negative thinking, you will miss out on the best that life has to offer.

Dawn: Maximizing Your Potential

The Saturn meridian is your road to success. Its job is to guide your intuition to know what you can control and what you can't. The wisdom gained in this land of pragmatic realizations is priceless. It keeps you from having to repeat the same behaviors that have not served you well in the past. There is reality testing in this Saturn world unlike in any other. It keeps you on the straight and narrow road to the accomplishments you hope to achieve. The discipline offered by Saturn is without rival. Managing your time becomes masterful.

A deepened sense of making commitments is part of this meridian package. Your relationships find stability and meaningful togetherness. People appreciate your being there when they need you. Perceiving whom you can count on grows in awareness.

Developing a new openness to learning and dropping rigid ideas creates an opening for an evolutionary intuitive synchronicity. Past negative thought patterns can be relinquished. Redefining a bigger and more flexible reality promotes happiness and a great chance for opportunities to present themselves.

Future Goals and Inventiveness: Uranus Meridian Activating Your Virgo Intuition

Light: Strengths

You have a natural affinity with this meridian. Why? It is because the ruling planet of your sign is Mercury, a very mental planet. It just so happens that Uranus is a quick-insight planet offering great mental perceptions. Astrologers have referred to Uranus as the "higher octave" of Mercury, because it influences you to have a larger look at the future rather than only being concerned about all of the Mercurial specific steps to getting there. The two planets work hand in hand to

guide your intuition to accurately make choices that make for fulfilling prophesies.

You perceive refreshing ideas from the exciting Uranus. Thinking
in unique ways is part of the package delivered by this upbeat meridian. Walking into this land feels like a whirlwind of energy has
swooped you up into long-range goals. Walking out of limiting situations seems more plausible. What seemed like a daydream only days
before breaks into pursuing a new direction now. Your intuition will
tell you there is no time like now to bring the future into the present.

As a Virgo, you may be accustomed to playing it safe. There is
nothing wrong with this. You may feel that a sense of order must pre-
vail at all times. When Uranus comes into your life, it disrupts life as
usual. This releases great intuitive power from deep within your soul.

Spicing up an existing relationship is easier to do when making use
of this meridian. New experiences together prolong the vibrancy of
your togetherness. Awakening a deeper connection to loved ones and
friends is revived by this dynamic planet. Making new connections
through the Internet and all kinds of networking can occur in a big
way. Business concepts manifest in alternative formats, stimulating
you to move forward with greater enthusiasm.

Freedom takes on new meaning. Finding paths that give you a sense
of liberation can be entertained by your mind. Gaining clearer objectivity about problems lessens your anxiety level. Balancing your mind
and emotions promotes good health. Your intuition finds greater
chances for being used clearly when you find an inner calmness.

Shadow: Challenges

There are ways you could not be in tune with this meridian. One is
refusing to change your normal way of thinking to the point that your
mind is not as sharp. Routines are fine if they keep you focused, but
never changing your way of operating is limiting. You may need to
bring something new into a relationship to keep it growing. Not doing

this weakens its strength and is not so good for closeness. Even in your business dealings or career decisions, always staying with the same formula limits growth potential.

There is a chance that you could be rebelling against situations or people that with more patience would not be a problem. Headstrong ideas create power struggles you don't need. Refusing to see someone else's point of view causes disagreements that you may regret later.

What if you are not pursuing your own goals to avoid displeasing someone else? This causes you unhappiness and a lot of internal confusion. Your sense of direction gets foggy. The future may seem not so important if you don't feel free to make your own independent choices.

There is the potential for not knowing how to slow down. Your nervous energy is out of control. If you don't learn how to handle stress, it detracts from your mental clarity and health. Burnout could result.

Dawn: Maximizing Your Potential

The Uranus meridian puts you into a totally inventive state of mind where you perceive ways to make your goals come into reality that much faster. This is a no-nonsense energy that allows you to think three steps ahead of everyone else in executing a plan. Having the patience to wait for others to catch up might be required. Your ability to sort through emotional problems objectively is guided intuitively when you connect with this maverick planet.

You can still be as organized as you ever have been. But when you look through eyes open to alternative ways of seeing the world, an evolutionary intuitive synchronicity comes forth. It is then that you have greater freedom to walk through more creative doors.

Making a friend of Uranus ensures that you never have to fear having insights to live out your own ideas about the future. This is the meridian that makes your relationships come alive with lively exchanges of information. Once awakened by this unique terrain, your intuition inspires you to never go back to limiting experiences. On the contrary, you will want to keep breathing this new air. Your mind, body, and soul know it is the reason you incarnated.

Creative Imagination and Idealism:
Neptune Meridian Activating Your Virgo Intuition
Light: Strengths

Your earthy Virgo nature, with its pragmatic logic, meets a very different energy in this meridian. Neptune takes you into intuitive realms that have you traveling along highways that lift your imagination into magical experiences. You get a chance to get the best of two worlds, one being the mundane, everyday opportunities to explore your skills. The other is to discover ways to express your ideals. Neptune is the essence of romanticism. The quest for love in relationships and a deep sense of purpose in a career is guided by this meridian.

Life feels more inspirational when you follow your heart toward goals that fill you with an inner satisfaction. Being a Virgo, you tend to trust your ideas, which are practical. Getting results is important to you. Neptune energy fills in those places that you don't always see or consciously notice. It is the faith to believe in your highest values. Following the highway laid out by this meridian takes you to places you may not have known existed. It is the mystical side of Neptune that brings out your greatest creative instincts.

Tuning in to the collective unconscious puts you in touch with symbols that stimulate you to rethink your future plans. Helping you find the inner strength to make your dreams come true is Neptune's job. You might work for a cause that enlarges your vision of how you need to live your life. An artistic ability might become highly marketable. The healing arts may become part of your career plans.

Searching for a soul mate is the language of Neptune. The motivation to seek unity in relationships and to find work that allows you to feel valuable intensifies in importance. The longing for a community and home with an atmosphere of harmony becomes just as vital.

You experience that your emotional and mental anguish from previous experiences is healed when you make contact intuitively with Neptune. People will sense you are there to be of service and have their best interests in mind. You attract the good things of life rather than having to worry your way from one day to the next. Releasing your negativity opens the door to great creative power.

Shadow: Challenges

Excessive worry removes you from a positive Neptune ride. As a Virgo, you have a natural attention to detail. There is nothing wrong with this and it can help you to stay on top of difficult jobs. It is when you obsess over what you can't control that you lose the Neptune experience. Rather than having faith that you will eventually be successful in an undertaking, your doubts are in the driver's seat. You are missing out on the relaxing trip that Neptune has in mind for you. Your intuition is only operating at about half the strength when high anxiety is your reality.

Perfection drives you toward great work or makes you miserable. If you don't get good at knowing when to stop trying to make something perfect, you won't be happy. Your relationships and work situations will never live up to unrealistic expectations. Living in a world of divine discontent will keep you in a state of unhappiness.

Low self-esteem could attract the wrong types of friends and lovers. You will be doing all of the giving and very little receiving. You will need to live in denial to maintain the relationships with those only wanting you to serve their needs, with little regard for yours. This same theme could put you into groups where you are not getting a chance to empower your own identity. The collective purpose is swallowing too much of your own goals.

Doubting your intuitive capability is another potential problem when not making the Neptune connection. Your conscious mind can be so strong that your more intuitive right brain is left out in the cold. Rather than utilizing the two brain hemispheres to your advantage, you are selling yourself short.

Dawn: Maximizing Your Potential

The Neptune meridian is a paradise that can be lived by you here on Earth. It transmits an energy that is easier to integrate into your mind when you take the time to reflect and meditate. The energy is more ethereal than in the other meridians but can still be translated into meaningful reality. It is especially wonderful when influencing your creativity. If you are attracted to aesthetic creative expression, Neptune empowers it. Intuitive ideas about a business or job can be discovered. Your healing energy is replenished and deepened.

The love you want to find and express is amplified in this meridian. A deep yearning to meet a soul mate is accelerated through encountering Neptune. This meridian awakens your highest ideals and desire for greater meaning.

Neptune rules Pisces, the opposite sign of Virgo. This opposing factor puts Neptune in the position of acting as a cosmic mirror, or mirroring agent, reflecting back to you how to balance your ideals with your need to satisfy your fondness for logic. These two worlds can coexist in your life and point you to ways to put both to work for you. One does not have to be done to the exclusion of the other. Each carries equal weight. If you are getting too dreamy, your reality-oriented tendency keeps this in check. If you are focusing too much on the details, trusting your intuition comes to the rescue.

When you choose having faith over worrying, it allows greater possibility for an evolutionary intuitive synchronicity to manifest. Your insights into situations sharpen with greater accuracy, helping you stay clear of obstructions to your happiness. Neptune is the great reliever of stress. Under this planet's guidance, you will find techniques to relax your mind and perceive the wonder of living with less apprehension about the future.

Personal Empowerment and Passion: Pluto Meridian Activating Your Virgo Intuition

Light: Strengths

Are you hoping to empower yourself? Then you are in the right meridian. Pluto adds to your inner resolve to master skills and channel your energy powerfully into creative pursuits. The passion you want to feel is awakened by this emotionally intense planet. There is a strong business dimension to the Pluto meridian with which your intuition can make a partner. Knowing how to survive any challenge is a Pluto offering. The best way to handle adversity is something you learn here.

You transform negative impulses into positive insights under this planet's guidance. It only takes a willingness to let go of what is not working favorably and join forces with a new way of doing business in the world. Past painful experiences are integrated into a happier present. Focusing more on putting your energy into productive outlets releases you from the bondage of concentrating on the past. When you face your inner conflicts and don't blame others for your problems, you open the door to new fulfillment.

Giving yourself permission to trust someone deepens the relationship. Sharing your inner secrets brings a lover close to your heart and even makes the sex more powerful. The bond you create is hard to break when you communicate honestly. Building a partnership is as enjoyable for you as working on a career.

Getting over a fear of failure unleashes your creative power. Pluto tells you there is nothing impossible to accomplish. Taking one step at a time shows you the way to stare into the future with intrepid eyes. Pluto teaches you to be patient and trust your intuition. Be content with reaching self-mastery, for it is the door to your abundance and good fortune.

Shadow: Challenges

What might occur when you are not flowing with the Pluto meridian? Getting close to people could be a challenge. Trust issues become large. If you don't take a chance on a relationship, you won't ever know if you have found the right person. A fear of losing your power to someone else may be the real issue, or it could be that you have difficulty communicating when it gets to the feeling level. This will keep you from experiencing the type of intimacy that brings a person closer to you.

Another problem area is power struggles. You attract people who are not willing to compromise. They always want their own way. Or it could be you who is having difficulty walking in someone else's shoes. Finding common ground is impossible if you stubbornly hold on to having things on your own terms.

Self-doubt will keep you from moving into rewarding circumstances. Not giving yourself the chance to try new experiences holds you back. Your options to find happiness in relationships and careers could be hampered by not believing in your ability.

An obsession with concentrating on a problem makes you a nervous wreck. Refusing to back off and tackle the situation later might cost you more time, energy, and money. Patience and trusting your intuition to take a break are denied.

Dawn: Maximizing Your Potential

The Pluto meridian takes you out into the deep water of self-exploration and at the same time delivers experiences to confirm your personal empowerment. Your emotional intensity is channeled passionately into your relationships and your favorite ways of expressing creativity. You discover new meaning in your career goals. You might even go in a new work direction and learn new skills.

Your intuition shows you how to stop worrying about the little things. Self-mastery keeps you focused on the details without losing sight of a bigger purpose for your actions. Your highest beliefs attain renewed energy in this domain.

Overcoming past emotional pain frees you to break new ground in an evolutionary intuitive synchronicity. Communicating honestly with those you love gives these relationships an enduring quality. New insights open your perceptions to more creative possibilities. This meridian is the land of rebirth. Hold the hand of Pluto as you embark on future goals and you will attract the abundance you desire.

—— *Chapter 8* ——

LIBRA

Libra (9/23–10/22)

Archetypes: Lover, Marriage, Partnership, Mediator, Peacemaker
Key Focus: Social Awareness and Forming Partnerships
Element: Air
Planetary Ruler: Venus
Cosmic Mirror Planet: Mars

Welcome to your Libra sign chapter. Your Libra intuitive social instincts find great stimulation when joining forces with the planetary meridians. Your intuition will guide you to clearer perceptions about people. There is a wealth of self-exploration and widening social circles waiting to be investigated by you.

Intuition moves strategically through your airy sign. This coexists compatibly with your Libra natural tendency to weigh decisions carefully in an attempt to give fair consideration to opposing viewpoints. Your artistic side and your desire to find peace of mind are encouraged by the intuitive guidance offered by the planetary meridians.

Your hope to find harmony in your relationships, work, and goals is strengthened by listening to your intuitive voice within.

Your Libra Dashboard Meridian Summary

It is important to remember that you have the freedom to choose which meridian to call on to make the choices that best suit a situation. It often happens that you will be simultaneously connecting with more than one of these ten intuitive highways that are constantly available to you That is the way your creative consciousness works.

Your Libra Sun meridian ignites your creative imagination in wonderful ways. The Moon meridian helps you stay in touch with your deepest feelings and maintain a clear sense of security. The Mercury meridian is there to guide your desire to perceive your everyday dealings with the world accurately. The Venus meridian helps you make wise relationship choices and keep a sense of inner peace. The Mars meridian pumps you with assertiveness and courage. The Jupiter meridian fills you with faith in your beliefs and encourages you to expand your knowledge. The Saturn meridian aligns you with the right career and helps you follow through on your important commitments. The Uranus meridian accentuates your need to be a true individualist and to pursue your goals with excitement. The Neptune meridian is your gateway to finding an inspiring cause and living out your highest ideals. The Pluto meridian points you toward empowering relationships and work opportunities.

Enjoy your tour through the planetary meridians. Each has their own special way of activating your intuition. Keep an open mind to discover more about yourself through your life travels and experiences.

Creative Expression:
Sun Meridian Activating Your Libra Intuition

Light: Strengths

The creative vitality of the Sun moves breezily through your birth sign, Libra, arousing all types of social urges. You belong to a section of the zodiac that is people-oriented more than many of the other signs. It is not that you cannot survive alone, but the motivating force of the public awakens your intuition in a very creative way. It is as though your mind and feelings go into other states of consciousness when interacting with others.

The Sun sign of Libra solarizes you with a socially curious spirit lighting you with a deep desire to form key alliances. Your inner being senses that you thrive on the support of important allies. Your ideas become electrified when communicating your most heartfelt goals. When you are in love with a person or a career, your intuition gets energized. It is this connecting with a lover or profession that moves your energy powerfully into the intuitive realm.

You are a natural mediator. That knack for seeing both sides of an issue is what gives you the ability to help two opposing sides find a compromise. Your mind is rich in diplomatic skills as well. If a peacemaker is needed, you might get the call.

Your creativity can be marketed in the aesthetic world. If you develop a passionate interest in the arts, you could excel. Even as a hobby, these types of pastimes accelerate the growth of your intuition. Your consciousness is directed by this meridian to discover you have abilities that you never knew you possessed.

When acting decisively, you are usually more at ease. Staying clear of overly stressful relationships and job situations puts your mind at ease and promotes good health. You are happiest when feeling free to express your opinions openly. Living life at your own pace rather than on someone else's terms is likely what you prefer. You attract abundance by putting yourself in circumstances where you don't feel under great pressure.

Shadow: Challenges

Indecisiveness is one way you can be out of rhythm with this meridian. This comes from being able to perceive more than one way of doing things. Also, you may be feeling too much that you need to please someone else. This causes you to delay going after what you really want, which puts great stress on your nervous system. Your intuitive power is lessened.

There are instances where you may be fighting too hard for an idea. Not being willing to compromise puts you right into a power struggle that with some patience you could have avoided. It is when you don't listen to conflicting viewpoints that you are seen as obstinate. Standing up for your beliefs is a good thing, but not being open to alternative suggestions may get others angry.

Hiding your talent due to a fear of ridicule holds back your chances for greater opportunities. Your inner voice guides you to create great things. Self-doubt due to negative thinking might lead you to be reluctant to make your ideas known.

Dawn: Maximizing Your Potential

The Sun meridian is a big superhighway that your intuition expresses itself through with tremendous willpower. Self-confidence gets lit when you believe in your creative ability. You don't have to change the world. You only need to fall in love with the creative process.

Taking some recreational time gives you a chance to rebuild your ego strength so that you manifest the goals that mean the most to you. Going on vacations and visiting your favorite spots for escape is a good way to bond with lovers and family.

Maintaining an emotional and mental balance keeps you ready to respond to life's challenges. When you don't run away from adverse circumstances, you grow mentally and spiritually. When you courageously step forward and show your talent to the world, an evolutionary intuitive synchronicity comes bursting through. It is showing the world you know how to act decisively that propels you into new growth.

Creating a Home and Expressing Feelings: Moon Meridian Activating Your Libra Intuition

Light: Strengths

The Moon works with your socially adept Libra Sun sign to establish even greater instincts about people. Your ability to move in and out of various types of interactions with individuals from diverse backgrounds is enhanced by the intuitive power found in this meridian.

Another key theme for you is knowing how to maintain a state of peace in your life. This is not always easy to do. You have a more delicate nervous system than is found in many of the other astrological signs. This meridian will try to send you messages from time to time indicating that it is time to slow down to rest your mind and body.

Your home needs to provide a retreat from stress. You may enjoy entertaining people at your residence because, after all, you are a Libra. But the main point is that you must feel your living quarters reflect your way of staying centered. The atmosphere created in your home will likely reflect your beliefs and especially your sense of style. The colors and scents that emanate throughout your house need to be soothing to your mind. You require a geographical location in the world that gives you many chances to connect with a wide variety of people. This is what stimulates your thoughts to be vibrant and active.

You tend to trust people who don't pressure you to reveal your feelings too fast. Lovers and friends who communicate openly eventually find their way into the deeper canyons of your thoughts. A soul mate who shares your inner and outer vision of beauty wins your admiration. A person who helps support your mental and emotional balance becomes a friend for life.

Shadow: Challenges

When your intuition is not flowing with the Moon meridian, you may have trouble establishing clear boundaries in relationships. If you grow too dependent on others, you become emotionally confused. The balance is difficult to find when you don't communicate your needs clearly. Denying your own goals to please others is when you get into trouble.

Libra is an air sign, denoting that you often lead with your intellect. There is nothing wrong with this, but if you hide your feelings on a regular basis behind an intellectual wall, it distances you from others. You are perceived as aloof and sometimes cold. This keeps you from enjoying the closeness you secretly cherish.

Your moods are your best friend in tuning in to your intuition. They let you sense the best choices to make. If you let the stress in your life grow too dominant, it distorts the accuracy through which you need to make the right decisions. It is only when you don't take the time to calm down that you jump from a frying pan into a fire.

Dawn: Maximizing Your Potential

The Moon meridian entices you to relax into its mystical way of getting you to let go of your worries and look at the world through replenished eyes. There is a rich emotional body of water in this lunar domain that takes you out of past problems and guides you into a new river of happiness. You have to tune in to your instincts to find your way into the deepest part of this meridian. You will learn to have more faith in your intuition as you see life confirming the choices you make.

The Moon guides you to believe in intimacy and not fear the closeness you can have with those you love. This meridian discloses how to keep your mind and emotions balanced. There will be times when you will need to declare your space. Meditation and reflection initiate an evolutionary intuitive synchronicity. When your mind finds stillness, the magic comes into your life. This even helps you clarify your goals. Why? Because you are then able to separate your mind and emotions clearly and hear an inner voice trying to help you make the best decisions.

Mental Insights:
Mercury Meridian Activating Your Libra Intuition
Light: Strengths

Mercury is perched anxiously in its meridian ready to come your way instantly to help you make the best choices to accomplish your goals. If you are looking for new learning material, this planet is your best ally. Your intuition enjoys aligning to the mental swiftness offered by this quick-witted celestial wanderer. If you are needing to adapt to new situations, then it is this meridian energy that comes to your aid.

How do you activate this meridian? The best ways are to read, write, teach, and share ideas. Keeping your mind active and alert is a surefire way to bring Mercury down into your mental sphere. This is a planet that instills curiosity into your entire mental circuitry. The purpose is to keep you learning throughout your lifetime. In Mercury's world, there is no such thing as boredom.

Your relationships are strengthened by making use of this meridian. When you are determined to know what is going on in someone else's mind, Mercury energy will help you figure out how to make the best approach. You can't force others to open up, but you can be a diplomat and convince them it will improve the communication between you. Your mediation ability comes through and sells the idea that mutual understanding is in both of your interests.

It is easy to get scattered in a busy schedule. The organizing mechanism built into this meridian keeps you focused. The trick is slowing your mind down long enough if you get hurried to let this energy work on your behalf. It is easy to feel panicked when meeting a deadline. Taking a brief pause to collect yourself allows your intuition to help you see that time is a friend rather than an adversary. You can slow time down when having the faith that the details will get done if you stay centered.

Shadow: Challenges

What happens when your intuitive connection to this meridian is not sharp? You are not as poised in making decisions. It is difficult to perceive the right relationship partners and could cloud your judgment in making business deals. You may not be getting what you want from negotiations. Self-doubt could be the real problem. Your emotions and thoughts could be on a collision course. That very clear Mercury razor-like thinking is clouded.

A too-passive nature in asking for what you need causes missed opportunities. What produces this behavior? Usually it is due to trying to please others a little too much. It's that need to be liked at all costs that gets costly. Rather than being direct, you are avoiding the conflict.

You thrive on peaceful situations. Your mind does not handle stress very well, as a general rule. That is typically true of Libra. This is not saying that you can't tough your way through a demanding project or a challenge in a relationship. It is only saying that prolonged worry wears you down in ways you may not be aware of until you are totally exhausted. Emotional confusion and bad choices are the result if you allow yourself to be drained.

Dawn: Maximizing Your Potential

The Mercury meridian is a multidimensional vista with stimulating energy to awaken your deepest insights. Whether you are a nine-to-five working person or an independent entrepreneur, this is a place that enhances your learning ability. Sizing up the bottom line of situations to see if they are worth entering is part of this package.

Your communication skills grow by leaps and bounds when your intuition links with Mercury. Explaining complicated concepts in simpler terms becomes a talent. Your ability to see more than one side of an issue makes you a natural mediator of disputes. There is a legal mind within you that serves you well in defending your point of view.

You can show an innate desire to deepen your awareness of how to improve your relationship prowess. Maintaining an independent attitude about your own life goals can be interwoven masterfully with those of your most intimate partners. It is in deep emotional exchanges with friends and lovers that an evolutionary intuitive synchronicity finds birth. Your mind can be influenced through the sharing of ideas with others to adopt a more open perspective in enlarging your vision for what you would like to accomplish in this incarnation.

Relationship Tendencies:
Venus Meridian Activating Your Libra Intuition

Light: Strengths

Have you ever wondered what gives you that social ease in connecting with people? It is the Venus meridian that gives you that extra edge in mixing comfortably with the public. Your ruling planet is Venus, which means you have a special association with this heavenly body. Your aura has an intuitive presence of being a diplomat. You can enter any situation and be appreciated as a helper rather than an adversary.

It only takes showing the face of a social worker or adviser for you to be perceived in a favorable light.

Making people feel at ease comes naturally. You have the capacity to arouse anger if that is what it takes to get a strong reaction for a proposal, whether in business or to settle a dispute. Your ability to sense the mood of a group or an individual is an intuitive gift wrapped magically for you by this meridian.

Your self-esteem rises to high levels when you are in harmonious relationships. You thrive on attention received from those you love. Falling in love with a soul mate adds to your self confidence and stimulates your creative power. It isn't that you must have a partner, but when you join forces with empowering individuals, it infuses your mind, body, and soul with a feeling of constant renewal. The life force seems to generate greater enthusiasm in your mind when you form compatible friendships and romantic partnerships.

You have an inner antenna that guides you to seek beauty and comfort. It is the Venus meridian that helps you to remember to take time to smell the roses. Some stress keeps your mind sharp. Too much anxiety requires some rest and relaxation. You are at your best when combining work and play. Rewarding yourself with material possessions you need is stabilizing. It makes hard work seem worth the effort. People who share their emotional and material resources win your trust.

Shadow: Challenges

What might be an indication that you are not intuitively making the right connection with this meridian? Your relationships won't be as rewarding. You could be giving a lot more than you are receiving. Why might this occur? Probably you don't want to see the reality. Your own happiness is playing second fiddle to what others keep taking from you. Your mental, emotional, and material well being is suffering the consequences. You are trying desperately to hold on to a person you really don't need.

You could fail to reward yourself for all of your hard work. This may be due to low self-esteem. Or you may not believe enough in abundance. You keep thinking that there is something wrong with spending money on yourself or even on those you care about. This is not the road to happiness.

There is the possibility that you lack the effort to take a creative risk for various reasons. One is that you think good things will come your way without needing to take greater initiative. Another is a fear of rejection. These behavior patterns hold you back from bigger opportunities.

Dawn: Maximizing Your Potential

The Venus meridian is your gateway to enjoying all of your relationships. This is essentially a launching pad into an expanded social life. In the eyes of Venus, there should never be a social situation that a Libra like yourself cannot handle. You are fully armed with an arsenal of the right things to say at the right time.

This is the land of good and plenty, meaning the law of abundance is alive and well. If you have a positive attitude regarding wealth and money, you will never go without enough to live comfortably. If you walk with a firm belief in your values, your life will be a rewarding and fulfilling experience.

It is when you make a creative, bold move out of your comfort zones that an evolutionary intuitive synchronicity comes forward. It is then that your mind looks at the world with a new outlook full of hope and enthusiasm. You benefit from having friends and lovers with shared beliefs. You enjoy having special people in your life with a deep commitment to achieve great things together.

Initiating Action:
Mars Meridian Activating Your Libra Intuition

Light: Strengths

There are occasions when you will reach a fork in the road and can't make up your mind which way to go. If you are needing to be decisive and straightforward, this is the meridian that gets you there. Mars is taking the bull by the horns, as the old saying goes. This means you are determined to get through an obstacle and take control of a situation.

As a Libra, you have a tendency to weigh a decision carefully before making a choice. You have a natural instinct to consider all of the options. There comes a time when it is in your best interest to get moving. That is where Mars comes to your aid. This meridian is full of fiery enthusiasm. It rekindles your courage like no other meridian can do. In ancient times, Mars was known as the god of war. In your life, it brings out your need to be a warrior when required.

Your career aspirations can get ignited. Going in a direction that before seemed impossible may now seem within sight. If someone or something was holding you back, it no longer is going to be considered an impediment to going after a dream.

If you are already too bold, Mars can guide you to direct your aggressiveness with more insight by pointing it at more appropriate targets. It is taking a strong desire to prove your capabilities to others with less forcefulness but rather with a well-timed, patient thoughtfulness. If you are less bold as a regular rule, then Mars can push you to be more willing to let the world see what you have been hiding. An inner confidence can be displayed.

Entering romantic or business relationships with an air of self-assuredness comes standard when you tune in to this meridian. Your intuition rides the brave electrical currents generated constantly by Mars energy into an exciting new social arena. The stimulation of new people in your life motivates your creative energy.

Shadow: Challenges

What happens when you are not expressing this meridian in a positive way? You lack the assertiveness you need to get goals finalized. This might be due to talking yourself out of an idea before it has a chance to come to fruition. You are aware of too many options and can't pick one to pursue to the end. Or it could be that you are letting people influence you too much. This means your own volition is being watered down by the opinions of others.

The intensity of Mars to get you moving may find you showing too much impatience with yourself and other people. This is a high-energy meridian that does require some restraint. Anger in itself is not a bad thing. Your anger could get out of control if you are holding on to a lot of hurt feelings and not letting someone know it. This produces sudden angry explosions. If you never let your anger out, it is not good for your mental or physical health.

A fear of taking a risk causes you to miss out on opportunities for a more abundant life. There are times when you will wish, with twenty-twenty hindsight, that you had taken a leap of faith, realizing that there was not much to lose but a lot could have been gained.

Dawn: Maximizing Your Potential

The Mars meridian fills you with courage like no other meridian can. It has a presence that instills a new boldness in your thinking that takes you to wonderful creative heights. Your passion for what you love is a winning formula that attracts success.

Mars rules the sign Aries, the opposite sign of Libra. Mars is the cosmic mirror, or mirroring agent, for your sign. This opposing influence allows Mars to ruminate back to you that it is okay to act swiftly on a choice after weighing it carefully, like you prefer to do as a Libra. This balancing act of Mars action and Libra contemplating is the back-and-forth negotiation going on in your mind. The two forces work together to get you positive results.

Your intuition is strengthened by the feisty power embedded in this meridian. The decisiveness you hope to find is only one breath away when you tune in to this energy. It is in taking a bold risk that you can be swept spontaneously into an evolutionary intuitive synchronicity. It is then that your dreams will become an exhilarating new reality.

Expanding Knowledge:
Jupiter Meridian Activating Your Libra Intuition

Light: Strengths

Your good fortune takes a turn for the better when your intuition connects with this meridian. This is the terrain that expands your opportunities for growth in a big way. Having faith in your ability pays off greatly when acting with confidence. There is no time for extreme caution or worry when Jupiter is in the driver's seat. People may perceive you as overconfident, while you say that the odds are in your favor to be successful.

A desire to widen your social circles comes under this meridian influence. You only need to exude a persona of openness to attract new friends. Your communication ability expands immensely. New experiences keep your mind invigorated. Foreign people and countries may intrigue you as never before when you tune in to Jupiter.

Your legal knowledge sharpens. Jupiter is associated with law and the courts. Your ability to argue for what you need in everyday business affairs can be shown off through using this meridian. Seeing opposing viewpoints is a Libra talent. Jupiter shows you the way to defend your principles and morals in a lively manner.

If people look to you for advice on a regular basis, you are likely tuning in to this meridian. Your profession can involve teaching, sales, and working with the public in some form when you tap into this meridian. An endless drive to learn more information keeps your mind open to new ideas. Traveling to various locations awakens your creative energy.

Shadow: Challenges

What are indications that you may not be in sync with the Jupiter meridian? You could be leaving a good relationship too soon without giving it enough time to develop. There is a lot of restlessness in this meridian, which causes impulsive actions. Your mind can fool you into thinking that there is greater happiness to be found with someone else you have not even met yet. The hidden reason for the behavior may be escapism and fear of commitment.

If you lack assertiveness, you could stay way too long in a relationship, denying your own happiness. You don't want to face the fact that there are major problems for fear of losing your partner. This is compromising too much of your own needs to please someone else.

You could be trying to do too much at once. There is such an expansive nature in this meridian that it motivates you to put too much on your plate. This will result in a lot of loose ends without any productive results. You might be promising too much to too many people.

Dawn: Maximizing Your Potential

The Jupiter meridian inspires your most confident creative energy. There is no end to the enthusiasm you derive from tuning in to this planet's generous gifts. All it takes is an open mind and an eagerness to explore new possibilities. You activate this energy through travel and exchanging ideas with others that stimulate positive thinking.

In Jupiter's world, it is okay to give yourself permission not to take no for an answer when you are trying to make a dream come true. This is the meridian that keeps hope alive if you are willing to play your role and not give up. It helps to keep a sense of humor and learn to laugh if you make a few mistakes. After all, nobody is perfect.

Having an endless faith in your potential will one day germinate into an intuitive evolutionary synchronicity. You can count on it. This is the promise of the Jupiter meridian that making the effort to put your highest beliefs into action will bring you the abundance you want to come your way. Past memories will empower you, the present will uplift you, and the future will become fulfilled ideals if you maintain a positive spirit.

Career and Ambition:
Saturn Meridian Activating Your Libra Intuition

Light: Strengths

Saturn is the great focusing agent of the sky, so you can expect this meridian to offer you a more serious tone. This does not mean you cannot enjoy yourself here. The success and milestones you achieve in life can be traced back through the door of this ambitious meridian.

If you are seeking clearer definition in your relationships, then you have come to the right place. Saturn penetrates your mind with clarifying instincts that infiltrate your intuition. Solidifying your commitments comes under the gaze of this earthy planet. This influence makes you want to reality-test your ideas.

Your career plans are pinned down when tuning in to Saturn. Putting a plan together for the future is encouraged by this pragmatic meridian. Your determination to finish a project will not get any stronger when utilizing the resources of this meridian. The term "true grit" was invented for this planet.

Taking small steps toward a goal helps you overcome your fear. Chipping away at a tall order a little at a time is the secret to creating winning situations in this world. When you overcome anxiety about failing, your creative power gets released with great energy. It can knock down any obstacle in your path.

Karmic patterns are associated with Saturn. Perhaps in some past lives you were too controlling. Your mission in this incarnation is to let go and let others be self-determined. Let them make their own choices. In other lifetimes you may have been too willing to let others make your important decisions. Finding that right balance between personal autonomy and compromise is the wisdom that frees you to enjoy a fulfilling present.

Shadow: Challenges

If you grow too guarded, it is a sign that you are not expressing this meridian energy as smoothly as you could. There can be a tendency to keep others from getting to know the real you. Fear causes you to tighten your grip and want extreme solitude. Privacy or time alone is a good thing to recharge your mental and physical energy. It is only when you are hiding yourself from others on the emotional level that people may sense they can't come close.

Running away from commitments keeps you from enjoying relationships. It may even interfere with staying on a job. You are keeping yourself away from potentially fulfilling experiences by constantly starting over.

Another indication that you may be out of step with this meridian is unclear definition in your relationships. The give and take is out of balance. If you become too bossy, someone will pull away. You might be the person getting controlled too much of the time. A lover or friend may be usurping too much of the power. Your ideas are undervalued.

Dawn: Maximizing Your Potential

The Saturn meridian is there to guide you to fulfill your highest ambitions. Your goals crystallize into long-lasting milestones. Rugged determination comes standard with this stabilizing meridian. Career focus gets serious in a hurry.

If you overcome a fear of redefining your identity and life purpose, an evolutionary intuitive synchronicity becomes a reality. It is in letting go of rigid ideas that you stay young. Creative pleasure is more likely when you stay open to new ideas. "You are never too old to learn new skills or subjects" is a Saturn slogan.

The longevity of your relationships and most cherished ideals gains power in this meridian. Your past experiences make empowering memories. The wisdom you discover in Saturn's world has no rival. Staying flexible keeps you ready to adjust to any changes you need to adapt to and maintains a mentally alert mind ready to latch on to new challenges.

Future Goals and Inventiveness:
Uranus Meridian Activating Your Libra Intuition

Light: Strengths

This meridian spins you into a new direction faster than any other. Uranus will excite your perceptions with great force. The wake-up call of this planet is meant to shake up your current reality. Your intuition will be guided to look into the future with greater hope for fulfillment in the presence of this forward-looking meridian.

New friendships begin suddenly in unexpected ways. This meridian likes to surprise you. Why? Because it awakens your intuition to unique new insights. Breaking free from limiting situations is what Uranus delivers. You will possibly desire greater stimulation in current relationships. You and a partner might want to explore a subject of interest together. If you feel you are spending too much time together, each of you may cultivate an independent study.

Change seems more welcome when your mind interfaces with Uranus energy. Living in a new location releases a more intense creative energy. It might be easier to increase your social life in new surroundings.

The inventor in you comes alive boldly when you are immersed in the spirit of Uranus. Your intuition guides you to add something new to your creative expression. This live-wire planet sends you off into a new career direction.

The idea of reinventing yourself opens your eyes to new opportunities. Old problems will no longer hold sway over you. People will perceive a different you. An entirely new peer group might inspire you to be more risk-taking and assertive.

Uranus is an air-type planet, and your Libra Sun sign belongs to the air element. So you and this meridian have a curiosity about people in common. Communicating ideas with others helps you clarify your goals.

Gaining greater awareness of situations as they unfold is offered by this meridian. Seeing the whole picture faster makes it easier to plan for the future. Greeting new experiences with an open mind and heart leads you to the abundance you crave.

Shadow: Challenges

Rebelling without any real purpose in mind occurs if you are not expressing this meridian positively. You can be a disruptive force in a relationship or work situation without getting productive results. Rather than looking to create harmony, you end up with discord.

Remaining in unfulfilling relationships proves frustrating. Your goals are squashed by the strong egos of others. You are not getting the equality and respect you deserve.

Refusing to leave limiting jobs leads to missed opportunities elsewhere. Your nervous system becomes difficult to manage if you procrastinate for prolonged time periods. This may result just as well if you put yourself in extremely stressful situations and forget to take time to rest and relax. This meridian works better when you allow yourself time to pull back and look at things objectively. You get in over your head if consistently under the gun of anxiety.

Becoming too impatient with the present causes your actions to be haphazard. If you don't channel your energy with discipline and forethought, it is difficult to reach your goals.

Dawn: Maximizing Your Potential

The Uranus meridian fills your mind with an exhilarating glimpse of your future. Your intuition has a scintillating feel inside of you when Uranus pays a visit. You are supposed to pursue new adventures when this planet comes calling.

Freedom from limitation is the flavor of this meridian. People willing to experiment with refreshing ideas capture your attention. These are the days to walk hand in hand with stimulating friends and lovers. A sense of liberation permeates your consciousness.

It does not hurt to keep at least one foot grounded while the other walks in search of alternative ways to express your ideas. You still have to pay the bills. Being open to paths that free your creative power ignites an evolutionary intuitive synchronicity. Your life may never be quite the same. The odds are you won't want to go back to life the way it was before. After all, that is what happens when your intuition joins forces with this meridian.

Creative Imagination and Idealism: Neptune Meridian Activating Your Libra Intuition

Light: Strengths

Falling in love with a person, career, or life purpose occurs under the mysterious guidance of this meridian energy. Neptune appears in mystical ways. You may receive messages in your sleep in the form of dreams that transform your mind. Your creative imagination finds inspiration in this territory like in no other meridian. Your ideals get energized in such a way that they are a catalyst to take you into a bold new life direction.

Having greater faith in your intuition is what Neptune really wants to deliver. When you take a chance and go with a feeling, you may be delighted to see how it takes you to greater abundance. Libra, being an air sign, will influence you to rely on your intellect to solve problems and make choices. This is fine, but Neptune will splice some emotion into your intuitive wiring to get you to act with more passion. Growing comfortable with feeling your intuitive power goes far in supporting your creative success.

Your healing energy multiplies when you connect with Neptune. This means you will be a more sensitive individual to invisible forces waiting for you to interact with them. You may be sought out for advice from friends and family members in a bigger way. Your profession could make use of metaphysical subject matter. Even if you are in a traditional job, your understanding of how the mystical energy of the universe operates develops. Your spirituality becomes more important to you. It is possible that you may turn a craft that was a hobby into a business. Neptune has a way to tempt you into expanding your creative instincts into a large format. Whatever type of creative expression you are performing, this meridian will encourage you to integrate other ideas into your thinking.

Finding a soul mate is part of this meridian's world. Looking for someone who shares your beliefs and ideas becomes a strong urge. Your heart wants to be in a relationship with someone who makes you feel alive and valued. If you have already found that special someone, Neptune deepens the love you feel for each other.

Shadow: Challenges

How might such a wonderful meridian energy not work in your favor? One way would be forgetting to reality-test your idealism. This causes you to take chances that later you see were not well thought out. You may enter a romantic relationship that is not in your best interest. If you deny what the other person is really like, you get into trouble.

There could be a tendency to want to look only at imagined good qualities in an individual and ignore their many bad behaviors. Your need for a partner could become so strong that you don't want to face what might be the problems.

Dedicating yourself to a cause that takes up your whole life may turn out to be a bad choice. You may not be getting in return what you had hoped to experience. Serving a leader or group without any regard for your own needs may prove exhausting in the end.

Your emotions might confuse your thinking. This meridian produces a lot of feelings. It is a watery atmosphere. It does require sorting out the details and having some objectivity. If you don't balance your intellect and emotions, they tend to collide. If you neglect to take some quiet time away from stressful situations to reflect, you may wind up with making the wrong choices.

Trying to appear helpless to get others to do things for you in the end takes away from your personal power. When you act like a victim to manipulate others, it backfires because you are throwing relationships out of balance. Your identity gets weakened.

Another theme is not saying what you really need. Hiding your real feelings and insights interferes with clear communication. Rather than talking out a problem, you are only prolonging it. This creates distance rather than the closeness you need.

Dawn: Maximizing Your Potential

The Neptune meridian enlarges your imagination to release great creativity. Your intuition will not find a finer bridge to cross over from your conscious mind to a whole new way of perceiving the world as though it is from your soul. The healer, artist, and visionary in you will come alive when making contact with Neptune. This is a chance to not fear trying to make your dreams come true.

Having faith in your belief system lights the way to new abundant paths. A desire to live out your ideals brings forth an evolutionary intuitive synchronicity. The courage to believe in your intuition attracts the relationships and professional life you seek. Balancing your ideals with a firm sense of reality keeps you focused and on track to attain the fulfillment you hope to establish.

Personal Empowerment and Passion: Pluto Meridian Activating Your Libra Intuition

Light: Strengths

Are you looking to improve your negotiating skills? Then this is the meridian you need to look into. Sensing the best way to intuitively create win-win strategies is part and parcel of this landscape. The soil is rich with business material for you to use. Personal empowerment on the mental, emotional, and spiritual levels is possible when playing the Pluto card.

Passion in your romantic relationships increases in intensity under Pluto guidance. Finding a person you trust is a road to happiness. A partner who is not fearful of your more intense emotions deepens your bond. Your intuition finds confirmation when you find a lover who will be there through the good and bad seasons.

Finding friends and allies who enjoy living life to the fullest comes naturally when tuning in to this meridian. Forming close connections to people who support your need for mental and emotional balance is aided by Pluto. Exchanging ideas with others sparks your creative insights. Pluto brings out your curiosity about people and wanting to know what motivates them.

Your career goals receive refreshed energy. The stamina to make a job or business work in your favor is enhanced by tuning in to Pluto energy. You experience a rebirth in discovering how to utilize your talents and skills.

The Pluto meridian magically transforms your negative thoughts into positive energy. Facing your personal fears and feelings of insecurity makes relationship and professional harmony more likely. An inner clarity is your constant companion when you courageously link with Pluto's powerful life lessons.

Shadow: Challenges

What does your life look like when you are not intuitively in harmony with Pluto influences? Balancing your own power with others gets trickier, especially in your closest relationships. You become too demanding and overpowering. It is usually an inner anxiety over losing control that brings out this behavior. You won't truly enjoy a relationship if you don't share the power.

It is possible that you are the person giving up your power too easily to others. The result is that your own goals get diluted and may never be accomplished. Low self-esteem or insecurity could cause this to occur. Your dependency needs are in a state of confusion.

Another clue that you are out of sync with this meridian is if you are not communicating. Using the silent treatment to manipulate others will not bring you the happiness you need. Holding back your real needs will cause confusion in relating to people.

If you spend more money than you can afford, it could cause severe financial problems. Pluto is a money planet. Ignoring common-sense budgeting leads to problems. This causes great stress in your relationships and taxes your nervous system.

If you refuse to reward yourself with adequate material things, you throw your life out of balance. The leisure you lack keeps you from the peace you cherish as a Libra who is entitled to some creature comforts. Not believing you deserve to have the right amount of abundance takes away from your creative power.

Dawn: Maximizing Your Potential

The Pluto meridian empowers your intuition to pierce through the armor of any obstacle you need to overcome. This is a great energy field in which to problem-solve and do research. Your psychological strength is a match to compete with anyone when your mind is doused with Pluto's wisdom.

Your relationship clarity finds a wonderful ally in this meridian. The staying power of your partnerships finds renewed commitment. Trust deepens when you tap into Pluto guidance. Your resolve to be there for someone you care about intensifies.

A powerful rebirth occurs when you process the past honestly. It is then that the present is highlighted with clear new insights. When you face your inner shadows, those places where you might lack confidence, an evolutionary intuitive synchronicity emerges.

—— *Chapter 9* ——

SCORPIO

Scorpio (10/23–11/21)
Archetypes: Researcher, Detective, Entrepreneur, Shaman
Key Focus: Empowerment and Self-Mastery
Element: Water
Planetary Ruler: Pluto
Cosmic Mirror Planet: Venus

Welcome to your Scorpio sign chapter. Your Scorpio passion to make a bold statement about your abilities finds intuitive guidance in the planetary meridians. Directing your emotional intensity so that it can be used clearly occurs when you let your intuition guide you. Experiencing a feeling of rebirth is possible. Empowering insights are a reward for embracing your intuition.

Intuition moves forcefully through your watery sign. This equals the passionate way you are able to display creative power. When you link with the energies of the planetary meridians, you are likely to experience harmony in relationships, work, and your most cherished dreams.

Your Scorpio Dashboard Meridian Summary

The meridians are always ready to serve you. Don't ever forget this. You are often using more than one at a time at any given moment. It is how the universe manifests itself through you. Your intuition is a wonderful vehicle to enjoy the dance of these lively forces as they ask for you to express them.

Your Scorpio Sun meridian is a key to your creative self-expression ready to fill you with self-confidence. The Moon meridian is your inner portal to establishing a sense of security and finding a location that produces harmony in your life. The Mercury meridian is at your disposal to sharpen your mental perceptions and communication skills. The Venus meridian helps you express your social skills and find compatible friends and lovers. The Mars meridian accentuates your assertiveness and need to courageously pursue your goals. The Jupiter meridian encourages you to expand your knowledge and hold on to a strong moral compass. The Saturn meridian enables you to search for meaningful work and to be true to your commitments. The Uranus meridian stimulates your sense of individuality and need to be inventive. The Neptune meridian activates your awareness of invisible forces and asks you to have faith in your highest beliefs. The Pluto meridian offers you a chance to find rebirth and to discover your personal power.

Enjoy your tour through the planetary meridians and observe how you can make use of each of them. There is no end to the insights and creative expressions available to explore. Always remember that these friendly forces are ready to be put to use so you can find the harmony you wish to create.

Creative Expression:
Sun Meridian Activating Your Scorpio Intuition

Light: Strengths

The creative vitality of the Sun moves passionately through your birth sign, Scorpio, coloring your personality with a deep, inquisitive disposition. There is a deliberate way your intuition operates. Why? Because you want to make sure you understand all of the dynamics at work in circumstances you encounter. You tend to show more spontaneity when feeling in control. People may describe you as secretive, but you see this as being cautious. Your trust must be pursued and won.

The Sun sign of Scorpio solarizes you with an emotional spirit, yet you may hide these feelings. Why? Because you don't reveal your inner world and deepest motivations to someone until you really get to know their own reasons for wanting to know you on a deep level. You are capable of sustaining long-lasting relationships. It is loyalty you value. You have no use for someone who betrays your trust.

You have a strong business side. Management positions suit you well. People in authority know you will leave no stone unturned. Getting your work done thoroughly feels like it is a mission. You can do quality control with the best of them.

You find great joy in winning others over to your ideas. There is a strong determination to see a goal through to the finish. This is especially true if it is connected to your livelihood. Helping others get through a crisis makes you a friend forever.

Your intuition builds strength as you proceed through a project. It is the challenge that stimulates your intuitive power. Taking the time to reflect or pace yourself makes your actions that much more fulfilling.

Learning to forgive yourself or others deepens your mental perceptions. Not dwelling on past mistakes but rather viewing life as a series of lessons to be learned is a road to harmony.

Love and friendships keep you energized. You are drawn to people who share your interests. Someone who does not fear your emotional intensity is preferred. These are the type of friendships that excite your mind.

Shadow: Challenges

When you are out of rhythm intuitively with this meridian, how might it manifest? One indication is that you are bottled up emotionally. Your creative power is more like a powder keg ready to explode if someone makes the wrong move. Your stress levels are high, even if this isn't evident to others. Your energy gets burned out.

You become so passionate about accomplishing a goal that it becomes an obsession. You will neglect important people in your life if you are not careful. It is like your whole being is totally focused on the outcome of a project and the rest of the world does not exist. Your perspective about keeping a balance gets lost.

Power struggles result if you become too stubborn about always having your own way. Your ego grows too attached to your own ideas and you lose sight of everyone else's viewpoints.

There is a possibility that you could resist peace. It may sound strange to read this. The emotional intensity aroused by the sign Scorpio gets further fueled in this meridian. You create a crisis just to start one. This destabilizes relationships and your work life.

Dawn: Maximizing Your Potential

The Sun meridian produces combustion in your creative engines like no other can do. Self-confidence permeates your entire being. Your intuition finds a renewed energy that ignites your sense of purpose. The ego strength you require to feel good about yourself has a happy home in this sunny terrain.

A powerful rebirth comes when you let go of your worries. Opening your heart to greater love is the way to bring forth an evolutionary intuitive synchronicity. Your entire consciousness is raised to a determined level to attain your goals. A new heartfelt pride is born when you entrust your intuition to the solar blaze of light found in this meridian.

It is okay to want things on your own terms, as this is a Scorpio trait that has existed since the beginning of time. Acting with flexibility brings the harmony you seek in relationships and in work in a magical manner.

Creating a Home and Expressing Feelings:
Moon Meridian Activating Your Scorpio Intuition

Light: Strengths

There is a valuable partnership formed between the Moon and your sign. The Moon operating from the comfort of its meridian works to get you to trust your intuition. How might it go about doing this? The Moon is a water planet, just like your Scorpio Sun sign. So there is a natural kinship between the Moon and your sign. Finding an inner sense of security is the first step to tuning in to your intuitive power.

A second step is letting your lunar instincts guide you to find a home and community that support your search for personal power. This is vital to relaxing into your intuition. Your Scorpio love of privacy will filter over into your home life, as the Moon rules this area in astrology. You may be seen by many as a private person even if surrounded by a wealth of friends. It is your inner world that only those very close to you will come to know. The Moon meridian assists you to discern the people you can trust in love and business and the ones you need to stay from. Balancing closeness and distance is part of this meridian package deal.

You probably prefer to take your time before making major decisions. The Moon will help you decipher which goals are worth the time and effort. Think of this meridian as an inner barometer that lets you know how you should really feel about a choice.

When you lend your emotional support to a lover, family member, or friend, it wins their loyalty. People want to feel that your mental intensity is working on their behalf as well as your own. It makes them want to give the same energy back to you.

Shadow: Challenges

When you are not intuitively reading the messages from this meridian accurately, there will be indications. What might they be? One is that your moods grow extremely intense. This might be due to unresolved anger issues. Your emotional intensity builds if you don't communicate directly. It results in blaming others for your problems without giving it enough forethought.

You become too private an individual, not trusting anyone. You won't receive the love you need if you put up a wall around yourself. Privacy is a great way to rebuild your inner strength and achieve clarity. But if you use it as a defense mechanism too much, it will alienate the people you would like to get closer to.

If you become too dependent on others, you could lose your own sense of personal empowerment. Your identity gets lost in trying to fulfill the goals of others and neglecting your own. The reverse is true as well. Letting people lean on you to the extreme is burdensome. Taking on too much responsibility weighs down your mind, body, and soul. This produces total exhaustion.

Dawn: Maximizing Your Potential

The Moon meridian powers your intuition with great imagination. It leads your Scorpio passion to be a creative negotiator, manager, problem solver, and entrepreneur. You feel the confidence to master a field of study, whether it be traditional or alternative. The thoroughness you desire to put into a job or project follows the instinctual intuitive guidance of the Moon.

This is the meridian that aids you in putting together the right home atmosphere. You build healing energy and a secure feeling in your residence. This is your refuge to recharge your mental, emotional, and spiritual bodies. The Moon energy sends you messages to find the community in the world where you will find inner and outer harmony.

Trusting the innate power of your intuition opens doors of opportunity. Having the faith to venture beyond the borders of your comfort zones is the surest path to an evolutionary intuitive synchronicity. New adventures excite your intuition to act with courage and attract abundance.

Mental Insights:
Mercury Meridian Activating Your Scorpio Intuition
Light: Strengths

This is the meridian where your perceptions get sharpened. This is Mercury's job. Your mental intensity to master skills and to perform with excellence finds plenty of stimulation in this home of Mercury. The world of information is at your fingertips in this meridian.

Your intuition links with Mercury to empower your communication ability. You write or speak with convincing force when tapping into this wealth of word power. Your ideas penetrate the minds of those whom you want to believe in you. Selling an item or plan gets a boost from this mentally imaginative meridian.

You gain greater objectivity about a situation. Your intuition guides you to follow Mercury's footsteps to distance yourself from the heated emotion of a decision. Staying clear-headed and calm is the payoff when you embrace the essence of this meridian.

Maintaining organization even in the midst of a hectic pace is easier when tuning in to Mercury. As a Scorpio, you probably prefer to finish one job at a time. Mercury will show you how to diversify without missing a beat.

Transforming negative thinking into positive energy occurs when you intuitively accept the wisdom of Mercury. Overcoming a preoccupation with worrying over what you cannot change liberates you. It might take a lot of patience and practice, but continuing to accent the positive will erase those negative thought patterns. You will have more time to enjoy a happier and more creative present. You will be opening the door to greater abundance.

Shadow: Challenges

What might happen if your intuition does not connect accurately with this meridian? You could find yourself stressed out by endless worries and not taking the time to calm down. Your mind races endlessly due to the mental intensity of this meridian. If you don't have methods to get back to your center, you become mentally and physically tired.

You could run from the truth. Not being willing to deal with problems as they occur in relationships or at work makes your troubles even larger. Avoiding direct communication by denying the reality of situations compounds the dilemmas. Your lovers, friends, and business associates will become disappointed in you.

Negative thinking causes missed opportunities. This is not good for your mental or physical well-being. Your goals will lack the faith you need to have in them to make a better life for yourself. If you resist developing a more positive mental approach, you will lose out on the harmony you would enjoy experiencing.

Dawn: Maximizing Your Potential

The Mercury meridian ignites your brain power. You tap into the mental toughness needed to handle many life challenges. Your intuition surfs the waves of exciting new goals with great anticipation of a brighter future. Your insights into people and your work gain clarity when aligning with this mentally crisp meridian.

It often only takes a slight tweak in your perceptions to stimulate an evolutionary intuitive synchronicity. Shedding the hold of negative thoughts that have plagued your happiness will allow you to ride the wings of Mercury to new horizons. Believing that you deserve more harmony in your life goes a long way in attracting good fortune.

Your communication skills grow immensely when allowing Mercury to be your guide. There is a greater promised land awaiting you in relationships when you communicate with confidence. You reach your highest goals when you fill your mind with positive energy. In Mercury's world, there is no time like the present to go forth and seize the opportunities that life is wanting to give you.

Relationship Tendencies:
Venus Meridian Activating Your Scorpio Intuition

Light: Strengths

Venus helps you project your Scorpio passion toward people. This is the meridian that expands your social circles. Your intuition is guided by Venus to establish important people connections. The search for a soul mate begins early if you are so motivated by this love goddess. Picking the right friends who have similar values is inspired in this domain.

An inner intuitive radar for attracting empowering people makes for relationship fulfillment. Learning to be firm in knowing what you need from a lover or friend maintains your independence. You are happier when a relationship is based on equality.

Your need for inner peace finds its roots in the gentle atmosphere of this meridian. Venus will help you preserve your emotional and mental balance. Your spirit is nourished by entering relationships and work that raise your self-esteem. You feel more whole when being in the company of people pursuing similar goals. Your work environment is enjoyable if it feels like it is leading to a more abundant life.

Your love of music and the arts arouses your creativity. You may possess talent in these areas. Your intuition links powerfully with the artistic world, whether in the form of an appreciation or expressing this in a career.

Business instincts can be highly developed. A knack for knowing what people want to buy makes you a success story, and you know how to market your skills. Working in fields that manage investment funds or money could be a talent. Your dedication to excellence makes you a valuable asset in any type of work.

Shadow: Challenges

How could such a promising meridian not go in your favor? One possibility is that you are too possessive of someone. You lack the trust needed to make for a happy partnership. Manipulating someone is not the road to happiness in the end. Or you could be with a person who doesn't trust you. Your own power is being pushed back to stay in the wrong relationship. You think you have to deny your own needs to keep the partner in your life.

Your intuition is not working clearly to pick the right job. You could remain in positions thinking you can't improve your opportunities. This is a case of not valuing your abilities enough or at least not giving yourself a chance to get a better job. Another possibility is simply indecision. The influence of Venus gets you to weigh choices carefully. Trouble sets in when you refuse to jump off the fence and make a final committed decision.

Low self-esteem manifests for different reasons. You could be buying too much into the opinions of others about you. Or you could have too many negative thoughts in your head about yourself. If you refuse to have a positive approach, you will limit your chances for relationship or work fulfillment.

Dawn: Maximizing Your Potential

The Venus meridian activates your intuition to broaden your social circles. As a Scorpio, you have a no-nonsense approach to relationships, meaning you like people who will say what is on their mind. You prefer lovers and friends who let you reveal your deepest secrets on your own terms. Passion is awakened by those who share your love of life. An adventurous person stimulates your desire to try new experiences.

This meridian encourages you to find a soul mate with whom to join forces. You fall in love when knowing you can trust someone on the deepest of levels. This is when you feel that your commitment is real. Having friends whom you know you can count on is something you likely value.

One of the two signs Venus rules is Taurus, the opposite sign of Scorpio. Venus is the cosmic mirror, or mirroring agent, for your sign. Venus mirrors back to you a softer expression than the more intense one found in Scorpio. This does not mean one is better than the other. Scorpio influences you to have an innate need for dealing with conflict by trying to overpower it. Venus asks you to weigh a situation carefully before responding with too much force. Together, when combined into a cocktail, they produce successful results.

When you have the faith to put your values into action, an evolutionary intuitive synchronicity occurs. This opens a door to your creative power. You then attract the abundance and personal power you desire.

Initiating Action:
Mars Meridian Activating Your Scorpio Intuition

Light: Strengths

Mars was considered the ruler of your Scorpio Sun sign until 1930, when Pluto was discovered. So there is an affiliation between Mars and Scorpio. Think of Mars as a cousin. This gives you somewhat of an edge in tuning in to the intuitive energy of Mars. How might this manifest? One form it could take is a feisty self-confidence to pursue your goals. A spontaneous burst of energy pushes you over the finish line in getting a project done. Your Scorpio emotions and Mars raw energy combine into great courage and the ability to stare down any obstacles in your path.

Mars arouses assertiveness and even anger. Channeling your intensity into productive outlets is the key to utilizing this dynamic energy expression. Your intuition gets motivated in a hurry when aligning with Mars to take you to new creative heights. Past fears can be faced and conquered to set a new plan into motion.

Your identity feels stronger when connecting with this planet. Your mind and actions are in sync in such a way that you can sell your ideas to others. There is a charismatic spark lit that is contagious when your intuition links with this fiery meridian.

A new boldness in relationships is displayed. You attract the lovers, friends, and business associates who are more in line with the person you are now when embracing the power of Mars. You observe that people notice a more energized step in your future plans. Your enthusiasm brings the results you are hoping to attain.

Shadow: Challenges

If you are not moving forward with much energy, it could be because you have a block in your intuition regarding this Mars meridian. The assertiveness you need is asleep. It could be due to emotional confusion or decreased self-confidence. You may be facing a roadblock due to sorrow over a loss or relationship trouble. Doubting the clarity of your decisions has you going around in circles and not getting anything important done. You could be overly influenced by negative individuals who are giving you the wrong input about yourself.

What if you are too angry too often? This might be due to not really expressing hurt feelings at the time you have been slighted by someone. What happens is that you retain anger for so long that it finally comes out like an erupting volcano. The problem here is that it may be directed at the wrong people or for an inappropriate reason. Your timing is off due to repressing how you really feel.

Impatience can get the best of you. Not seeing a goal through to the end occurs if you get overly restless and lack discipline. It leads to missed opportunities in relationships and jobs. This is a meridian that pushes your impulse buttons, so some restraint is necessary. You can't get your way all the time or when you want it in the moment.

Dawn: Maximizing Your Potential

The Mars meridian picks you up in ways that no other meridian does with such force. If you need extra adrenaline, you have walked into the right world. This fireball of a planet was put into the universe to get you moving forward with courage. Your intuition develops the insight to get what you need without being overly demanding. Assertiveness is better than all-out aggressiveness as a general rule. As a Scorpio, you may like moving slowly to ensure your actions will deliver the desired results. Mars gives your intuition an internal prompt that now is the time to act.

Moving fast without rushing is an art that you can master in this meridian. You can exhibit swift actions that make people want to hop on to your bandwagon of enthusiasm. Your passionate Scorpio nature when joined with Mars inspires you to take bold actions. Your identity experiences a great rebirth that catapults you right into an evolutionary intuitive synchronicity.

Expanding Knowledge:
Jupiter Meridian Activating Your Scorpio Intuition

Light: Strengths

The Jupiter meridian gives you a large target of optimism to send your most inspiring dreams toward. This is a never-ending oasis to stimulate your most enterprising energy. Yesterday's shortcomings don't matter to Jupiter. This lively planet is just waiting for you to take the dare and leap forward with faith. Your intuition encounters a benevolent friend when you knock on this door of opportunity.

Increasing your knowledge about the world expands your vision of how to make your luck happen. Jupiter says there is no need to wait for the right time. As a Scorpio, you may be reluctant to listen to an inner voice advising you that the promised land is here now. Jupiter will entice you to walk confidently. It is okay to proceed slowly. This ball of bliss knows you will run enthusiastically when you see the chance to make a goal come true.

Those who doubt your ability will hold less sway over you. Jupiter will help you loosen their grip. Your intuition locks on to a higher belief in your talents. Negative thought patterns are converted into positive insights.

There will be occasions when taking a trip will give you clearer thinking about a decision. Travel comes under the rulership of Jupiter. While you are in motion, Jupiter elevates you to a higher plateau, where you find clearer sailing. Distancing yourself from immediate dilemmas could be the way to solve their puzzles. The time away gives you perspective.

You discover new empowering rituals or symbols when tuning in to this meridian. Your Scorpio energy blends with Jupiter to walk your talk forcefully. Mastering new skills can be your path to self-mastery.

Shadow: Challenges

If you deny there is a more abundant life possible, then you get stuck in limitation. Your jobs and relationships lack the fulfillment you would like to experience. Jupiter is supposed to expand your self-confidence. Your intuition may actually know this is true, but your conscious mind needs convincing.

Your mind is glued to the same daily routines and resisting change. Your creative power and passion for life will take a dip. Your insights into situations lack crispness if you don't allow new knowledge to infiltrate your thinking. A lack of mental stimulation dulls your mind.

Overconfidence is another potential theme. You lack a sense of boundary or reality. You enter relationships in the heat of the attraction and later wish you had slowed down to get to know the person better. There could be a tendency to overindulge in pleasure or material things to the point of spending your way into financial trouble. You lose sight that the expenditures on a charge card will need to be paid eventually. Your wonderful Scorpio commonsense budgeting awareness is too dormant or missing in action.

Dawn: Maximizing Your Potential

The Jupiter meridian gives you renewed confidence whenever you call on it. Your intuition knows the number to dial to get this activated. You only need to let it happen. This friendly giant of the universe broadens your philosophical understanding quickly. You only need to keep an open mind and fill it with knowledge. When you fall in love passionately with a subject of interest, an evolutionary intuitive synchronicity could occur. This is your portal to a greater faith in your talents.

When you let your spirit explore the world from a fresh perspective, you open the door to new relationships and career opportunities.

There is a tireless student within you wanting to stay energized. There is even an inner teacher wanting to share the information you have gained. Let Jupiter guide you to a fulfilling abundance. This is the meridian that teaches your intuition how to create its own luck.

Career and Ambition:
Saturn Meridian Activating Your Scorpio Intuition

Light: Strengths

Saturn beams tremendous focusing power to you. This meridian has a great grounding force. Your emotions are pointed seriously at your goals when your intuition interacts with this energy field. Saturn's earthy pragmatism influences you to stay committed to a plan even if it requires your greatest determination.

With each milestone in life that you reach, this planet will be there to guide you to the next one. This in many ways is the work meridian. Your management capability will attract recognition when you make friends with Saturn.

Learning from the past is wise. One Saturn motto is that you don't have to be ruled by previous mistakes. You get stronger by facing where you went wrong and being willing to view experiences as life lessons.

Saturn assists you in knowing your boundaries in relationships. Sharing power with others is the best scenario. It is more likely to yield win-win results for you with your friends and lovers. Being able to make compromises is a sure-footed way to find relationship success in love and business.

Your instincts to serve the public get stimulated by this meridian. Your intuition senses how to make customers happy. Being flexible is the lubricant needed to ensure this meridian works in your favor. Learning new skills increases business and career potential.

Saturn points to karmic patterns you need to work out in this incarnation. In some past lives you may have usurped too much power. You did anything necessary to win. Being in control was too important to you. In other lifetimes you did not assume enough power. Your own goals lagged behind what others expected from you. Authoritarian types controlled you. This life is asking you to balance your power. Your personal fulfillment is easier to reach when you have equality in your relationships.

Your creative power builds confidence when you don't surrender to your fear. Breaking through an inner resistance to pursuing your most heartfelt goals sets you free. This is a key to redefining your reality and feeling in harmony with life.

Shadow: Challenges

How do you know if your intuition is not making a solid connection with this meridian? It will show up in various ways. One is you will lack flexibility. People will perceive you as obstinate. You may even appear cold and intolerant of opposing viewpoints. Your emotions are missing. This leads you to become too controlling.

A failure to communicate honestly will distance you from those you love. Even in business relationships, this behavior will prove problematic. The underlying cause is often a lack of trust. This makes getting along with others a rough ride. Hidden fears you won't reveal to anyone make for a lonely existence.

Depression occurs if you feel your goals are not being realized. The worst part of this is feeling frozen in mind, body, and spirit. It is hard to move forward if you don't like yourself. Positive energy is overshadowed by the negative thoughts in your head. Positive affirmations are very far from your mind.

A past-life pattern of rigid thinking could resurface. Living in this type of world does not take you on a successful highway. You feel like you are pushing three cars uphill.

Dawn: Maximizing Your Potential

The Saturn meridian is a large territory in which your intuition helps you glide safely into your goals. Your desire to climb the mountain of ambition intensifies if you walk into this reality-oriented land. This is a get-down-to-business terrain unlike any other. You can be a success in any profession. Letting go of your fear is accomplished by taking one carefully calculated step at a time. Before you know it, you will be wondering why you proceeded so slowly to the life that is making you happy.

When you learn to trust those you love, it stimulates an evolutionary intuitive synchronicity. When your deepest emotions and secrets are shared with a close confidant, your creative power grows. Finding the right work brings you into self-mastery. Following the guidance of this Saturn meridian will show you the way to success you only once dreamed about.

Future Goals and Inventiveness: Uranus Meridian Activating Your Scorpio Intuition

Light: Strengths

If you want to break away from your usual way of operating in the world, then this is definitely your meridian. When your intuition links with this maverick planet, you embrace the spirit of reinventing yourself. You can distance yourself from the past very quickly, as though it was a long-lost memory. The future calls to you to let it guide you toward future goals by grabbing the hand of Uranus.

You don't need to burn all of your bridges, only the ones that take you back to nowhere. Adding some stimulation to your routines keeps your brain sharp and ready for action. This is a wakeup call to ensure you will take advantage of a new opportunity for growth should it come knocking on your door.

As a Scorpio, your emotions run deep, right into the caverns of your soul. This is true of most people born under your zodiac sign. Uranus gives you a mental touch to look more objectively at situations that stir your emotions. You then ascertain more clearly how to react when your feelings are upset by someone. Uranus allows you to step back before overreacting to a situation.

Freedom is found throughout the halls of this meridian. Liberation from negative thinking is possible. Your intuition wants to merge with your mind and walk you toward a sense of independence. Your intuition knows the route to travel to get you to a new life. Just follow it.

Experimenting with creative projects is activated by this meridian. Something you have already mastered integrates with another format. Your marketing ability is inspired by the insights found in Uranus energy. You want the world to notice your talents and discoveries.

Uranus brings new people into your life. Meeting a lover or even connecting with a new circle of friends occurs suddenly. Your inner being feels ready to leave the familiar and seek a new peer group.

Fresh ideas crop up and lead you to find a different type of job. Alternative professions could get your attention. Thinking out of the box is a nourishing diet presented by this meridian. When your intuition feasts on the food of the Uranus domain, your mind, body, and spirit become electrified with new innovative thinking.

Shadow: Challenges

Your mind feels like a ball being batted around inside of a pinball machine if you take a wrong turn in this meridian. It might even feel like an emotional rollercoaster ride. Your mind feels like it is all over the map, with no focus. Your mental center is out of sorts. Your patience with yourself and others is short-fused. Not knowing how to slow down in the middle of stressful situations leads to bad results.

What if you are stuck in past problems and cannot proceed forward? This could be due to stubbornly resisting change. Or it might be caused by a strong skepticism about future goals to the point of not giving them a fair chance. A hidden fear could be holding you back.

Your relationships lack stability due to extreme restlessness. You avoid commitments because it seems like too much is expected of you. There is the possibility that you may lose out on a valuable lover or friend by not following through. Refusing to give a relationship a real chance will often prove to be a problematic pattern.

You could be too reluctant to voice your own ideas and to push your own goals. Being around negative individuals who criticize you repeatedly leads you to give up on your own unique insights. Serving the wrong people keeps you in limiting circumstances.

Dawn: Maximizing Your Potential

The Uranus meridian launches your Scorpio creative passion into exciting directions. Any fears of the future and its challenges need to be cast aside. Your inventive insights make for great self-discovery and stimulating career changes.

New relationships can begin suddenly. Your identity feels refreshed and is a big reason you are searching for like-minded free thinkers. People who are not afraid to allow for innovative perceptions attract you. Unconventional thinkers get you to see the world through brand-new eyes and are a catalyst for an evolutionary intuitive synchronicity.

If you want to reinvent yourself, then this is the meridian to champion. You will undergo a transformation that will change your life forever. A boldness will color your thinking and guide you to a new mental frontier.

Creative Imagination and Idealism:

Neptune Meridian Activating Your Scorpio Intuition

Light: Strengths

The Neptune meridian makes it easier to put your intuition into creative action. You are a Scorpio, which makes you a "show me" type of person. You want to see proof that something is real, whether in matters of love or business. Neptune asks you to show faith first and wait until later to look at the results. If you like to feel totally in control, this Neptune process does take some practice. You will like the relaxed energy this meridian puts into your mind, body, and soul. Neptune has a way of dancing with your aura and guiding you toward tuning in to the essence of your ideals. It is not your logic that impresses Neptune. It is your intuition that grasps the Neptune language. Your higher self or soul loves bathing in this mesmerizing energy waterfall.

Finding a soul mate is aided by Neptune. This mystical force will attempt to lead you to someone with similar beliefs. You could meet a lover and it seems as though you have known each other all of your lives. If you are currently in a long-term romantic partnership, this meridian teaches you how to renew your vows and fall in love all over again.

A profession or cause might capture your entire being. Your ideals and work join at the hip. A deeper spiritual awakening is often part of the Neptune gift package. Tuning in to the collective unconscious unlocks your inner fears and allows you to transcend them. You can discover new inspiring symbols, whether they appear in your dreams while asleep or through intuitive experiences. Expressing the arts creatively may become marketed into a career. Your healing energy might be discovered.

You feel a renewed sense of purpose. Yesterday's disappointments and disillusions are traded in for today's new goals. An inspiring energy engulfs your being, telling you anything is possible. The love and fulfillment you hope to attain are only a breath away in Neptune's world.

Shadow: Challenges

You become a ball of confusion if you make a wrong turn in this meridian. Your emotions run contrary to your logic, causing you to tread water in an ocean of internal conflict. Your goals keep evaporating. It might be due to running away from reality. Your problems enlarge quickly if you don't face them.

Your relationships get into trouble if you don't talk. There is a tendency when connecting with Neptune to assume that others can read your mind. Or you could be involved with someone who refuses to communicate. It is difficult to establish a commitment when you cannot clarify what you need from each other.

Too much idealism with no reality testing causes you to lose time, energy, and money. You can fall in love with the wrong person, job, or cause. The service and empathy dimensions of Neptune are getting the wrong interpretation by you in not knowing your boundaries.

You may refuse to acknowledge the mysteries of life. Logic only takes you so far in Neptune's world. Denying there is an energy trying to guide you that your eyes can't see or your hands can't touch limits your intuitive opportunities. Your intuition is not being given the freedom it longs for to swim in the miraculous energy in this meridian taking you to inspiring experiences.

Dawn: Maximizing Your Potential

For some, the Neptune meridian is only a fairy tale that should be avoided. For a Scorpio like you, this is a terrain with an ancient, myth-like presence full of inspiration. Making use of Neptune magic enhances your love and professional lives. Your creative power blossoms in ways you never imagined.

Putting Neptune into practice only takes a little bit of faith, as this planet knows how to do the rest for you. When you acknowledge that there is a higher power working little miracles every day, an evolutionary intuitive synchronicity occurs. Your eyes see a new set of possibilities. Your mind finds new hope. Your emotions feel cleansed. Your spirit is replenished. Your ability to attract what you need intensifies in intention. Faith in your talents strengthens. You work hard and relax into inner peace at the same time.

Personal Empowerment and Passion: Pluto Meridian Activating Your Scorpio Intuition

Light: Strengths

If you are looking for a boost in marketing your skills, then you have come to the right meridian. Pluto is the ruler of your astrological sign, Scorpio, giving you a natural affiliation with this planet. Both Pluto and Scorpio give you a penetrating laser-like focus to get a goal accomplished. Sensing how to influence others to your way of thinking is guided by this territory. Your intuition locks on to the intensity found here to burst through any obstacles in your path to success.

You figure your way out of just about any problem. People look to you to help them find solutions. This is a talent you display in your work or when helping a friend. There is an inner tenacity you possess when linking with this meridian that gives you great perseverance. Some might accuse you of stubbornness, while you see this as rugged determination.

Your intuition makes regular visits to this land of passion. You search for lovers and business associates who share your enthusiasm to launch an idea into wealth. Trust is something you care deeply about. Loyalty from others makes you want to know them on the deepest of levels. You are not going to share your secrets with just anyone.

Pluto holds the key to your self-mastery. Channeling your energy wisely is learned when making use of this meridian. Finding the confidence to show your ability to the world attracts greater abundance. Your intuition senses the right time to invest in a business or to make a career change.

You experience a rebirth when you shed your inner fears. It is as though a new identity has been discovered. The past no longer need haunt you. Facing your negative thinking makes it easier for your intuition to move into positive new thoughts. Being grateful for what you have paves the way for harmony.

You cherish authenticity. People who speak the truth and do what they promise win your support. These are qualities you hope to find in a soul mate. You are more capable of long-lasting relationships when you are willing to work though problems and learn the art of forgiveness.

Shadow: Challenges

What happens when you don't make a clear connection with this meridian? You start blaming others for your own problems. Being overly critical doesn't win the support from people you need. Power struggles interfere with the harmony you would prefer.

If you don't assume your own personal power, there is the possibility that you will attract individuals who are too controlling. Your goals won't get accomplished because you feel a need to please someone. This could be due to a fear of losing the relationship if you try to be yourself. The problem here is that you must deny your own needs to stay in this type of partnership.

Manipulating others to get your own way will eventually backfire. Resentment will set in by those you are using this type of behavior on. This is usually due to a lack of trust. Your relationships with friends, lovers, or family members will lack the depth you need.

Obsessive behaviors could be due to refusing to face problems. Taking any desire to the extreme throws your life out of balance. There could be a work, food, or sex obsession as a way not to deal with personal problems.

Dawn: Maximizing Your Potential

The Pluto meridian is a launching pad to empower yourself. It offers an intensity to get a plan moving forward like no other meridian does with such force. When channeled productively, your emotional energy gives rise to a new career or business. There is a wonderful passion for life that gives you a feeling of renewal.

Undergoing an inner transformation deepens your psychological strength and is a catalyst for an evolutionary intuitive synchronicity. You have a lot more to give to a relationship when you go through this process. This is an intuitive rebirth that takes you to the abundance you hope to find. Your relationships and professional experiences seem more rewarding. This is a meridian that opens you up to the mysteries of life and a greater awareness of invisible forces at work. Your personal power finds a magical confirmation here.

—— *Chapter 10* ——

SAGITTARIUS

Sagittarius (11/22–12/21)

Archetypes: Teacher, World Traveler, Student, Philosopher
Key Focus: Expansion and Quest for New Knowledge
Element: Fire
Planetary Ruler: Jupiter
Cosmic Mirror Planet: Mercury

Welcome to your Sagittarius sign chapter. Your Sagittarius fondness for travel on both the mental and physical levels gets further intuitive inspiration when connecting with the planetary meridians. Your intuition can guide you to explore life with an open mind eager to exchange ideas with others. This maintains that natural tendency you possess to expand your options for success.

Intuition moves restlessly through your fiery sign as though it can't wait to take you on the next adventure. This goes well with your innate desire to keep your mind stimulated with new ideas. There is no time for boredom. When you make a solid connection with the planetary meridians, the doors open to new relationships, exhilarating work opportunities, and renewed faith in your goals.

Your Sagittarius Dashboard Meridian Summary

You like to move in more than one direction at a time, which is typical of a Sagittarius. It is predictable that you will pull from more than one meridian at a time. It is what makes life interesting. Exploring these wonderful energy expressions expands your horizons and opens up your perceptions to a wide variety of opportunities.

Your Sagittarius Sun meridian is a chance to display your creative self-confidence and to let the world see your abilities. The Moon meridian shows you how to tune in to your feelings and find the right location for success. The Mercury meridian is there to enable clearer mental perceptions and accelerate your learning processes. The Venus meridian guides you to establish meaningful relationships and find a sense of peace. The Mars meridian activates your courage and the drive to initiate goals. The Jupiter meridian points the way to increase faith in your talents and expand your knowledge. The Saturn meridian helps you determine a career path and establish clearly defined commitments. The Uranus meridian excites your vision of the future and awakens your need to be an individualist. The Neptune meridian reminds you to be true to your ideals and to believe in your highest values. The Pluto meridian is your gateway to personal empowerment and self-mastery.

Enjoy your introduction to the planetary meridians. Each has a particular energy expression to help you find the happiness you are hoping to find. There are many paths awaiting you to explore. Never forget that these planetary forces await your call to assist you in realizing your highest potential.

Creative Expression:
Sun Meridian Activating Your Sagittarius Intuition

Light: Strengths

The creative vitality of the Sun moves swiftly through your birth sign, Sagittarius, coloring your personality with an upbeat nature. Your eyes will appear to many to be burning with truth oil. There is optimism running through every cell of your body. Your mind is usually optimistic. You don't like investing much time in negative pursuits, as this feels like death to you. Your intuition longs for adventure. Boredom seems like it is from another galaxy and does not belong in your world. You are a restless soul.

Sagittarius moves so fast that it appears actions and intuition occur simultaneously. It should be said that at times your fiery mind might not even be aware that intuition is leading the charge forward. Occasionally slowing down allows your intuition to make the right connection to this meridian and make the right decision in the nick of time.

The Sun sign of Sagittarius solarizes you with a curious spirit lighting you with a thirst for knowledge. How might the Sun go about activating your intuition? It is the anticipation of new experiences that stimulates your intuition. It makes you dream of a better tomorrow and put your ideas to work. It is when you tirelessly shoot your arrows toward a more promising future that your creative power manifests strongly. When you do focus on a plan or your favorite subjects, you attain high levels of self-mastery. A goal must be interesting enough to keep you desiring to follow it through to the end.

You are a student, teacher, and philosopher rolled into one package. It is your multidimensional mind that attracts lovers, friends, and business connections in a magnetic way. You talk about a wide variety of newsworthy items, as your mind is interested in the whole world.

Some people view you as a fascinating conversationalist, while others think you could not be aware of so many topics.

You will argue to prove a point. When you show you can listen, people are more receptive to your way of thinking. There is a fine legal instinct in your thoughts. Justice and truth are highly valued. Your favorite people like this about you. A keen sense of humor keeps life in perspective. It is your unrelenting great faith in your abilities that attracts good fortune and abundance.

Shadow: Challenges

How might you not be in tune with this Sun meridian? Overconfidence can be a haunting problem for a Sagittarius. That beautiful self-confidence snowballs into a complete exaggeration of your ability. It is a leap of faith that needs sound reality testing. When you don't know your limits, you promise more than you can deliver, which upsets people. Not gauging your boundary lines accurately gets you into trouble.

A lack of effort puts out your creative fire before it really gets going. You expect things to come too easily. There is a relaxed intuitive feeling running through your sign that can cause an illusion that time will wait for you. It isn't really true. Deadlines will come and leave you behind. Procrastination results, leading to frustration.

Another indicator you are off your game in this meridian is being overly opinionated. You refuse to lose a dispute. The spirit of agreeing to disagree is missing. This causes stress in your life and disrupts good relationships. People will perceive you as too judgmental if you are intolerant of opposing points of view.

A final symptom of being out of step in this meridian is not allowing for an expansion of your learning. Losing interest in staying aware of new trends causes missed opportunities for growth. That insatiable appetite for knowledge is not activated, and this makes your intuition dull and not ready to jump on new abundant dreams.

Dawn: Maximizing Your Potential

The Sun meridian lifts your creativity to new heights. Think of this energy as a cheerleader for your intuition. The Sun wants to guide you to the confidence to let your talent shine. Your optimism will never fail you if you keep believing in it. Luck and good fortune come your way when you keep a positive mind.

Allowing your mind to be exposed to innovative ideas is the surest key to unlocking an evolutionary intuitive synchronicity. You were meant to come into this life to never feel as though there was one ultimate truth or path. Your feet are supposed to walk an assortment of trails that offer information from a wide variety of sources. Your sense of well-being stays on high ground when you remain open to new learning. Your relationships and professional life remain inspiring if you share your resources happily and generously.

Creating a Home and Expressing Feelings:
Moon Meridian Activating Your Sagittarius Intuition

Light: Strengths

You were meant to roam. That is what being a Sagittarius is all about. Even if you are not well traveled to many scenic places, you are an inner explorer and still keep one eye on the world. Many people born under your astrological sign travel on the mental and physical levels.

The Moon accompanies your adventurous Sun sign with a security-oriented instinct. Sooner or later, you are glad to return home. The Moon influences your intuition to guide you to create a residence that supports your need for plenty of mental stimulation. You need to reside in a geographical location offering opportunities for growth. If you are in a remote location far from a city, your home must be filled with the right technology and books to keep your mind occupied.

Sagittarians are known to leave their hometown early in a spirit of looking for a new frontier and a desire to spread their wings. Lunar intuition inspires you to gaze at distant skies, feeling you belong there. Restless urges make you want to explore foreign frontiers.

The more you communicate your ideas openly, the more people like you. Romances and friendships flourish when you support the goals of others. This meridian brings out your emotional warmth. You are internally stronger when letting your closest allies know your inner thoughts. You tend to trust that people will do the same for you.

You like to feel needed but at the same time intuitively know you require a lot of breathing room. You enjoy a lover or friend who is not too demanding of your time. There is an independent side of you that must feel free to wander the globe, whether doing so physically or mentally.

This Moon meridian shows you to be somewhat hard to figure out emotionally until your identity is secure. You prefer to be perceived as an individualist and yet long to have your logic understood. When someone shows an ability and willingness to tune in to your mental framework, this individual is a friend forever.

Shadow: Challenges

You can be a constantly rolling stone if you miss the mark in this meridian. That in itself is not a bad thing. It is only if you have difficulty getting focused that it becomes a problem. Experimentation and self-discovery are great to explore through travel. It is when you are running away from responsibility and not facing problems that escapism becomes an issue.

Never expressing feelings is a form of denial. You stay on the intellectual level as a method of evading closeness with others. You are difficult to know if you do not reveal much emotion. This symbolizes a blocked intuition as well. You will be seen as impersonal and aloof.

Your moods can make you unpredictable, warm and friendly one moment and quiet and withdrawn the next. It makes it a challenge to maintain a clear communication with you. You may have anger brewing or pent-up feelings you are hiding.

Dawn: Maximizing Your Potential

The Moon meridian strengthens your intuitive confidence. When you walk into this lunar kingdom, your intellect softens and you find humility. The Moon asks your willpower to be somewhat reflective to gain greater emotional clarity. It is then that your fiery Sagittarius actions and moods combine to show off your creative expertise. Patience is not easy to come by for a fire sign like yourself. It comes with practice but is worth developing. It deepens the intuitive connection between you and lovers, friends, and family members. Even in the business world, you make sounder decisions when taking your time.

Letting the Moon guide you to deep instincts for self-discovery gives you a sense of inner peace. Knowing when to act on impulse is wisdom learned in this meridian. Opening your mind to knowledge from the four corners of the earth stimulates an evolutionary intuitive synchronicity. You came into this life as a seeker of truth and to share inspiring ideas. Let the Moon bring you home to this intuitive purpose.

Mental Insights:
Mercury Meridian Activating Your Sagittarius Intuition

Light: Strengths

The universe gave you Mercury to keep your Sagittarius mind as curious as it can be. The Mercury meridian complements your Sagittarius thinking perfectly. Why? Your intuition connects the dots between this mentally clever planet and your Sagittarius openness to new learning. This is a match that is as smooth as a captivating sunrise over an ocean.

If you want to sharpen your communication skills, this is the correct meridian. Your perceptions about people and business grow quickly when your intuition links with the fast-thinking Mercury. You can think your way out of any problem. Insight is at your fingertips.

Your writing and speaking skills get revved up in this landscape. Your intuition enjoys the many mental highways featured in this meridian. Your perceptions about life deepen. Sensing how to quickly take advantage of new opportunities is a gift from this domain.

Being able to prioritize the details in order of importance becomes an artform. Seeing your way through a maze of information is enhanced in this meridian. The little things seem to fall into place rather than distract you.

Tuning in to your ability comes with patience and practice. When you are able to consistently focus your fiery energy, there are no limits on what you can accomplish. Keeping a positive mind is vital to your success.

Shadow: Challenges

If you make the wrong turn in this meridian, how might you know? Your attention to detail will be diluted. You may be so concentrated on large dreams that you miss the key steps to getting them done. This feels self-defeating, which frustrates you to no end.

Your mind can be forever racing. This is due to excessive worry. If you don't learn how to stop and relax, it drains your energy. There is a tendency to act on impulse without thinking through your options.

You could become too critical of others by placing too much emphasis on your own opinions. That Sagittarius openness and humor are missing. An underlying negative outlook is driving this behavior.

Dawn: Maximizing Your Potential

The Mercury meridian entertains your Sagittarius mind in multiple ways. Your love of learning and sharing knowledge is accelerated in this fast-moving terrain. A desire to travel the world of books or the globe is stimulated by Mercury. Putting what you learn into pragmatic use is yet another dimension of Mercury's world.

Mercury rules Gemini, the opposite sign of Sagittarius. This opposing factor shows Mercury serving as a cosmic mirror, or mirroring agent, to reflect back to you how to keep one eye on details and the other on the larger goals you have. Think of Mercury representing the trees and Sagittarius the forest. You need both. Your ideas, when part of a larger plan, intensify your intuitive power.

Diversifying your skills makes them a marketable commodity. You detest and likely fear boredom. This meridian will keep calling to your intuition to cross into its borders with an open heart. Having your mind on ready alert for growth opportunities sparks an evolutionary intuitive synchronicity.

Relationship Tendencies:
Venus Meridian Activating Your Sagittarius Intuition
Light: Strengths

Venus blends right in with that part of your personality that's never met a stranger. Your intuition flies high in this meridian, interacting with people from many diverse backgrounds. In many respects you seem like a citizen of the world. The traveler in you is never far from your heart. Your soul-felt dedication to being a student of life will have you filling your mind with a multitude of experiences.

Venus is connected to what you value. Friendship is probably held in high regard by you. Your attraction to individuals with similar beliefs is strong. You sustain close connections with people having a far different belief system as long as there is a mutual respect for one another.

You are lost when your self-worth is low. It goes totally against the grain of your Sagittarius self-confidence. You came into this life with your inspiration levels soaring. You are at your best when acknowledging this.

A soul mate keeps you balanced mentally and emotionally. You may possess a ferociously independent streak, which comes standard with your sign. Yet there is a longing deep in your being to find a compatible lover. You feel empty when living only for yourself. It takes a cause or a special relationship to elevate your intuitive power. A marriage of the minds is more important to you than having to spend every waking moment together. You admire someone who gives you the space to discover your true potential. After all, you may feel it is your birthright to go off in search of a new, exhilarating goal. It is reassuring to have the encouragement and affection of a close, supportive partner.

Shadow: Challenges

The freedom urge could get away from you. If you don't link to this meridian accurately, your relationships become confusing. You get swept up into too much self-focus. This will derail important friendships. Or another possibility is that you are involved with a lover or friend who demands all of your attention. In this scenario, you are no better off than in the previous one described. If you are trying too hard to be a people pleaser, your own needs and goals get left out in the cold.

Another way you are off-center with this meridian is relaxing too much. Your ambition grows sluggish. It is difficult to focus on a serious plan. You might be expecting others to be too much of an inspirational force. They can't possibly live up to unrealistic expectations. Your self-starting drive needs a jumpstart.

Indecision results from creating too many options. Your intuition is not sure which direction to guide you. You become frustrated by being over-expansive and not getting far from the starting gate.

Dawn: Maximizing Your Potential

The Venus meridian spices up your social awareness. Your outgoing personality enjoys riding the relationship waves offered in this people-oriented terrain. Even if you happen to be a shy Sagittarius, your energy can connect intuitively to be more confident in making new friends and expanding a peer group.

Your communication skills may be shown more confidently to the public. People sense a new ease in your words. That is the reward for linking to this socially adept landscape. You can market your teaching, writing, sales, and consulting talents in a professional setting.

Being true to your belief system initiates an evolutionary intuitive synchronicity. Faith in your knowledge propels you into inspirational endeavors. You attract harmonious lovers and friends through adopting a philosophy containing an eclectic influence. It is your ability to walk in someone else's shoes that makes people want to remain close to you for a lifetime.

Initiating Action:
Mars Meridian Activating Your Sagittarius Intuition
Light: Strengths

A Sagittarius like yourself is right at home with the Mars meridian. You are a fire sign, so mixing with this fiery planet brings out your passion to act boldly. Obstructions better get out of your way. Blasting through obstacles is easier when your intuition links with Mars. Your self-confidence is lit fast in this hot domain that breathes courage. You don't have time to think about what you can't do.

Your idealism wants to influence others. You hope to motivate people to be as enthusiastic about their goals as you are about your own. Your intuition often finds optimism long before your mind figures it out.

Directing your energy constructively pays dividends. You get much work finished in a short amount of time. It is vital that if you are doing a job or learning a new skill, your interest is grabbed quickly. The connection needs to happen spontaneously before you move on to something entirely different.

You must have future goals. Why? It is what keeps you mentally happy and alert. You need the reassurance there will be opportunities for growth and expansion awaiting you. It keeps the pilot light of your intuition shining brightly and alert for that next chance to express your dream for success.

You are the defender of your principles and sometimes even for an organization. Your friends and business peers will appreciate this about you. Your feisty attitude to protect those you care about wins their loyalty and admiration.

You like the pursuit of love. Relationships need to have a bit of intrigue in them. It piques your interest in a person to know you must win their attention. There is a natural romantic in you that attracts lovers. When you show you can be trusted with feelings and resources, you never fear being alone for long.

Shadow: Challenges

What are the warning signs that you could be off-target in this meridian? One is becoming too expansive, which is an easy role for a Sagittarius to play. This causes you to have trouble getting a project started. Your mind is distracted by many other ways to be entertained. You might begin a job or move toward a goal but quickly lose interest. The idea of having to put all of your eggs in one basket is intimidating. You can't stand not having a convenient escape to greener pastures.

Angry outbursts are another possible negative expression of this meridian energy. You react too quickly to people disagreeing with you. There is a tendency to be too defensive of an idea. Fighting for what you believe is fine, but attacking someone for fear of losing an argument will cause great friction in your relationships. Communication breakdowns result.

Anger turned inward is self-defeating. It causes you to negate your chances for an abundant and harmonious life. Denying positive thinking causes sorrow and missed chances for success when they appear.

If you lack assertiveness, your needs don't get met. This is probably due to being easily talked out of your own ideas. Buying into negative input from critical tongues derails your hopes and wishes.

Dawn: Maximizing Your Potential

The Mars meridian elevates your creative power in a big way. Your charisma is enlarged when you take an intuitive plunge into this energy-producing engine. Your courage to pursue your dreams will not want to play second fiddle to anyone. The time is now is a Mars mantra.

Taking your knowledge into the world assertively ignites an evolutionary intuitive synchronicity. Your passion for your ideas will get the ear of others. It is your belief in an idea that makes people want to support it.

Expressing your emotional intensity with a great awareness of its impact is wisdom learned. Your honesty and integrity attract attention. You are at your best when sharing your insights with the world. Your favorite friends and lovers have a common interest in self-growth and are not afraid to experiment with a new adventure.

Expanding Knowledge:
Jupiter Meridian Activating Your Sagittarius Intuition

Light: Strengths

An enterprising spirit is what you gain when you tap into this gold-mine of optimism. Jupiter is the planet that rules Sagittarius. This indicates that you have the inside track in utilizing this good-luck planet. Thinking big is Jupiter language. Daring to fulfill your hopes for abundance is never truly beyond your reach. Staying positive in thought is the surest way to bring Jupiter into successful expression.

You are good at convincing others to invest in your talent. The art of persuasion is a gift from this meridian. When you fall in love with a profession, your drive to make it a success finds no rival when Jupiter is at your side.

Training others to learn your skills comes naturally when your intuition links to Jupiter. The teacher in you enjoys being displayed. Friends, family, lovers, and work colleagues will depend on your insights. Being generous in lending support makes you a special person in the lives of many.

Your creative power is inspired through travel and expanding your knowledge. Staying mentally alert by taking in information through books and other sources available to you opens doors of opportunity.

Your adaptability allows you to accept change better than many. Dealing with adversity by maintaining a calm and upbeat attitude keeps your problem-solving perceptions sharp. It is your faith that everything will turn out for the best that allows you to land on your feet.

You tend to stay in relationships that promise growth and stimulate your mind. Work that holds your interest by offering advancement or appeals to your belief system is more likely to keep you there. You have an insatiable hunger to move in multiple directions. An explorer's mentality drives you. You feel fulfilled when there is enough on your plate to keep you mentally challenged.

Shadow: Challenges

How could such a positive force go wrong for you? Your intuition can go too far with the "I can't lose" feeling that colors this meridian. Your boundaries grow cloudy, causing you to not accurately diagnose limits. This causes you to squander time and money in overestimating your ability. Blind faith with no reality testing gets you into trouble.

Becoming too judgmental is another potential negative theme. Being right becomes all too important. If you are too critical of others, it causes friction in your relationships. The wonderful tolerance for dissenting opinions is missing. Dogmatism causes you to be argumentative too much of the time. You will miss out on learning new ideas if you have tunnel vision.

An inability to focus can occur. You feel confined by a goal and therefore lack the discipline to see it through to completion. Commitments may scare you, making long-term relationships and work experiences challenging.

Dawn: Maximizing Your Potential

The Jupiter meridian is a place of never-ending inspirational energy. It allows you to stay motivated. Your ruling planet does not like you to ever give up on a dream. When your intuition locks on to this expansive planet, your mind tunes in to its creative power.

Your belief that anything is possible opens the door to an evolutionary intuitive synchronicity. You feel a pull to travel from one end of the globe to the other in search of a new vision quest. This is the awakening magic of this meridian. When you fall in love with a profession, you tend to excel in communicating the information to others. You make a great teacher, trainer, and consultant when you make use of Jupiter.

There is luck in Jupiter's world unlike in any other. This generous planet will guide you to harmonious relationships. Keep an open mind and look for the good in others and don't be afraid to praise it. This is the doorway to meeting the right people at the right time.

Career and Ambition:
Saturn Meridian Activating Your Sagittarius Intuition

Light: Strengths

A free-spirited Sagittarius finds great focus in this meridian. Saturn guides your intuition to accomplish your most heartfelt dreams. Your fiery spirit discovers a grounding wire in this landscape. You can be as expansive in thought as ever, plus have Saturn's pragmatic energy watching over you.

Sagittarius likes to know there are options to any plan. The Saturn meridian lends its solidity to ensure you make the most out of diversification and at the same time get desired results. Saturn instills a sense of commitment into your major life goals.

Your usual lighthearted humor meets a more serious tone in this meridian. Both your matter-of-fact approach and Saturn's reality-oriented influence can coexist. It is good to keep things in perspective. Rome was not built in a day, as the old saying goes. You can balance work and play in a balanced manner.

Finding a soul mate who shares your appreciation for learning and travel is a Sagittarius quest. Knowing you have a partner with whom to face challenges and adversity is more of a Saturn theme. You can have the best of both worlds in finding a pragmatic, fun-loving type. You would like to have this in one person. When you don't fear intimacy and choose to reveal your inner world, a lover may be with you through all seasons.

Karmic challenges are part of this meridian. In past incarnations, overconfidence may have put you into situations best avoided. Saturn is teaching you how to make use of reality testing in this lifetime. The daredevil in you may still be alive and well. The love of adventure is in your normal way of operating. Taking a more patient and sober approach keeps you from wasting time and money. There is a possibility that you lacked faith in your ability in some past lives. Saturn is asking you to trust in your talents. Getting over a fear of making mistakes is perhaps the solution. Taking small steps toward a goal to build confidence is wisdom learned through intuitively connecting with Saturn.

Shadow: Challenges

If you consistently experience a disconnect with this meridian, your sense of adventure may feel like it has hit an iceberg. Your intuition freezes and is in desperate need of a thaw. How might this occur? Your idealism may have run into a wall. A plan either delayed or given a thumbs-down can be what happened. Or a romance soured. You are not the same when not lit by that drive to seek new opportunities.

When a Sagittarius grows too cautious, it feels awkward. Patience is one thing, but fear is another. If you are afraid to risk failing, you will never know how successful you might have been. When you lose optimism, your momentum to push through obstacles or to start a new project weakens.

Running away from responsibility and commitments causes lost opportunities. You miss out on good relationships and jobs. Escapism is the underlying cause of this behavior. Your personal power takes a dip.

Ignoring that life has limits is likely part of a karmic challenge. You came into this lifetime to exercise the wisdom of the Saturn meridian. Saturn has been teaching people for centuries not to always go against the odds, especially when they are stacked heavily against you. Sooner or later you will lose. Not listening to that intuitive inner voice advising patience and taking it slower gets you into big trouble.

Dawn: Maximizing Your Potential

The Saturn meridian is solid ground for a Sagittarius philosopher and creative thinker to walk on. Your dreams find fertile and reliable soil here. This is a strategy-laden terrain. Your intuition easily finds a sure ally to make professional goals a reality. Determination will push you to climb a ladder of success when walking hand in hand with Saturn.

Staying open to new ideas and learning paves the way for an evolutionary intuitive synchronicity. Flexibility is far better to utilize than rigidity. You are meant to be an absorber of knowledge and to turn what you learn into something with your own original spin. Sharing your ideas with others is a way for you to enjoy yourself.

Saturn will teach you how to define your relationships into win-win partnerships. Keep your expectations within reason and you are a lot closer to happiness. Showing lovers, friends, and family members that they can depend on you keeps them close. Embracing commitments to people and projects with an optimistic mind brings you great fulfillment.

Future Goals and Inventiveness:
Uranus Meridian Activating Your Sagittarius Intuition
Light: Strengths

This meridian is similar to a bolt of lightning awakening your mind to a brave new future. You will feel like you have outgrown the present when your intuition connects with Uranus. You may be wanting a new job, relationship, or location from which to operate. The Uranus meridian has a tendency to ignite a sudden desire for change. Even if you make no major new moves, there will be a need to add something stimulating to spice up your everyday life. An innate sense that a greater exuberance is required is likely when you make the Uranus connection.

A quest for a goal that gives you a feeling of renewal could occur. Your Sagittarius need to experience the heartbeat of inspiration is enhanced quickly in this fast-paced terrain. Learning new job skills is exciting. Your creative self-expression breaks new ground.

New relationships open you to alternative ways of thinking when the Uranus influence strikes. Unconventional people can be frequent visitors. You are introduced to new lenses through which to view the world. You want to have the same shocking effect on the minds of others. Your mind is thrilled and startled at the same time with a new reality.

The freedom energy aroused by Uranus is well matched with your adventurous Sagittarius instincts. Tuning in to this meridian helps you break away from limiting relationships or jobs. The courage chip is inserted into your brain by this meridian, allowing you to move forward. Giving yourself permission to pursue your own unique goals is possible in this futuristic land. Having greater faith in your ideas is motivated by the Uranus meridian. It is waiting for your intuition to take the plunge into its stimulating arms.

Shadow: Challenges

The energy swirling in this meridian takes your intuition on a wild ride. The question is, to where? If you find you are constantly nervous, it is essential to learn to direct this energy productively. Concentration can be difficult, as is getting enough sleep. It feels like you are always in the fast lane. Following through on a plan is a challenge when you can't slow your mind down. Mental and physical exhaustion might result.

Becoming too self-centered will turn people off. Your relationships get out of balance. An equal give and take is missing. A rigid ideology runs contrary to the openness of Sagittarius. The liberating qualities of Uranus are not being interpreted by your intuition accurately. A refusal to listen to the ideas of others causes communication breakdowns.

It is possible that you could be on the receiving end of a person with a me-focused personality. In this instance you are not getting your own goals realized. Losing your individuality is disorienting. Your dependency needs are in a state of confusion. A Sagittarius who is not willing to experiment with new ideas limits their chances for success. If you get too attached to the same routines, it dulls your creativity and insights.

Dawn: Maximizing Your Potential

The Uranus meridian pours new ideas into your mind. The inventor and trendsetter in you comes alive. Your Sagittarius mental approach becomes even more impressive when interwoven with the Uranus landscape. Thinking out of the box points you into a new business or career.

Excitement is the energy that circulates throughout the halls of this meridian. If you welcome change, you will enjoy what Uranus does for you. A willingness to open your mind to fresh new perceptions will surprise you with an evolutionary intuitive synchronicity. It can happen so fast that your mind may not even notice when this happened. That's how swiftly this ambassador of innovative thinking brings you new, exhilarating insights. The future calls to you to come with a positive and open mental framework. Why? So this meridian can deliver to you the highest level of abundance and harmony possible that resonates with your goals.

Creative Imagination and Idealism: Neptune Meridian Activating Your Sagittarius Intuition

Light: Strengths

Welcome to the ethereal world of Neptune. This is the meridian where your intuition has fun displaying a vivid imagination. You are invited to wear many different masks and use the appropriate one for whatever situation you encounter. This is a landscape that keeps you young in spirit. It has a playful twist, yet you can get really serious here and discover your artistic side. This is a dreamy atmosphere full of muses that inspire a Sagittarius to dream big.

Neptune tugs on your intuition to guide it to take you to high creative levels. This is the energy that is utilized by healers and psychics. Your use of this energy definitely manifests in your communication skills. You intuitively know how to get ideas and information across to others in easy-to-understand language.

You are already somewhat idealistic in being a Sagittarius. Neptune intensifies the drive to put your beliefs into action. This mystical wizard, which inspired the likes of Merlin in ancient times to weave his magic, entices your own mind to have faith that invisible forces will guide you to success. Neptune says, don't doubt your capability, as the door you need to walk through is always closer than you think. The seeds of new goals get planted by intuitively linking to this wondrous planet.

The search for like-minded compatriots is stimulated by Neptune. The quest for a soul mate is encouraged by this romantic meridian that activates the troubadour in you. Finding someone to share your love and ideals with is driven by Neptune.

Neptune is a powerful force that appears subtle. The planet works behind the scenes, arranging circumstances to bring out your most intuitive qualities. Finding a spiritual connection and tuning in to your inner clarity is one way to link to this meridian.

A greater faith in your talent can be found. Your intuition knows how to summon Neptune to keep your idealism alive. Your most heartfelt search for a meaningful purpose attracts Neptune to work with you and point the way to the love and success you seek.

Shadow: Challenges

Looking at the world through rose-colored glasses and thinking this is reality is an indicator that you are not clearly expressing this meridian. Your mind is only perceiving what it wants to see. Your emotions are fogging up your clarity. Denying what are the facts to paint a fantasy gets you into trouble.

Falling in love is a great high. There is a possibility in this meridian not to be honest with yourself when in a romantic relationship. You can have an unrealistic assessment of someone and deny the truth.

You are doing most of the giving and very little receiving. Placing a person too high on a pedestal keeps you from an accurate perception of who the individual really is. Nobody is perfect. Your expectations of yourself and others are too high.

Perfection is a nagging nuisance. You might not pursue a goal, thinking it is not the right time. You talk yourself out of good opportunities, feeling there will be a magical moment to move forward. Your Sagittarius fire goes out if you wait too long.

Purposely not speaking the truth leads to confusing communication. You may be overly sensitive about hurting someone's feelings. Closeness might scare you and cause you to talk in circles. Or you are hiding information too much to avoid dealing with real problems. A lack of being direct causes others not to trust you.

Dawn: Maximizing Your Potential

The Neptune meridian elevates your Sagittarius zeal for being an optimist with an even brighter intuitive flare. If you are someone with a strong intellect, Neptune offers emotional energy to keep both expressions in balance. They play off one another, energizing each to work even sharper for you. Communicating with more feeling behind your words makes for a convincing force to get others to support your ideas.

When you have more faith in your creative power, it is then that Neptune brings you an evolutionary intuitive synchronicity. It is as though a new intuitive bridge has been made available for you to cross over into a magical world. At first you might not trust it. But then there will come the day when you will walk across this great intuitive walkway and be impressed with the gift you have been given.

A positive mind attracts the right people and job prospects. You appear charismatic when linking to Neptune. It seems to others like you have a vision of what you want from life. A sincerity is in your eyes that people feel they must trust. Sharing your knowledge wins friends. If you stay reasonable in your expectations, you find the love and harmony you desire. This is the wondrous manner through which Neptune's meridian operates. Immerse yourself in this magic and flow with your creative self-expression.

Personal Empowerment and Passion: Pluto Meridian Activating Your Sagittarius Intuition

Light: Strengths

Your ideals find great passion in this emotionally deep meridian. This is the land of finding the inner resolve to make your belief system a reality. When you are true to your personal power, your intuition will help you create a life that gives you a sense of pride. It is your ideas that attract attention and can be marketed into a valuable resource. Your fiery personality picks up extra doses of charisma when you bathe in this rich bastion of determined conviction to a plan. Your sign is not necessarily known for liking long-term goals unless there is an obvious reward at the end of the project. Pluto gives you that toughness to stick it out even when the going gets tedious.

Self-mastery is part of this meridian package. How does that occur? It is your extraordinary ability to see the positive in a situation where many others focus on the negative. Your mind finds magic in this Pluto land of metaphysical energy. A cosmic composting process of quickly converting your doubts into faith guides you to an inner knowing that you can succeed at whatever you really concentrate on.

Developing a more patient attitude toward those you love and care about strengthens these relationships. Nothing tears them apart. Believing impeccably in your soul mate gives that person the confidence to be all they can be. The beauty is that you will get the same in return. It is the Pluto wheel of life at work, the equal exchange of energy being mutually beneficial.

Learning to channel your emotional intensity takes practice. The payoff is that you will create harmony and abundance rather than losing what you hope to attain. Your intuition knows instinctively how to dance with Pluto processes. It is your mind that has to do the catching up. Eventually your mind and intuition will be on the same page, saving you much pain and frustration.

Finding the profession or cause you enjoy feels like a rebirth. Your mind and spirit are merged. When you find your niche in the world, your people connections flow better. It takes the pressure off of having to find all of your peace in a person. Your energy is channeled in a more balanced way. You are driven by a deep quest for self-understanding and to be understood. When you find there is no longer a need to prove who you are to the world, you feel liberated.

Shadow: Challenges

When you are not intuitively in harmony with the Pluto meridian, you will not have your usual self-confidence. There is a feeling that you need to manipulate people to get what you need rather than communicating honestly. Or you may have made the choice to be in a relationship with someone who is in the habit of withholding the truth from you. Either of these realities interferes with a road to harmony and wholeness.

Settling for jobs less than your capability could be due to a lack of not believing in your ability. It could be that you are afraid you do not have the determination to improve your skills. It is the length of time involved in a commitment that worries you. Sagittarius is a restless sign that likes to be constantly on the move. Harnessing this energy is not so easy but might be worth it if it would improve your earning potential.

Relationships are difficult to sustain if you feel too confined. Leaving a lover because you want your freedom is not a bad thing, but doing so because you fear closeness is another story. It is a pattern that will always come between you and another person if you don't deal with it. Running from fear only makes it bigger than it is.

Anger expressed inappropriately, as though it is an erupting volcano, is a sign that you have been repressing your emotional intensity
for far too long. When you hold back how you really feel, there is always the possibility that you will explode at the wrong people at the
wrong time. Hiding your real thoughts keeps your intuition less powerful and creative.

Dawn: Maximizing Your Potential

The Pluto meridian is a power zone where you can stop and fill your
mental and emotional tanks to no end. Your intuition finds rebirth
when blended with this passionate planet. Your personal power gets a
much-needed lift when you face adversity with a positive attitude. Life
is full of lessons. Pluto is there to help you process all of the big challenges you encounter.

Your Sagittarius love of adventure does not miss a beat in Pluto
land. Walking near the edge of a new goal just to see how it feels is a
Pluto theme. You can decide with wisdom if it is time to take a leap of
faith into a new opportunity. You like to spread those expansive wings
to fly high above the earth and gain new insights. Maintaining a broad,
refreshed outlook is the nourishment that keeps you stocked with
plenty of energized thinking.

Facing your inner fears releases an evolutionary intuitive synchronicity. Communicating your inner world to others strengthens
your intuitive resolve to act with decisiveness. Even your professional
life benefits. Freeing your emotions from one area where it is blocked
allows your intuition to move that much more freely through all of
the regions of your mind. Your creative power enlarges in ways that
serve only to make you happy. Self-confidence and fulfilling relationships will be the rewards.

— *Chapter 11* —

CAPRICORN

Capricorn (12/22–1/19)

Archetypes: Manager, Executive, Patriarch, Government, Business

Key Focus: Ambition and Serious Commitments

Element: Earth

Planetary Ruler: Saturn

Cosmic Mirror Planet: Moon

Welcome to your Capricorn sign chapter. Your pragmatic Capricorn mind merges with greater intuitive insight when utilizing the many possibilities offered by the planetary meridians. Directing your result-oriented thoughts is easier when you let your intuition guide you. Self-doubt turns into creative success when aligning your future plans with the power of the meridian energies.

Intuition moves with great focus through your sign. This serves you well, as you have a natural inclination to move carefully, one step at a time, to accomplish a plan. With the encouragement of the planetary meridians, you can create fulfilling relationships, discover rewarding work, and enjoy watching your goals come to fruition.

Your Capricorn Dashboard Meridian Summary

You can tune in to the meridians whenever you need them. That is what is miraculous about the universe. More than one of these forces are often working through you. Your intuition reaches for these energies spontaneously, guiding you to use the right meridian at the right time.

Your Capricorn Sun meridian activates your creative self-expression to fulfill your need to shine in the world. The Moon meridian helps you establish a home and tune in to your feelings. The Mercury meridian sharpens your mental perceptions and interest in learning new skills. The Venus meridian points the way to relationship harmony and abundance. The Mars meridian accentuates your courage and drive to face challenges directly. The Jupiter meridian brings out your quest for knowledge and helps you remain optimistic. The Saturn meridian helps in your search for career success and represents a determination to be true to your commitments. The Uranus meridian enlivens your hopes for a bright future and awakens your independent spirit. The Neptune meridian reveals your deepest idealism and need for a meaningful life purpose. The Pluto meridian instills a longing for personal empowerment and a wish to express your passion.

Enjoy your expedition through the planetary meridians. Each has a special way of helping you realize your true potential. It is important to remember that these energies are there for you to use at any time. You have the freedom to ride them to fulfill your most heartfelt dreams.

Creative Expression:
Sun Meridian Activating Your Capricorn Intuition

Light: Strengths

The creative vitality of the Sun moves in a very determined manner through your birth sign, Capricorn, coloring you with a down-to-earth attitude. People might perceive you as cautious, but you see this as wanting to be sure it is the safest time to move on a plan. Your earthy spirit gives you a pragmatic intellect. The universe is attracted to your structure-oriented mind because it knows it has found a reliable partner to make use of intuition.

The Sun sign of Capricorn solarizes you with the follow-through to finish what you begin. The challenge sometimes is relaxing enough into the intuitive experience to get into a creative flow. You don't enjoy having to do a task over and over again unless you know eventually you will be successful.

You can show great patience. Delayed gratification was probably invented by your sign. Your focusing power is often envied by the other signs. You have a natural instinct for outlining the solution to a problem to get it solved faster.

Ambition is never far from your thinking. Finding a job or profession that makes the most of your skills is what you desire. Your dedication to excellence earns you a great reputation. Being a mentor is something you excel at. You do attract responsibility. Your management ability is hard to beat.

You do better with relationships with people who give you a chance to warm up to them. You intuitively don't like to show your true self until you really get to know someone. You innately know that trust takes time. It is the slow building of partnerships that you prefer. Reliable friends, family, and lovers become strong connections for many years.

Shadow: Challenges

Your intuition's glow is missing when you are not connecting with this meridian. How might this occur? If you tighten your grip to control situations to the extreme, you lose that creative flair. Fear causes you to freeze and not enjoy life. It hampers you from thinking positively. A little caution is fine, because that is a card you naturally like to play. It is when you doubt your ability to perform at an adequate level that you miss out on opportunities.

Relationships run into trouble if you won't reveal any feelings. A lack of trust is the main culprit here. Carefully scrutinizing whom you should let get close to you makes a lot of sense, but never letting anyone get to really know you makes for a solitary existence. People cannot break through the wall that encloses you.

Your mind becomes too anxious about the future. Your intuition is not able to trickle through if you stay in a down state of mind. Your momentum is thwarted by self-imposed obstacles. You are working against yourself.

Dawn: Maximizing Your Potential

The Sun meridian gives you all of the tools necessary to put your creative power into action. With each little success, you build toward a bigger one. When you don't let fear interfere with your goals, there is no end to where your intuition can take you. Patience is the cornerstone of your Capricorn Sun sign. Staying the course to complete a plan gives you a great deal of personal satisfaction.

Flexibility is the key to your happiness. It allows your relationships to grow smoothly. Communicating your feelings as well as ideas generates greater harmony in your most intimate partnerships. Remembering to be harder on problems than on people enables you to maintain an open dialogue with others.

It is in allowing new ideas into your life that your vision in dealing with challenges strengthens. Surrendering worn-out, negative thoughts and self-doubts is the catalyst for an evolutionary intuitive synchronicity. Suddenly your life is redefined in ways to meet the needs of the present and future. The magic of the universe then works with your intuition to deliver the love and work your heart longs to find.

Creating a Home and Expressing Feelings:
Moon Meridian Activating Your Capricorn Intuition

Light: Strengths

The Moon travels with your pragmatic Capricorn Sun sign with an instinctive energy to allow you to get in touch with your emotions. This aids you in your relationships and even your working life. Balancing the demands of the world with a need to have a happy home life is how your Capricorn Sun and Moon meridians work together. This public and private balancing act is something you can learn to manage. You become so engaged with the responsibility that everyday dealings ask of you that it is easy to forget your inner world. The Moon's job is to remind you to tune in to the intuitive power deep within you.

Having a reliable support system is wise. People you trust and who have your best interest in mind are a key component to your success. The Moon is your gateway to finding a sense of security.

Listen to your moods. Why? Because they indicate how you really feel about situations. Capricorn is a sign that enjoys feeling in control. The Moon asks you to let go a little and not push yourself so hard. This subtle lunar entity will entice you to take the time to relax from nervous anxiety. Then your intuition gains clarity and strength to help you make better decisions.

Establishing a home is part of the Moon symbolism. This mysterious planet, which intrigued the minds of ancient people, is here to help you in this modern era. The Moon guides you to locations that are more favorable to start relationships and begin a career search. You require a location that gives you a retreat from stress and at the same time offers a chance to work in a stable job or support a successful business. You were born under an ambitious sign. The Moon meridian gives you the intuitive clarity to make the right professional choices. You likely enjoy living in a community with people who appreciate your talents.

Shadow: Challenges

Where could you go wrong in this meridian? The Capricorn drive for success could cause you to neglect your closest allies. Your job becomes all-consuming. Having ambition is a good thing, but if you get too caught up in work and ignore your lover and friends, it causes them to become resentful.

Your health suffers the consequences if you refuse to slow down. There is such a push to constantly be doing a project that you forget to rest. Burnout results and your actions are not as productive as they would be with a balanced pace.

There is a chance that you could go in the opposite direction and have a problem initiating a goal. You become stuck in negative thought processes. This could be due to being in the company of discouraging people or suffering from a fear of failure.

You might struggle with intimacy. Trust is usually the main challenge. Building a wall around you makes it difficult for others to really get to know you. Your business relationships are probably more comfortable than the personal ones. Closeness scares you. If you don't want a solitary life, you will experience a great deal of loneliness.

Dawn: Maximizing Your Potential

The Moon meridian sends you a wonderful intuitive breeze to tune in to choices that are in your best interest. The Moon feeds off your moods and feelings. When your mind is centered, it is easier to follow the guidance of this emotional powerhouse.

Having a home that provides you with a peaceful atmosphere helps you deal with stress. You may find that working at home suits you better than a job outside of your residence. The Moon rules the sign Cancer, the opposite sign of Capricorn. This opposing setup lets the Moon serve as the cosmic mirror, or mirroring agent, to help you balance your public and private lives. Your Capricorn Sun sign tends to lead you into commitments that require great focus. Your mind easily concentrates outward to respond to the demands placed upon you. The Moon energy stimulates your mind into a relaxation mode. There are intervals where taking a break from the action rejuvenates your spirit and clears your mind. You might depend heavily on those closest to you for emotional support.

Going beyond your fear to try a new relationship or job invites an evolutionary intuitive synchronicity. Surrendering a need to be in control attracts a whole new way of living. The Moon asks you to allow spontaneity into your life, as it is a door to greater creative power.

Mental Insights:
Mercury Meridian Activating Your Capricorn Intuition
Light: Strengths

You tend to be a logical thinker. This does come standard with a Capricorn Sun sign. The Mercury meridian is your chance to define the choices that best serve your life purpose. This god of perception links with your intuition to guide you to solid decision making. Mercury adds flexibility and adaptability to your thought processes. When you take your time and don't feel rushed into making decisions, your Capricorn mind finds this more agreeable.

There is a delicate line between relaxing into an intuitive flow and feeling like your mind must be in total control. Mercury helps you determine the happy midpoint between utilizing serious concentration and trusting your instincts to get a job done. You are more productive when you are not compulsively worried about details. Your intuition is a blessing in lightening the load you carry on your shoulders. This analytical planetary force serves you well in staying organized. It is in learning to try not being perfect that your intuition cruises high to give you innovative and creative insights.

You attract responsibility in being a Capricorn Sun sign. Your managerial and work talents get noticed by those with the good sense to make use of them. Delegating duties to others gives you more free time, which is good for your mind and body. Trusting that a job will get done when you give it your best effort, rather than worrying about the final result, is intuitive wisdom.

Shadow: Challenges

When your intuition is not flowing with the rhythm of this meridian, there will be signals. One is a tendency to think negative first and positive later. You feel stuck in a rut with this type of thinking. The details keep you too worried about the outcome of situations. You get worn out by refusing to relax or focus on something else.

Rigid ideas block your intuition from leading you to new insights. The Mercury meridian keeps sending you new, alternative perceptions. If you stay too attached to your ordinary way of operating, you miss out on new opportunities.

Communication with those you love lacks feeling. An inability to switch from business mode to intimacy creates distance that you don't want to have with a romantic partner. There could be an underlying fear of closeness that is a real problem.

You are trying too hard to be a success. All work and no play may dominate your thinking. Your life could be all about a career, leaving you wishing you had spent more time working on having a soul mate.

Dawn: Maximizing Your Potential

The Mercury meridian helps you make decisive decisions. Your intuition joins forces with this in-depth analytical planet to point you in the right career directions. Your preferences as a Capricorn to plan a careful strategy before embarking on a course of action does not miss a beat in this detail-oriented meridian.

Trusting your intuition as much as your concrete mental impulses opens the door to an evolutionary intuitive synchronicity. It puts your mind at ease when you find the faith to believe in your intuition. The winged messenger takes you on its mentally adept flight, showing you new, enlightening life paths.

Mercury is the communication wizard of the sky. Let this planet instill in you the confidence to speak from the heart and follow in the footsteps of your most stimulating ideas. This is a sure way to awaken your creative power.

Relationship Tendencies:
Venus Meridian Activating Your Capricorn Intuition

Light: Strengths

Welcome to the human relations department. The Venus meridian is the place to stimulate your social instincts. As a Capricorn Sun sign, you have a tendency to treat all relationships as negotiations. This is a natural inclination. The reason for this is that you are always looking for reliable commitments. Your intuition is on ready alert to guide you to stable partnerships.

Intuitively, this meridian serves you well in the business arena. You know how to make people happy in getting them what they need. Running a business or a department is in your range of expertise.

Venus sends you energy as a reminder to pay attention to those you love. When you share your emotional and physical resources, it builds higher levels of trust. When you showing emotional warmth to your closest people connections, they respond in kind.

Accepting life's successes and setbacks as learning experiences helps you maintain a positive attitude. Your self-esteem gets stronger with each role in life that you master. Being patient in adjusting to change makes you a happier person.

You thrive on recognition. When your skills and work performance are appreciated by others, it pleases you. Accepting criticism gracefully makes for a smoother life. Showing fairness to others when commenting on their abilities gets them to like you.

When you are true to your values, it gives your identity a sense of wholeness. You are attracted to lovers and soul mates with the same dedication to excellence. When a mutual respect is established, your relationships have a tendency to be long-lasting.

Shadow: Challenges

What will indicate that you are not making the most of the Venus meridian? Rather than experiencing inner peace, it is being overshadowed by stress. This is true for a variety of reasons. You are trying too hard to please others and in the process not enjoying the relationships. Or you could be in a job that is aggravating your nervous system and you don't realize you need a change. Then again, it could be due to working more hours than you really need to do. Your intuition is dormant or difficult to access in any of these circumstances.

If you don't live out your highest values, it takes a toll on your mental well-being. Settling for less than you are capable of doing impacts your feeling of self-worth. There is an underlying fear of being more assertive in order to be all you could be.

You may be too reserved in relating to others. Revealing emotions scares you. Making others guess how you are feeling about decisions makes clear communication a challenge. Holding back in making commitments causes you to miss out on promising relationships and career possibilities.

Dawn: Maximizing Your Potential

The Venus meridian is a lively, people-oriented atmosphere. You never feel completely alone when you allow your intuition to reach into the depths of this socially alive place. Whether you are a cautious or outgoing type of Capricorn, this meridian is ready to launch you into a new group of friends.

When you grow comfortable with creating abundance, your intuition links to Venus. It is then that you will find the doors to career and relationship harmony opening wide. Being at ease with your values sets your mind in a peace mode.

Having the self-confidence to pursue relationships and jobs that challenge you ignites an evolutionary intuitive synchronicity. Your intuition then puts in motion a set of circumstances opening your consciousness to a whole new range of options. Conquering your fear of entering new situations releases your creative power.

Initiating Action:
Mars Meridian Activating Your Capricorn Intuition

Light: Strengths

If you need some extra initiating energy, then you have come to the right place. The Mars meridian has all of the extra fuel you require to complete any project. Your Capricorn Sun sign and Mars work well as a team. Capricorn shows patience and Mars makes sure you don't wait too long to get going. This makes for great timing of your actions to get the best results.

Your Capricorn drive to be a success is ignited even further in this fiery meridian. A reluctance to try something new is quickly converted into a passion to dive in headfirst. You are a motivating force to excite others into working with you to get a job done. This meridian brings out your leadership qualities.

Mars is connected to raw emotion. If you channel this energy into creative endeavors, you show tremendous self-motivation. When you fall in love with a job skill or hobby, you can stay in this for many years. Self-mastery will come your way if you are committed to a creative interest. People will invest in your charismatic personality that manifests right out of your creative power.

Anger is another Mars theme. Getting a handle on angry impulses is wise. It's better to express your strongest feelings openly than keep them bottled up inside of you. Your relationships remain successful when you talk honestly. When you don't fear the emotional intensity of those closest to you, they will learn to trust you. The passion and bond in your romantic relationships deepen when anger and emotions are accepted as a reality. Being harder on problems than on people is a mantra to remember, as it will keep your partnerships balanced and on a road to harmony.

Shadow: Challenges

This meridian works against you if you freeze up in expressing yourself. Fear takes over. Your goals don't get realized. It could be unresolved emotional problems that are holding you down. Anger is turned inward because you are afraid to state your true feelings. There is a sensation of treading water, which runs against the true spontaneous energy of this meridian.

Intimidating others to get your own way is not in your best interest. People resent this type of behavior. It ends good relationships. An underlying issue of not trusting people is the root cause of this pattern.

An obsessive drive for success becomes all-consuming of your time and attention. You will find yourself living a lonely life as people drift away who were once close to you. They sense that you are not interested in supporting their goals as much as your own.

A lack of patience results in aborting goals that could have paid dividends. When you don't curb the adrenaline rush that emanates from the Mars meridian, you give up too quickly on people or a plan.

Dawn: Maximizing Your Potential

The Mars meridian will pump you up with stimulating energy. The attitude here is that there is no time like the present to put a plan into action. Why wait for permission? You have everything needed to put that strategic Capricorn mind to work. Your entrepreneurial spirit never felt so good. This is a self-starting landscape like no other.

Channeling your anger into productive activities serves you well. It keeps your stress levels in check. It is okay to express your most intense feelings. Your intuition is sharper when you don't hold on to old, unresolved issues with others. Making peace with the past is a doorway to an evolutionary intuitive synchronicity. This is the magical process to intuitively make a deep connection with your creative power that gets lit for a lifetime. It's then that your passion to walk in new life directions becomes your destiny.

Expanding Knowledge:
Jupiter Meridian Activating Your Capricorn Intuition

Light: Strengths

Your Capricorn seriousness meets humor and the lighter side of life in the Jupiter meridian. When connecting with Jupiter, your intuition is trying to tell you never to lose faith and that things will turn out for the best one way or another. This is the land of optimism. In Jupiter's world, there is no room for negativity. It only blocks your vision from seeing good opportunities wanting to make themselves known to you.

Making a strong effort is likely the method you are accustomed to using to get a job finished. Jupiter awakens your intuition to creating rewards for all of that work you do. The idea is to keep you inspired to finish what you start. Enjoying life is why the universe must have given humanity this planetary influence. Combining work and play is the Jupiter way of approaching a large project.

When utilizing this meridian, your intuition will attempt to point you toward mind-expanding experiences. This could come through books, travel, or taking some courses. If you have a business, you can discover interesting possibilities to increase the profits. This is an enterprising planet. It isn't beyond Jupiter to surprise you with insights that spur you on to new career goals.

Jupiter is a restless planet. Joining forces with this cosmic gypsy suddenly gets you thinking of faraway lands to visit. The habit of Jupiter energy is to come into your consciousness in a gentle way, followed by a jolt of energy to blow you forward into new experiences. This is a fire planet that gets your usual earthy, deliberate Capricorn thinking to act on a hunch. It is having the faith to trust your ideas so luck manifests before your very eyes.

Showing you truly believe in a lover wins their support for your own hopes and wishes. Making time to celebrate with those you love is wise. It creates memories that will be cherished as life goes on.

Jupiter is a planet of rituals. Your own belief system, whether traditional or unconventional, strengthens through a deeper understanding of symbols and mystical universal forces. This is perhaps the secret doctrine of this interesting planet. Being true to your highest beliefs attracts the abundance and harmony you will always appreciate.

Shadow: Challenges

You could forget that you have an intuitive Jupiter roadmap to seeing the cup as half full rather than half empty. It is okay to have a serious intensity to manage your life, but if you block out the Jupiter meridian, your mind loses self-confidence in trying new experiences. It could even cause you to negate the dreams of a lover or friend, which will disappoint them. Your relationships lose vibrancy when your mental outlook is to first think negative.

A lack of belief in your abilities causes you to miss out on chances for a more abundant life. You will never know how far you can take a creative idea if you don't let people see it. It might be that you are listening to too much criticism about your potential, which stops you from moving forward.

There is a possibility in this meridian of being too confident and losing sight of reality. The risk-taking push of Jupiter might cause you to take unnecessary chances. Rushing in where angels fear to tread, as the old saying goes, may prove disastrous. You lose a lot of time, energy, and resources without making use of forethought.

Dawn: Maximizing Your Potential

The Jupiter meridian lifts your self-confidence to such high ground that your doubts disappear. This is a terrain offering you inspiration in large quantities. It only takes believing in your goals so they catch the upward winds of this expansive planetary influence. The past is integrated harmoniously into the present, whether your memories are mostly happy or sad.

You cultivate new relationships that stimulate your insights to move in exciting directions. If you need more happiness, then you need to make frequent return trips to this meridian. Your intuition likes coming here. The refueling process is fast and furious. Your mind, body, and soul get recharged and get sent off to explore various sources of happiness.

Opening your mind to new knowledge is the key to an evolutionary intuitive synchronicity. The seeds of a new, miraculous beginning get planted. Jupiter awakens your mind to look for how and where you can operate in the world to find optimum success. Abundance and luck are closer than you think. They will come when your intuition guides you to an alternative vision, one that takes what you already know and gives it a new spin.

Career and Ambition:
Saturn Meridian Activating Your Capricorn Intuition
Light: Strengths

Capricorn is a Saturn-ruled sign, indicating that you have a natural affinity to comprehend the energy in this meridian. Your ability to hone in on a goal and make it a reality gets an extra boost in this get-down-to-business turf. Your take-charge attitude is even stronger when your intuition tunes in to Saturn's influences. Determination is the pervasive atmosphere in this meridian.

People probably perceive you as focused and never too lost in figuring your way out of a problem. As a matter of fact, you are often the person others come to when needing help in solving a dilemma. Saturn is the solutions planet, and your face may reflect years of solving problems in business and in your home life. Perseverance is in the very bones of this meridian, and it easily transfers over into your own.

As a Capricorn, you may not necessarily always feel ambitious, but your sign is known for this trait. Saturn will push you to take your skills to a higher level in the work world. Even if you don't feel the urge to be a boss, there will be authority figures anxious to promote you. Responsibility is easily attracted by Capricorn. Saturn ups the ante just like in poker, when someone matches or tops someone else's wager. You have the wisdom to know when it is worth the risk to take on a bigger job and when it is best to stay with the hand you have been dealt. Knowing your limits comes with practice, and Saturn is there to ensure you know the boundary line.

Commitments get serious when Saturn is in the picture. You like solid, hard-working people like yourself. Someone with a sense of humor does tend to lighten your spirit. There is an inclination to trust dependable types. You are attracted to someone who appears to take promises seriously. A person who honors similar traditions feels compatible.

Your lovers and friends stay loyal if they feel you are sharing your inner world with them. You may not talk about your ideals that openly until you really get to know someone. Your intuition knows who the right people are to keep close.

There are past-life patterns that can be tuned in to when linking intuitively to this meridian. In some incarnations, you were too driven to be in control. Power struggles resulted. Holding on to rigid ideas made negotiating with others difficult. In this lifetime, you came here to be more open to new ideas. Flowing with your intuition helps you see a better path to clearer communication. Another past-life theme is a tendency to dwell on a negative perspective. In the current incarnation, you are here to accent the positive. You don't have to be happy all the time, but you can learn to practice appreciating what is going right in your life. Your relationships and professional life attract greater harmony when you do this.

This is a great meridian energy for you to use to turn your ideas into a success. The pragmatic mind you have is right at home in this logical land of Saturn. Your intuition knows how to get back to this locale like a homing pigeon when you need to get grounded and to make sure you are on track for a plan. Whether you are a traditional type of Capricorn or lean toward the unconventional, there is nothing like this meridian to guide you intuitively to the harmony you seek.

Shadow: Challenges

If you have trouble connecting intuitively with this meridian, it will show in a few ways, one being that your perceptions seem too gloomy. This is a past-life pattern repeating once again. Your mind is struggling to see how to make a goal come true. It could be that you are too focused on the end result and are not looking closely enough at how to structure those first few steps. Your intuition is waiting for your mind to catch up with it and see that there is a methodology to getting a plan started toward success. You need to patiently start from the beginning with more hope.

You might be too fearful in letting a lover get to know you. Going slow makes sense, but never showing your more vulnerable side, no matter how long you have known someone, will lead that person to wonder if you will ever trust them. Your reluctance to make a commitment is another indicator that you are bumping into a wall in this meridian. Your hope to be in a long-term relationship could be dampened in this reality.

Becoming a workaholic is a possibility in this meridian. You have to keep a close eye on your boundary line. Your mental and physical health weaken if you don't make time for both work and a vacation. The harder you work, the more downtime you could require. If you lose that awareness of balancing your private and public lives, you may lose someone close to you for failing to pay attention to their needs.

The give and take in your relationships is a key to their success. You are not going to be happy in abdicating too much power to someone else. The other side of the coin is true as well in that you can't expect to always control someone else's decisions. If you become too dictatorial, you will get into power struggles. But in not speaking up for your own goals, you lose that sense of empowerment you need.

Dawn: Maximizing Your Potential

The Saturn meridian is a landscape that provides you with plenty of room to define your goals. This is a strategy-oriented atmosphere that matches your own mental approach to making decisions. Your intuition is strengthened when linking to Saturn. There is an extra added determination to accomplish a plan.

Balancing a need to feel in control of situations with the trust that your best effort will be good enough leads to great wisdom. You will discover an evolutionary intuitive synchronicity when you let go of negative thought patterns. This opens the door for new self-discovery.

Your creative power multiplies when putting more energy into what is possible than compulsively surrendering to what you can't do.

You are happier when you are willing to adjust to change. This does not mean that you have to compromise your own values and beliefs. It is just saying that adaptability keeps you feeling younger and happier. New ideas give you insight into better ways of marketing your skills.

This meridian ensures that your relationships have the element of permanence you want. When you communicate with openness and honesty, people want to remain near you. Your partnership commitments stay strong when you put as much dedication into them as you do your work. Maintaining a balance between your public and private lives is a road to abundance and harmony.

Future Goals and Inventiveness:
Uranus Meridian Activating Your Capricorn Intuition

Light: Strengths

As a general rule, a Capricorn Sun sign person like yourself does not like sudden change. You usually prefer to know what is coming. If you are looking for a surprise or two, this meridian will supply it. Uranus stimulates new ideas. You discover skills that you never knew you had or that you never knew could be put into action. This is the reward for tapping into this exciting planet with your intuition.

A renewed sense of energy to put a goal on the fast track is possible. The future calls when your intuition connects with this meridian. You are able to hot-wire a career you thought was ending or was badly in need of reviving. An existing business may quickly take on new customers. Your instincts about how to attract business are greatly enhanced by linking to Uranus.

It is okay to be true to traditional values or beliefs. You don't have to give these up. Uranus shows you how to incorporate unique insights into your thinking without necessarily upsetting the whole applecart.

New relationships burst onto the scene. This meridian has the capacity to widen your social circles if you so desire. Reinventing your usual way of interacting with people opens the door to new friendships. Think in terms of experimenting with alternative ideas.

Breaking free from the same old routines gives you extra vitality. Leaving behind limiting relationships, jobs, or even a city of residence allows you to find happiness in other situations. Uranus breaks the hold of self-defeating circumstances to give you a new lease on life. Your replenished creative power is the road to finding harmony and abundance.

Shadow: Challenges

There are ways that you could be out of sync with this meridian, one being that your nervous energy multiplies quickly if you are staying in a situation that you should be leaving. Your intuition is reading the Uranus energy as an indication that it is time to move forward, but your conscious mind is stubbornly resisting this message. An internal tug of war will persist until you do something about it.

Completing a goal or project is very challenging if you can't get a plan organized. Your mind is racing so fast that you can't get focused. It is like a runaway train. You might be trying too hard to force something to happen before the time is right. Refusing to rethink your approach proves frustrating.

Breaking away from a relationship or job due to impatience causes you to miss out on promising possibilities to be happy. Remember that this is a race car–like meridian that speeds up your mental impulses. It does require that you step back and pause to gain objectivity. You could be ending a good thing without giving it enough time to come to fruition. This may be due to a rebellious urge like the one the actor James Dean acted out in real life and in the movie *Rebel Without a Cause*. Just make sure the changes you want to make are in your best interest and are based on logic. You might be burning bridges that later you will regret.

Dawn: Maximizing Your Potential

The Uranus meridian takes you quickly along paths of wonderful self-discovery. This is the land of freedom and inventiveness. If you want to chase after a new goal, then this is your meridian to make it happen.

New learning material keeps your mind alert. The courage to break away from your normal way of operating in the world gives birth to an evolutionary intuitive synchronicity. Being open to alternative thinking makes life interesting and allows you to see a bigger picture in how to find the doors to the best opportunities.

When your intuition links to this meridian, you meet people with unconventional perspectives. Exposing your mind to new ideas triggers stimulating career directions. Uranus has the capacity to change your life forever. If you are ready to see the world through an innovative lens, then ride this energy to creative heights. The sky is the limit.

Creative Imagination and Idealism: Neptune Meridian Activating Your Capricorn Intuition

Light: Strengths

The Neptune meridian was created by the universe to make it easier to access your intuition. Although as a Capricorn, when you get busy in the everyday world, it is not evident that Neptune is nearby. The demands and distractions of life fog your awareness of this invisible energy. How might you make contact with this subtle planet that often stays hidden behind the scenes? When you are true to your ideals, Neptune comes forward to assist you in manifesting them. It does require you to have the faith to put your beliefs into action.

Neptune symbolism is associated with meditation and reflection. Taking the time to pause and practice centering techniques energizes your intuitive power in this magical meridian, which even Merlin in ancient times loved. Your soul or higher consciousness knows the roads that lead to Neptune even though your conscious mind can't perceive them.

This meridian sends you messages packaged in dreams while you sleep. This is when your resistance to ethereal energy is at its lowest. These forces then penetrate your psyche, delivering new, inspiring information. Balancing stress and rest allows the Neptune processes to work in your favor.

Finding meaningful relationships that light up your romantic feelings is yet another Neptune theme. Finding a compatible soul mate and forming deep friendships are stimulated by coming into this love-potion meridian. Your feelings are easier to communicate, as is affection, when your intuition links to Neptune.

There is artistic talent awakened by Neptune. This planet points to the creative energy swirling around in your mental processes that only needs to be channeled outward. Your Capricorn fondness for structure just needs to find the commitment and discipline to make this creativity a reality.

Healing energy is made available through accepting what this meridian has to offer. Old, painful memories can be healed. Your emotional body feels repaired. People become attracted to the sensitivity you show for their problems. This makes you a good counselor or confidant.

Career ideas surface as if they were there the whole time. This is the manner in which Neptune operates. This seductress of the sky drops hints in front of you to see if you will pick up on the clues. Success is often closer than you think.

Shadow: Challenges

If you are not in the flow with Neptune's meridian, there will be indications. You could find your usual Capricorn reality-testing switch turned off. This will be likelier to happen the more emotional a situation becomes. For instance, if you are denying how you really feel in a romantic relationship, you probably are not facing reality. Denial does occur in connection with this meridian more than in the others. There are no perfect people. You are expecting too much from someone. The idealizing tendency sparked by Neptune may lead you to expect too much from an individual. The person is not able to be what you desire them to be.

Another problem you might face in this meridian is a lack of faith in your ability. Your goals get watered down by not having enough positive belief in your capabilities. You are waiting for the perfect time to initiate a plan, but it never comes if you don't take that all-important first step.

Your dependency needs being out of balance is another trend related to this meridian. If you are always doing all of the work in a relationship, it enables your partner to be helpless. Or if you act too much like a victim, you lose your creative power. The equal taking of responsibility is missing.

One other trend that could manifest is leaving a good job to follow a dream. The problem comes if you haven't got a solid plan to make your new direction work. Your head is too high up in the clouds.

Dawn: Maximizing Your Potential

The Neptune meridian paints lofty pictures of new possibilities that you can aspire to. Dreams are manufactured in this wonderland that are as plentiful as the very air you breathe. Your intuition finds inspiration in this colorful landscape, which has motivated artists, musicians, healers, and dreamers for centuries. The faith you require to march toward an envisioned goal gets energized here.

Crossing over the borders of your past disappointments into the hope of a brighter present invites an evolutionary intuitive synchronicity. Your creative power climbs to higher levels, trading in yesterday's thinking for the chance at an inspired and renewed self-confidence. This strengthens your intuition. Letting go of self-doubt ushers in greater abundance. The gates to relationship and professional harmony are more likely to swing wide open.

Personal Empowerment and Passion: Pluto Meridian Activating Your Capricorn Intuition

Light: Strengths

The business side of your thinking is at home in this meridian. Pluto meshes well with your Capricorn Sun sign in knowing a good deal when you see one. Your negotiation skills intensify when your intuition links with this fierce business-oriented planet.

You wear your problem-solving hat confidently when making use of Pluto energy. You have more determination to make a goal turn into a reality when tuning in to Pluto. Analyzing a situation from top to bottom in order to be well prepared to handle it is strengthened in this meridian.

Your passion to pursue a meaningful career goal is ignited when joining forces with Pluto. You enjoy showing the world that you have mastered the skills you perfected. People perceive you as a charismatic personality. A feeling of success lifts your self-esteem to a high level.

Pluto takes you deep into yourself. This is the planet that reveals your deepest emotional issues. Facing your past problems releases great creative power. Your intuition knows how to do this for you. It is up to you to relinquish the tendency to hide your fears. A wonderful rebirth will then manifest. You will find that you have even more mental and physical energy to live out your plans for the future.

Your relationships are more enjoyable when you communicate honestly. Your lovers and friends trust you when they sense you are being real with them. Your romantic relationships have greater passion and harmony when you talk from your heart as well as your mind.

Pluto helps you survive and process a crisis. Make time for fun and relaxation no matter your current life challenges. Balancing work and pleasure keeps you happy and healthy. Remember to think positive. This allows your intuition to tap into abundance and peace.

Shadow: Challenges

When you combine your Capricorn focus with Pluto passion, you do need to watch out for extremes. You can lose your sense of balance quickly in this meridian. The emotional water gets deep as you walk out only a few feet. If your drive to finish a project does not know when to quit, you get burned out. A love of sex or food could become an obsession. You lose perspective if your desire nature gets out of control.

A tendency to hold back anger or emotional intensity causes you to eventually explode. It wears down your mental and physical well-being to sit on your true feelings for prolonged periods of time. Your communication becomes cloudy. A relationship grows apart if you can't really hear each other. You don't do well being involved with a partner who is not willing to talk out a problem. The solution never comes.

Learn to forgive. Old grudges serve no purpose. They weaken your intuition and creativity. You are your own worst enemy if you can't get past unresolved issues. They eventually need to be surrendered or they will be extra baggage wearing you down.

Negative thoughts that play like a continuous tape recording in your head interfere with your happiness. Abundance and harmony elude you due to this behavior. This is a self-defeating pattern.

Dawn: Maximizing Your Potential

The Pluto meridian takes your personal power to new levels. Self-mastery is a big item presented in this terrain. If you have been lacking determination, your intuition links with this meridian and pulls you magically forward. Letting go of a fear to initiate new goals paves the way for Pluto to guide you to newfound self-confidence.

Finding a new lover or a stimulating job gives you a feeling of re-birth. Allowing yourself the freedom to redefine your identity ignites an evolutionary intuitive synchronicity. The past no longer controls you. The present is more invigorating and intriguing. The future is perceived by your mind as a promise of good fortune and new growth.

---- *Chapter 12* ----

AQUARIUS

Aquarius (1/20–2/18)

Archetypes: Inventor, Activist, Trend Setter, Rebel
Key Focus: Freedom and Independent Spirit
Element: Air
Planetary Ruler: Uranus
Cosmic Mirror Planet: Sun

Welcome to your Aquarius sign chapter. Your Aquarius gaze at the future discovers intuitive sparks when you interact with the planetary meridians. You stay mentally alert and ready to embark on new adventures when following your intuitive guidance. A spirit of feeling reinvented and filled with replenished energy can be your reality.

Intuition moves with great speed through your sign. This resembles the way your mind looks to the days ahead because it fills you with anticipation for new excitement to come into your life. When you partner with the planetary meridians, you find greater stimulation in your relationships, work, and serious plans.

Your Aquarius Dashboard Meridian Summary

Remember that the meridians are your doorways to self-discovery. You always have freedom of choice to tune in to whichever one is needed or more than one at a time. The universe is always ready to respond to your intuitive power.

Your Aquarian Sun meridian moves quickly with you to put those stimulating goals into creative action. The Moon meridian is your emotional vehicle to make your feelings known and to create a stable home environment. The Mercury meridian works with you to keep you learning new skills and stay mentally alert. The Venus meridian points you toward the right people to find harmony with and to seek inner peace. The Mars meridian challenges you to come out of the world of ideas and courageously show your talents. The Jupiter meridian activates your thirst for knowledge and encourages you to stay open to new ideas. The Saturn meridian focuses your mind to commit to your most sincere ambitions and relationships. The Uranus meridian excites your perceptions of the future and adds inventive thinking. The Neptune meridian strengthens your faith in your ideals and belief in your intuition. The Pluto meridian empowers your identity and encourages you to act with passion.

This begins your tour through the meridians. They are each unique in their own way. Your intuition is eager to dance with each one. Make them your friends and you will never feel alone.

Creative Expression:
Sun Meridian Activating Your Aquarius Intuition

Light: Strengths

The creative vitality of the Sun moves through your birth sign, Aquarius, with a curious interest about the future. It is not that you can't live in the present or have no concerns about the past. The future excites your mind into an energized enthusiasm. Anticipation of finding new, stimulating experiences keeps you an engaged player in the game of life.

The Sun sign of Aquarius solarizes you with a ferocious intellect. Being an air sign, you don't always like to get too emotional, as it may get in the way of your thought processes. Your intuition and mind sometimes wonder if life can keep up with the fast pace you prefer. There are times when you enjoy slowing down to catch your breath. It is your way of reclaiming your energy.

Some people likely perceive you to be stubbornly determined to have things on your own terms, but you see this as simply knowing what you want. Once you head down a path to pursue a goal, it is not so easy to get you to change direction.

Freedom is your lifeline. Without it you feel lost. Lovers, friends, and family must accept this part of your identity. You get along better with individuals who honor your need for personal autonomy. You are apt to have a wide circle of friends. Getting input from various types of people makes life interesting. You value friendships. People you trust are your favorite companions.

You have an inventive mind. A job has to offer a challenge to your intellect or you soon outgrow it. Patience may be needed to ensure that you don't grow too restless. You are happier when there is hope of finding a more challenging career. Starting your own business is exciting. In a work environment, you require the freedom to be your own person. Intuitively tuning in to new trends helps you learn skills that are highly marketable and profitable.

Shadow: Challenges

How would you know if you are not making a positive intuitive connection with this meridian? Your emotions feel locked away. This prevents your creative power from expressing at optimum intensity. You lack the self-confidence associated with this meridian.

You are too fixed in your opinions. A cold logic is too dominant. The Aquarius love of freedom is not being shared with others. Rather than engaging in an equal exchange of ideas, you are too attached to your own way of thinking.

Letting someone else make too many of your important decisions interferes with your personal growth. Without your own unique goals, you are lost. Your sense of direction is going in reverse. A lack of assertiveness confuses your identity.

Dawn: Maximizing Your Potential

The Sun meridian replenishes your mental energy as fast as you use it. It is that quick. Your intuition loves coming here because this terrain raises your whole being to very confident levels. Promoting yourself and those you love happens powerfully. Your pride in self and others intensifies. Even your immune system benefits from the heartfelt atmosphere found in this meridian.

Falling in love with a compatible person is stimulated in this landscape. Your intuitive professional instincts get pushed forward with great enthusiasm. Following your heart when it is merged with your goals gives birth to an evolutionary intuitive synchronicity. When you don't doubt your ability, the Sun meridian guides you to the harmony and abundance waiting right around the corner.

The Sun rules Leo, the opposite sign of Aquarius. You have the distinction of being the only sign to have the Sun acting as your cosmic mirror, or mirroring agent, for your sign. What does this indicate? Whereas Aquarius lives very much on the intellectual level, the Sun inspires you to take action on your ideas. Aquarius is busy seeking objectivity, while the Sun instills dramatic feelings. These opposing forces strive to work in unison to show your intuition how to take you along the paths that will deliver the happiness and success you desire.

Creating a Home and Expressing Feelings:
Moon Meridian Activating Your Aquarius Intuition

Light: Strengths

The Moon works as a close ally with your mentally adept Aquarius Sun sign, weaving in a feeling-oriented energy. At first glance there seems to be an apparent conflict in the natural rhythms of the emotional Moon and detached Aquarius. With practice and patience, you see that the two quickly make friends, allowing your lunar intuition equal time with your immediate impulse to trust your conscious awareness first. This back and forth arrangement comes in handy in situations where you need to communicate emotions and in circumstances where you need to stay on top of your strictly mental fortitude.

You thrive living in a community that allows you to interact with a wide variety of minds. People fascinate you, whether you have one close friend or several. It is in figuring out what gets someone to think the way they do that interests you. The Moon meridian lets you tune in to the inner world of someone. Your geographical location must be progressive and innovative. Your restless mind needs this in a big way.

People who understand your need for closeness and distance win your friendship. You are somewhat complicated in that you learn to appreciate someone caring about you, but then again, you like time apart so you can miss them. You attract individuals who are fond of such an arrangement. Your freedom drive is strong. You feel secure in knowing you have the right to say what is on your mind.

You don't always have to be upfront about your feelings, but allowing your romantic partner to hear some emotion as well as your intellect maintains clearer communication. When you are in touch with your inner landscape, this magical lunar world serves you well.

Shadow: Challenges

If you are not flowing with this meridian, there will be signals telling you this, one being that you refuse to express feelings. How will this impact you? It distances you greatly from someone you want to have as an intimate partner. Your intuition is not as powerful either. There is a block in your psyche when you hide from your emotions. Aloofness reigns.

Dependency needs get out of balance. You are either depending too much on someone else or letting people lean too heavily on you. The boundary lines are blurred. You lose your sense of direction, and personal goals grow foggy. You are looking at life through someone else's eyes too much rather than manifesting that Aquarian need to be an individual.

You might live too much for the future and forget about the present. Acting irresponsibly won't win admiration. Your restlessness for excitement is out of control. You are rebelling without a clear plan. This behavior causes stress in your relationships. Your commitment to a professional life is on shaky ground if you are not focused.

Dawn: Maximizing Your Potential

The Moon meridian supports your intuitive grasp on establishing a sense of security. You are able to attract the right people into your life who share your need for a stable private life. Closeness is easier to accept, even for an Aquarian like yourself, when you embrace the Moon's gentle guidance. You don't really like to act vulnerable. You have a fierce independent spirit. Letting a special someone into your inner world makes being with a soul mate possible.

Your home needs to feel safe from the outside world. It probably needs to be filled with new technologies and the people you enjoy. Your residence must be a castle, enabling you to be the true individual you came into the world to be. Your intuition flows more freely and harmoniously when your emotions are calm.

Mustering up the courage to pursue your most emotionally intense goals is often the catalyst to bring about an evolutionary intuitive synchronicity. It isn't what comes easy that brings about the most powerful intuitive qualities hidden in the labyrinths of this meridian. Rather, it is reaching deep within yourself to tap into those inspiring symbols that get you to rise above caution and fear to put those magnificent Aquarian insights into practice.

Mental Insights:
Mercury Meridian Activating Your Aquarius Intuition
Light: Strengths

Your intuition gets a spark of excitement in this meridian without really having to think about it. It is an automatic response to the energy in this lively information-packed meridian. The ruler of your Aquarius Sun sign is Uranus. This planet has been referred to as the "higher octave" of Mercury, and therefore these two planets and your Sun sign have an affinity for one another. You are never at a loss for words when you link to the quick-thinking influence of Mercury. Your communication skills can impress others. It is that refreshing, unique perspective you give to a situation that people like. Your insight, when offered generously to your closest friends, is looked upon favorably. Individuals who do not fear to speak their minds win your admiration and often your loyalty.

You get bored easily, so learning patience comes in handy when you need to tough out a job or project. It helps if you know that your actions will actually lead to a rewarding result. Having more than one major life purpose keeps you motivated. It may be that you need a career and a passionate hobby.

Your favorite partners in life are not bothered by your frank opinions. You have a generous side if someone acts like they respect your intelligence. You accept different points of view as long as someone does not demand that you stay silent about your own. It is equality that you value and, right behind that, tolerance.

You stay fairly organized even if to an outside observer your life looks like chaos. There is an intuitive internalized sense of order not far from your awareness. You can get moving fast toward finishing a project. The closer you get to a deadline, the more focused you get.

Staying true to your most heartfelt goals keeps you the happiest. This is how you maintain a sense of direction. Moving toward the future with a positive attitude is your barometer to let you know your intuition is on target.

Shadow: Challenges

How would you know if your intuition is not working in harmony with this meridian? Your mind is racing out of control. You can't slow down. Your nervous system is letting you know you have lost your center. Frantic actions result from not being able to get focused. Refusing to take a break from what is worrying you keeps you in this cycle.

You can be too critical of others. Perfection expectations may be beyond reason. That detail mechanism offered strongly by this meridian has to be used carefully. If you put others or even yourself under a microscope, you become too preoccupied with what you observe to be wrong. Forgetting to get back to positive thinking gets you into trouble.

Doubting your goals before they have had a fair chance to take off causes you to give up too soon. You dig up the seeds before they get an opportunity to grow. Patience and follow-through are missing.

Communication disconnects result with people if you get too headstrong. That open exchange of ideas is not in the picture. This causes arguments and misunderstanding in your key relationships.

Dawn: Maximizing Your Potential

The Mercury meridian is your gateway to keeping your perceptions sharp. Your inventive ideas get energized here. A sudden move into a new field of study is possible. Your ability to adapt to change is easier when your intuition taps into this terrain. If you like the path you are on and want to maintain it, Mercury lets you see easier ways to operate.

Changing your usual routines occasionally alters the normal way your mind thinks just enough to ignite an evolutionary intuitive synchronicity. This shift in your usual schedule could be just the thing to let you see the same situations in a new light. Your creative power increases when you allow for new experiences to occur.

Communication flows more smoothly with others when you listen as much as you speak. Mutual respect for one another's ideas ensures that your important relationships stay in harmony. Thinking positive thoughts attracts the good fortune you hope to achieve.

Relationship Tendencies:
Venus Meridian Activating Your Aquarius Intuition

Light: Strengths

This is the meridian that helps your intuition keep up with all of your people connections. Venus is the social-planner planet. If you are not the type of Aquarius who enjoys mingling with others, this planet still comes in handy in handling your negotiation strategies. Whether it is in playful activities with others or dealing with more serious business associates, Venus is there to be utilized.

There will be those accusing you of being too aloof. You probably see this as being cool and logical. Venus guides you to be more personable and affectionate. That side of you that is mentally detached as an Aquarian gets mixed with showing greater emotion. This does allow your intimate partner and friends to know you value them.

Tuning in to this meridian helps maintain balance in your relationships. Knowing you are being treated as an equal by someone is what gets you to trust them. You appreciate teamwork. It means a lot to you if a partner or friend supports your goals.

You like a job where you have room to operate freely. Working independently suits you. Your ideas can be out in front of an organization or culture. Intuitively, you learn patience in order to fit into a company and to best serve the needs of others.

People with innovative ideas stimulate your own inventiveness. Your friends are likely from diverse backgrounds. You have the capacity to relate to a wide variety of people. Your romantic relationships often begin in a surprising way. It is the sudden meeting of a soul mate that changes the direction of your life unexpectedly. You are attracted to a lover with a shared spirit in welcoming the future.

Shadow: Challenges

How might the Venus meridian and your intuition not be on the same wavelength? One way is being in a relationship where you are not being treated as an equal. Your goals flatline. Your self-esteem bottoms out if you remain in such an arrangement.

If you become too unpredictable, a lover, friend, or supervisor will get frustrated. A lack of consistency in your actions makes cooperation with you a challenge. People are looking for reliability so they know what to expect. Being an individualist is fine, as that is being true to your Aquarian tendencies. It is erratic behavior that is the problem. A lack of shared goals with a romantic partner eventually pulls you apart.

Working against rest and inner peace is another potential manifestation of not being in the flow with this meridian. As an Aquarian, your mind can race toward one goal after another, making it hard for your body to get any breaks in the action. Nervous anxiety exhausts you. Resisting a need to get centered is taking a wrong turn in this peaceful meridian.

Dawn: Maximizing Your Potential

The Venus meridian is an island in the midst of everyday living where you find your balance. Your values are strengthened by the energy in this landscape so they will better integrate into your hopes for a successful future. This is a nourishing oasis available to massage your feelings of self-worth. Your intuition attaches itself to your career plans, attempting to signal to you the right moves to make to obtain the best results for your talents.

The unique people you encounter are the catalysts for an evolutionary intuitive synchronicity. Your life is enriched through the insights swapped in these valuable relationships. You are meant to be a free-spirited Aquarian mind calling most of your own shots. Sharing your resources with a trusted partner fills you with a treasure chest of love and emotional support that even an Aquarian will learn to appreciate. You attract the abundance and good fortune you desire by being true to your highest beliefs.

Initiating Action:
Mars Meridian Activating Your Aquarius Intuition

Light: Strengths

If you are looking to get your energy motivated in a hurry, then this is the right meridian to put to work for you. Your intuition knows the way here when trying to guide you to take brave action. The aura of this place is colored with boldness. If you don't believe it, just dare Mars to give it a try. Before you know it, you are well on your way toward getting deep into a project that perhaps once intimidated you with its magnitude. Fear has no relevance in the Mars world other than to scare you into acting with courage.

Your Aquarius Sun sign is fast-paced mentally, so making friends with this swiftly moving meridian is not so foreign to your thinking. You might be cast into a leadership spotlight suddenly in a role you have never played before. Your instinct to show others how to move ahead assertively comes spontaneously when you trust Mars to lead the way. You can wonder later how you pulled this off.

Aquarius is an air sign, which means you live a lot in your head. A key Mars theme is expressing anger. It may make you nervous to get into a heated argument, although expressing your feelings dramatically, even if it gets messy, could be in your best interest in that this does clear the air. Clearer and calmer communication then follows and you feel better getting strong feelings off your chest and out in the open.

Learning patience does keep you from having to repeat the same actions over and over again. Your timing of major decisions will yield more productive results when you take the time to look at the details carefully. People will like you more if you don't rush them into making fast choices and respect their need to reflect first and act later.

You tend to concentrate better in jobs that hold your attention and show a promise for growth. Being employed in progressive work environments keeps you loyal and with greater passion to be creative. You get bored easily, so you need to feel challenged in your work life.

Shadow: Challenges

What happens if your intuition is not making a clear connection with this meridian? You will find that you can't get yourself to take the steps needed to get a goal started. It could be you are fearful of the size of the project or doubt your ability to get the job done. Another possibility is staying on the intellectual level and not getting your feet moving. In other words, you are visualizing what you want to do accurately but are procrastinating in getting started.

Impatience can be a haunting problem. This could be lacking patience with yourself or others. Failing to realize that it is better to pace yourself might end up in you not having the energy to follow through on your actions. Stopping and starting will frustrate you and aggravate the important people in your life.

Your identity gets confused if you allow someone to influence your decisions too much. The Aquarian need for originality and freedom becomes diluted. Trying to be what someone else says you should be causes mental confusion. Your future will become blurred.

Dawn: Maximizing Your Potential

The Mars meridian is the fast track to put your goals into fast forward. If you need an energy wake-up call, this is the right place to visit. Bold actions are manufactured here in great supply. Your intuition will bring you here when courage needs to be summoned quickly. This is a spontaneous world not so unlike the Aquarian one you already know so well.

Expressing your most heartfelt feelings directly keeps your anger in check. There is a natural competitive drive in this meridian. If you need to put your best effort out there for the world to see, this terrain makes it happen. There is no need to worry about yesterday's setbacks. The present and future are the proving grounds for your courage. Your intuition knows the world is a stage to showcase your ability. Your mind catches on quickly if you take a well-timed leap of faith. An evolutionary intuitive synchronicity will appear suddenly as though it was there all the time. A brave new insight will be the gift if you don't doubt the path your intuition is taking you on.

Expanding Knowledge:
Jupiter Meridian Activating Your Aquarius Intuition

Light: Strengths

Your intuition considers this meridian a home away from home. Why? Because both your Sun sign Aquarius and the planet Jupiter have an avid interest in the future. Both of these influences in their own way act like they are already sitting in your future saying, "Just get here." In Jupiter's world, there is a restless urge to move forward no matter the obstacles. After all, the grass might be greener elsewhere—which, by the way, is a favorite Jupiter motto.

The desire to keep your brain stimulated gets an expansive lift from Jupiter. This might occur through travel to faraway places or by reading interesting books. The idea is to remain open to new sources of knowledge.

The Aquarius tendency to want things on your own terms learns how to adopt flexibility in this land of Jupiter. Taking a broad perspective allows you to be inclusive of differing opinions.

The educator and counselor in you is awakened when your intuition links with Jupiter. Sharing your understanding helps others find solutions to their problems. Selling ideas to promote a business concept or to land a job is part of the good luck that Jupiter delivers.

Optimism reigns in this meridian. Transforming negative thinking into productive creative power is something your intuition keeps telling you is possible. Good fortune and abundance are the rewards for letting go of negativity. Your belief in your ability opens doors for creative opportunities.

Shadow: Challenges

How might you be off-target with this meridian? One possibility is being too concerned about the future and neglecting obligations in the present. Having dreams is a good thing, but the restless energy in this meridian needs to be carefully channeled. Otherwise, your actions will be counterproductive to your hopes to accomplish goals.

Another potential theme is being too judgmental. A "my way is the only way" mentality does not win any friends. You will alienate the very people you hope to reach. The support you want for your own goals will disappear, making you a lone wolf. Tolerance for alternative views is not in the equation.

Mental curiosity is not a high priority. This runs against the natural rhythm of both Aquarius and especially Jupiter. The inventive gifts available to you from this meridian are turned off. This causes missed opportunities. You remain in a stagnant lifestyle. Your creative imagination is not as bright as it could be.

Dawn: Maximizing Your Potential

The Jupiter meridian blends well with your freedom-oriented mind. Your inventive streak gets inspiration from a positive blast of upbeat energy that is constantly circulating throughout this lively meridian. Thoughts of future goals are never far from your intuitive gaze when entering this airspace.

Independent study could be the catalyst for launching an evolutionary intuitive synchronicity. Or it might come when you break away from a confining situation. Suddenly you are filled with energizing insights. You find the stimulating growth hoped for in an adventure that opens your eyes to new possibilities. Travel to other locations takes your mind out of the everyday grind and endless routines. A change of scenery could be just the thing to show you the methodology to reinvent yourself. Don't be afraid of change. It will sometimes startle you into an exciting new reality.

Career and Ambition:
Saturn Meridian Activating Your Aquarius Intuition

Light: Strengths

At first glance this would appear to be a meridian that conflicts with your powerful urge to spread your freedom wings wide. But with further investigation, you and this Saturn meridian have something in common. What might that be? Before Uranus (the modern ruler of your Sun sign Aquarius) was discovered in 1781, Saturn was assigned rulership. So you essentially have two planets co-ruling your Sun sign. You can consider Saturn a cousin. Saturn represents your instincts to preserve the past, and you will soon see that Uranus pushes you to break away from tradition. Saturn is the grounding force your intuition comes to greet when needing to stay determined. This is the terrain that provides plenty of perseverance. Saturn tries to convince you that hard work pays off. There may be a bit of delayed gratification, but eventually you will get your just rewards.

If you are an Aquarius who considers yourself a patient person, you can thank Saturn. You are a fast-thinking individualist, whether you are in the habit of displaying this or not. Saturn focuses those quick insights into pragmatic winners. Your business skills flourish from mixing your energy with the essence of this meridian. Career aspirations get disciplined and reality-tested here like in no other planetary meridian. Saturn manufactures ambition.

Past-life patterns can be integrated harmoniously in this incarnation. Perhaps you were such a free spirit in previous lives that you came here to take greater responsibility. Overcoming a fear of commitments is part of the challenge. Being supportive of those who need you brings these past tendencies into enlightenment. In some past lifetimes you may have been too timid in asserting your own goals. This is your chance to step up to the plate and make a strong statement about your own needs. Saturn is guiding your intuition to help you balance these old karmic patterns into a favorable expression.

Shadow: Challenges

Where could your intuition run off course in this meridian? One potential area is becoming rigidly attached to one way of doing things. It is next to impossible to talk you out of a decision even if someone is trying to warn you of the risk ahead of time. Inflexibility causes your internal sensor trying to guide you around an iceberg to become silent.

One failure could depress you for a long time if you dwell too much on what went wrong. An inability to move forward is due to a fear of failing again and forgetting what you know how to do well. Refocusing on an alternative route is blocked when your brainpower is frozen.

If you lose your self-reliance, this shows that a past-life pattern is occurring again. Your Aquarius ingenuity weakens. That forceful, empowering drive to express your creative talent is in low gear and comes to a grinding halt. Allowing others to be too dominant in making your decisions confuses your identity. Your Aquarius sense of direction is lost in trying too hard to please people. This is not you at your best. Another past-life theme of recklessly taking chances with little forethought will cost you time and money and could even show you losing key people in your life.

Dawn: Maximizing Your Potential

The Saturn meridian gives logic to your ideas. You can be as spontaneous as needed in your Aquarius personal style. Your intuition links to Saturn to make sure your decision making has a solid foundation. After all, this is a meridian built with walls of stable thinking behind them.

Saturn guides you to believe in your leadership skills. Managing a business , department, or family is aided by this ancient god of taking control of a situation. This is the ultimate planning planet that combines beautifully with your goal-minded thought processes. The strategic talent furnished by this meridian serves to help you negotiate for what is in your best interest.

An evolutionary intuitive synchronicity bursts into your life when you let go of a fear of change. Occasionally, in losing control, it allows you to experience a transforming energy that permeates your consciousness. Your perceptions are stimulated to perceive a new reality, one that rises above negativity into a horizon filled with abundant opportunities for success.

Future Goals and Inventiveness:
Uranus Meridian Activating Your Aquarius Intuition

Light: Strengths

Your intuition visits this meridian frequently, the reason being that Uranus is the ruler of your Aquarius Sun sign. This gives you easy access to the brilliant insights offered by this inventive meridian. You can reinvent your identity when walking the halls of this free-thinking landscape. Your persona that you want to show the public has a carefree appearance, as though it knows something the rest of the world does not.

People will take notice of your progressive ideas when you make use of Uranus energy. The future calls to you often. Career dreams suddenly come alive, and your intuition points the way to make them come true. Your goals get stimulated here like in no other meridian. If you are looking for a catalyst to lift you out of your current circumstances, then you have come to the right place.

A group with a similar purpose may suit your needs at times. The support that such an atmosphere provides gives you a secure feeling. Even an Aquarius individualist appreciates the company of like minds.

Equality is first and foremost in your thoughts. If it isn't, it doesn't take long for Uranus to beam you a signal to remind you how important it is that your own opinions are valued. Being with friends and lovers who respect your intelligence is highly valued.

Your professional life must be mentally interesting. You require a job with a lot of autonomy to express yourself. If you don't have a work arena that does this, you will seek outside interests or other employment opportunities that provide you with this. In many ways, this meridian is the gatekeeper watching over you to guide you to information and people who expand your mind.

Romantically, you enjoy someone who is both a lover and a friend. This is influenced by the impact of this Uranus meridian, which emphasizes friendship. You like a person who has an open mind and wants to grow with you. Your independent soul attracts individualists and unconventional types when your intuition basks in the aura of this highly imaginative meridian.

Shadow: Challenges

What are indications that your intuition is not in harmony with this meridian? You become too distant emotionally from those who care about you. Your intellect is used more as a defense rather than a positive communication tool. There is a possibility that you will lose key people in your life due to this behavior.

There are times when rebelling against those who abuse their authority is a good thing. But if you are in a constant rebellious mode, you lose your focus toward important goals. Your stability is visibly shaken if you don't get back to more consistent actions. Your creative power is not as sharp in the long run.

Too much dependency on a group or person for your identity causes confusion. You are not expressing that wonderful Aquarius need for freedom and independent thinking. Your unique insights lessen in intensity.

Becoming too eccentric or out of the mainstream works against you. Uranus energy can be utilized to shock others. You can take those inventive and alternative ideas right into a business or hobby. However, it is when you are being different just to be different that you get into trouble.

Dawn: Maximizing Your Potential

The Uranus meridian is a true home for you. The sign Aquarius and the planet Uranus make a dynamic duo. Your mind is on ready alert to try the latest technology available. Progressive ideas turn on your creative buttons. It excites you to let go and run with the mentally exhilarating energy found here.

Giving yourself the freedom to experiment with new alternative thinking brings you an evolutionary intuitive synchronicity. Getting away from the same routines elevates your perceptions into a reinvented reality. Even if you don't make any major changes, your mind is reinvigorated with great insights.

This meridian attracts a wide circle of friends. You enjoy the company of people from diverse social backgrounds. It is in exposing your world to fresh ideas that you never have to worry about boredom or stagnation. You remain forever courageously marching forward with an eager quest for knowledge.

Creative Imagination and Idealism:
Neptune Meridian Activating Your Aquarius Intuition

Light: Strengths

When Neptune was discovered in 1846, it was moving through the sign Aquarius. It was actually Neptune's gravitational pull on Uranus, the ruler of your Aquarius Sun sign, that gave clues to astronomers of its position in the sky. Therefore, Aquarius, in a sense, is a cousin to Neptune. If you really try, you can tap into this elusive planet with your intuition, which in many ways dodges the radar of your conscious mind. Don't feel bad. It does this to all of humanity. Why? Because it can. Neptune travels along mystical pathways that only your intuition is able to accurately interpret.

As an Aquarius, you belong to the air element. This indicates that you rely heavily on your intellect. Your insights come in a flash when your mind puts new perceptions to work for you. Neptune sends messages in a different sort of manner. This information comes through dreams and sometimes when you are in a meditative type of state. Have you ever had a thought that seemed to come from some place other than your normal mental processes? If you have, it very well could have been the Neptune influence. The universe works through you in mysterious ways. This ethereal energy is what might make you an artist, psychic, or healer. It will inspire your highest ideals. Whatever creative expression you undertake, don't ever forget that Neptune is ready to guide you to an inspiring and enlightening experience. This energy has a transforming quality that lifts self-doubt into positive creative manifestation.

Locating that faith within you in order to exhibit those Aquarian goals powerfully is possible. When you find that sacred and quiet space inside of you, anything can occur. The universe will open abundant doors if you knock loudly enough and follow those internal Neptune hints being dropped in your path periodically. The reward is often a new uplifting career, connecting with a soul mate, or tuning in to a cause that fuels your spirit with a never-ending inner peace.

Shadow: Challenges

Neptune will bring out the helper in you who wants to alleviate the emotional problems of others. It could just as well find you enabling negative behaviors in people by not wanting to confront them. An overly passive approach works against the Neptune meridian flow. Rather than empowering someone by believing in them, you are doubting that they can overcome negative patterns. This behavior is not good for you or those you care about.

A loss of boundaries occurs if you lose clarity about self-definition. You are not as mentally sharp when not utilizing your reality-testing ability. Your closest relationship encounters are not as harmonious or productive. The passion eventually evaporates.

If you overly idealize people, you will expect too much from them. You can't let someone project the same illusion upon you. Perfection is impossible to live up to and will disrupt relationships in a big way.

The emotional power found in this meridian is immense. It will cloud your wonderful Aquarian intellect if you deny your feelings. Communicating your emotional intensity feeds your creative power. Denying it takes away from your confidence to achieve your goals. Your relationships lack the trust you so badly desire.

Dawn: Maximizing Your Potential

The Neptune meridian accelerates the growth of your intuition quickly. You are already mentally fast. Mental lightning bolts ignite your perceptions to see situations unfold before others do. It gives you an edge in managing your profession, family, and love life. Neptune does the same for you with its intuitive magic. These two energies unite, giving you the success you hope to achieve.

When you take an extra moment to reflect before moving too fast with choices, it gives Neptune a chance to add its voice. It is then that an evolutionary intuitive synchronicity may slip past your conscious awareness to give you an inspirational awakening that rocks your soul into a state of joy. The universe calls on you to show your creative talent when you have the faith to follow your idealism forward. There is no need to look back, because the abundance and love you seek have already arrived.

Personal Empowerment and Passion:
Pluto Meridian Activating Your Aquarius Intuition

Light: Strengths

This meridian is a roadmap to empowering your Aquarian goals. Your career drive intensifies when your intuition links to Pluto. Actually, your whole being finds a renewed passion for your life pursuits. If you need a rugged determination to push forward toward success, you are in the right neighborhood.

Pluto deepens your emotions. Expressing them openly stimulates your mental energy. Your mind and feelings need to play off one another to maximize your intuitive power. This is a big secret to your relationship and professional success.

As an Aquarius, you depend greatly on your intellect. Pluto awakens your mental curiosity to keep adding knowledge to help keep your options open. This is a research meridian guiding you to delve deeply into your favorite subjects.

Self-mastery comes through not fearing new challenges. In dealing with conflict by looking for real solutions, you become internally stronger. Your success in the world may come right out of being a great problem-solver.

Trust means everything to you when it comes to forming significant partnerships. You remain loyal to people who are willing to generously lend their support to your highest dreams. Individuals who walk their talk win your loyalty and friendship. Someone willing to give you enough breathing room to establish your own unique identity is what you prefer.

You sometimes demand a lot from lovers and family members. They probably perceive you as shockingly outspoken, but you see this as saying what you mean. Developing an intuitive awareness of the impact of your actions and words on others is part of this meridian package deal. Your closeness with those you love deepens as you talk as much from the heart as the mind. Being there when someone really needs you wins their admiration and desire to be a friend for life. This is the message of the Pluto meridian.

Shadow: Challenges

What could go wrong if you don't make a clear intuitive connection to this meridian? There is a chance that you will become too obsessed with a goal, whether it is beneficial for you or not. Walking near the edge of a dangerous cliff is exciting when you are feeling Pluto intensity. It draws out your passion. The question then becomes, is this decision in your best interest? It might be hurting you and people you are close to. An unwillingness to change direction might lead to disastrous results. Flexibility is absent.

Another issue that surfaces in a negative manner is bottled-up emotions. You won't say how you feel about situations. Your quietness leaves people wondering what is going on in your mind. Silence is a way to manipulate others into agreeing with you or even punishing them. This does cause problems in your relationships. Sooner or later, resentment settles in and a lover or friend will want to end the relationship.

Surrendering too much of your personal power to an individual or group causes you to lose your identity. Your own goals are being sacrifices to serve others in an extreme way. The Aquarius equality you value and the freedom you cherish are lost.

Dawn: Maximizing Your Potential

The Pluto meridian is a wonderful place for self-discovery. Your creative potential is awakened as you search for ways to express your skills. Your intuition finds a strong ally here to empower your belief in your abilities.

Facing your fears shines a light on them and points you toward mental clarity. Dealing with adversity opens your perceptions to greater self-confidence. Believing in your insights and showing them to the world ignites an evolutionary intuitive synchronicity. It is that meeting of your mind with the ideas of other individuals that stimulates your creative thinking.

Your intuition will guide you to the love and friendship you need to be happy. Taking the risk to trust someone you love is scary and exciting all at once. Sharing your inner world with the same intensity that you act with in the outer world keeps a lover as close as you would ever want them to be.

—— *Chapter 13* ——

PISCES

Pisces (2/19–3/20)

Archetypes: Idealist, Healer, Mystic, Spiritualist
Key Focus: Developing Faith and Inspiring Ideals
Element: Water
Planetary Ruler: Neptune
Cosmic Mirror Planet: Mercury

Welcome to your Pisces sign chapter. Your Pisces goals find intuitive inspiration when connecting with the planetary meridians. The inner strength to follow through on a plan can come forward when listening to your intuitive guidance. A renewed belief in your abilities is possible.

Intuition moves dreamily through your sign. This matches the introspective and reflective way you pursue your goals. Your idealism can tap into the fortitude to make your highest aspiration for success come true through linking with the planetary meridians. You will then create harmonious relationships, find meaningful work, and rejoice in seeing your dreams become a reality.

Your Pisces Dashboard Meridian Summary

The meridians are part of your everyday self-expression. Remember that you always have the freedom to choose how you want to use these celestial gifts from the universe. They are ready to serve your intuition to make your dreams come true.

Your Pisces Sun meridian is proud to help you show the world you have ideals that make a strong statement about your creative drive. The Moon meridian is your gateway to establishing a home base and aids you in tuning in to your feelings. The Mercury meridian stimulates your mental sharpness and encourages you to adapt to change. The Venus meridian points you toward relationship harmony and guides you to find inner peace. The Mars meridian activates your courageous competitive spirit and encourages you to initiate spontaneous action. The Jupiter meridian awakens your desire to explore a wide range of knowledge and to operate from your highest level of integrity. The Saturn meridian intensifies your ambition instincts and shows you how to honor your commitments. The Uranus meridian excites your independent streak and speeds up your desire to move in new reinvented directions. The Neptune meridian increases your belief in your ideals and deepens your understanding of love. The Pluto meridian enlivens your passion to find creative outlets and to embrace your personal power.

This begins your excursion through the meridians. Enjoy each of these paths to self-discovery. One is not better than the others. They work together with your intuition to make your life experiences that much more meaningful and rewarding.

Creative Expression:
Sun Meridian Activating Your Pisces Intuition

Light: Strengths

The creative vitality of the Sun moves fluidly through your birth sign, Pisces, infusing your personality with a highly imaginative flair. You are able to display a whimsical mind that sometimes appears to others as not being focused. You see this as your own way of processing information and gazing at the world around you. It likely does not matter to you if others understand your logic or reasoning method.

The Sun sign of Pisces solarizes you with a sensitive spirit that has a great capacity to tune in to the mood of a person, group, or organization. This serves you well in business dealings, as you sense what is expected of you. Your intuition can push for a winning negotiation.

Your artistic instincts are highly evolved. It does not matter if you engage in artistic activities professionally or as a hobby. You simply just know good aesthetics when you see, smell, or hear them It is in the depths of your soul to channel creative impulses, while many in the world stumble through this experience. Finding routes around your conscious mind is an artform your intuition developed early in life. This is your magical way of bypassing what your mind says is not possible. Your creative imagination prefers a lot of room to roam freely.

You can work a nine-to-five job but need something extra in life to keep those creative imagination juices activated. Your talent need not be hidden. This meridian builds your self-confidence. Finding the ego strength to show everyone your ability comes with patience and practice. Not waiting for the perfect time to arrive to put your creative power in action builds your self-confidence. Trusting your instincts strengthens your creative power.

Shadow: Challenges

What happens if your intuition does not get into the right step with this meridian? Your emotions seem and feel like a large ocean of confusion. Land is not in sight. This usually occurs if you are too sensitive to criticism. Your feelings get upset too easily. Staying in a relationship with a person who negates your every idea is like drinking poison. Remaining on a job that does not match up to your potential could be equally as problematic.

A fear of people not appreciating your talent or ideas holds you back. This is hiding an ability that might take you to a more abundant life. Your self-esteem is not as vibrant as it could be.

This meridian provides a forceful thrust of self-confidence. If you keep waiting for the perfect time to arrive to put a plan into motion, you are working against the natural atmospheric pressure in this terrain. You will feel a lack of inspiration in playing the waiting game as your enthusiasm evaporates.

Dawn: Maximizing Your Potential

The Sun meridian helps you keep your life in perspective. There is no need to worry excessively about trying to make something too perfect. The Sun says give it your best shot and the details will fall into place. Believe in your intuition! You can make the necessary adjustments later.

This meridian allows even a Pisces dreamer with a vivid imagination to hold their feet on the ground. The Sun's radiance will reward your willingness to trust in its guidance. Creativity is manufactured here in large quantities. You only need to tap into this wondrous wealth.

Putting your ideals into action is what gives rise to an evolutionary intuitive synchronicity. This is the secret to keeping your mind young and your heart happy. There is no need to hide your feelings. Extending out into the world intuitively has its roots in being clear about your emotions. When you rise above the fear to show your ability and creative power, you find the harmony you want.

Creating a Home and Expressing Feelings: Moon Meridian Activating Your Pisces Intuition

Light: Strengths

Your Sun sign, Pisces, has a lot in common with the Moon in that both belong to the water element. This makes for a promising partnership, as both your Sun sign and the Moon blend well together. The Moon meridian is a crucial component in guiding your intuition to clarity. Finding a secure place within yourself and a comfortable niche in the world is influenced by the Moon energy.

This tends to be a moody meridian. It is made from rich emotional soil. Your inner world is easier to stabilize when your relationships are defined clearly. You are happier when feeling free to express your feelings. This empowers your intuition. Roles that let you live out your ideals give you a sense of renewed faith.

Your home does not need to be as quiet as a monastery, but you probably prefer it to be a tranquil place. Living with a soul mate and surrounding yourself with items symbolizing your beliefs are encouraged by this meridian. Residing in a location that offers you the possibility of showing your intuitive creative power is music for your mind and soul.

You like individuals who are able to read your moods. It is as though you communicate an unspoken verbal language with one another. It builds trust. But in the end, clear spoken communication is your best bet to relationship success. A lover who shares your need to escape occasionally from the same daily routines warms your heart. This is your way of establishing intimacy as well as recharging your mental and emotional batteries.

Shadow: Challenges

What could indicate that you are not in sync with the Moon meridian? Your emotions may regularly flood your thoughts. You could feel too responsible for someone else's problems. Guilt detracts from your intuitive clarity.

Losing sight of your boundaries makes it extremely challenging to keep balanced in relationships. Your dependency needs are out of alignment. Wanting to be needed and needing someone else is fine. It is when you are afraid to be alone or compulsively dependent on a person that you get into trouble. A person who constantly weighs you down with their problems will wear you out.

Staying in comfort zones all the time prevents you from experiencing new opportunities in jobs or relationships. Settling for situations that don't meet your needs confines you to limiting situations. You lack the belief in your own ability to take on a new challenge.

Holding back strong feelings for too long will make you very moody. Your decisions become foggy. This causes angry outbursts as you boil over with resentment. Your mind and emotions stay in a tug of war.

Dawn: Maximizing Your Potential

The Moon meridian is an energy that guides you to create a life that feels in harmony with your intuition. It is your inner landscape to find the right paths to give you a sense of security. Your Pisces idealism is very much at home in this terrain. Linking to the Moon meridian allows you to be clear about your inner motivations for action.

In venturing out beyond your comfort zones, you make the possibility of an evolutionary intuitive synchronicity more likely. Why? Because this is when the universe sees that you have serious intentions in wanting to engage in new experiences. Familiar routines do give you stability, but taking alternate routes with new scenery lifts your intuitive power to new, energizing insights. The Moon meridian will be inspiring if you have the faith to follow your higher values to greater abundance.

Mental Insights:
Mercury Meridian Activating Your Pisces Intuition

Light: Strengths

Your emotions find mental focus in this meridian. Your Sun sign has a great capacity to make use of intuitive right-brain instincts. In this left-brain landscape, you make those brilliant intuitive right-hemisphere energies reach pragmatic results.

Mercury is the king of details. Your big dreams find better planning in this meticulous environment. Your Pisces water sign is assured by Mercury that you are walking on stable ground when linking to this get-down-to-business planet.

If you need to reach back for mental strength, then this is your meridian. Your intuition knows to knock on Mercury's door when guiding you to put your ideas to work. There is a time and place for the precise conscious-mind awareness offered by Mercury.

Maintaining a sense of order when taking on a major project is another great perk found in this meridian. Let your intuition have its freedom. Don't try to rein it in too much. Mercury will help you put the pieces together in a clever way later on.

Learning new skills keeps your mind alert and maximizes your earning potential. Tweaking your talent occasionally expands your marketability. The versatility featured in this meridian influences you to be diversified.

There are two key dimensions to Mercury, because it rules two astrological signs. As the ruler of Virgo, Mercury gives you an in-depth analysis of details. As the ruler of Gemini, Mercury spreads its restless wings to take you on a multidimensional path. So you are able to get the best of two worlds here. One is knowing that Mercury has your back to give you the step-by-step discipline to finish what you start.

The other is the way it fans your intuition to lead you into a variety of new experiences to excite your mind.

Adapting to change is a breeze when you connect with this meridian. It is as though your intuition was trying to tell you all along that changing circumstances need not be feared. You have this insightful Mercurial eye watching over you.

Shadow: Challenges

How will you know if you are not in step with this meridian? One signal is that you will not trust your intuition. Extreme worry about the outcome of situations blocks your intuitive flow. That Pisces faith in your ability is missing. Believing you can make a plan come to a positive conclusion is lost to self-doubt.

Trying to be too perfect is a nagging potential impediment to your happiness. Not knowing when to stop obsessing over making something perfect makes for frustration. You are forgetting to put your best foot forward and edit your plan later.

Staying on the intellectual level to the exclusion of emotional expression makes you appear aloof. It is difficult to establish intimacy if you can't communicate feelings. This is fine in business dealings but not good in your love relationships. You will appear too insensitive to romantic partners, friends, and family.

Dawn: Maximizing Your Potential

The Mercury meridian helps you maintain a steady and clear direction to put your goals into concrete action. Your perceptions get a tune-up here regularly. It is Mercury's job to make sure you don't lose sight of the details as you complete a project. This ensures that your intuition has the freedom to roam without getting too preoccupied by the little things.

An evolutionary intuitive synchronicity will be discovered when you are in the midst of learning a new skill or off on a wonderful, exhilarating adventure away from stress. Your insights get rejuvenated by these transformative experiences. Your ideals and hopes for the future become energized.

Mercury rules Virgo, the opposite sign of Pisces. Mercury is the cosmic mirror, or mirroring agent, for your sign. How might this play out? With its emphasis on paying close attention to details, this Mercury energy complements your Pisces desire to flow intuitively while accenting the need to grasp the big picture. Mercury mirrors back to you the need to look for stable paths to fulfill your idealism. The happiness you desire finds a good ally in this meridian, one that keeps one eye on the road, allowing you to enjoy the inspiring, beautiful scenery. Your ideals and dreams for the future become enlivened.

Relationship Tendencies:
Venus Meridian Activating Your Pisces Intuition

Light: Strengths

Your intuition is a frequent flyer in this meridian. Venus knows your relationship hopes and dreams well. It is your idealism and belief in others that attracts this love goddess planet. When you reach out to help people, this meridian sends its blessings. It does try to remind you in the process of helping others not to forget to water the soil of your own goals.

Your social instincts find great stimulation in the land of Venus. You need not ever feel alone. This meridian tries to let you know that you have an invisible friend here. Venus will guide you to relationships that promise harmony.

There is a business dimension found in this meridian as well. The drive to be able to support yourself and establish a comfortable life is part of the Venus package. Finding a job that allows you to express your values is like earning a bonus. A greater reward is finding work that strengthens your self-esteem and also pays the bills.

You likely value friendships. Individuals who don't wear you out emotionally are your favorite people. Those who share your ideals and goals win your support. You especially enjoy the company of people who naturally tune in to your inner world without needing a great deal of explanation.

Escapes to movies, restaurants, and relaxing travel getaways inspire your imagination. This is your way of revitalizing your mind, body, and soul. Balancing work and pleasure helps you maintain your appreciation of life.

When you fall in love with someone, it ignites a special purpose. Romance is like a religious experience to your inner being. It transforms your mental processes. Your consciousness feels as though it is dancing.

Some people view you as hard to please. You see this as having high expectations of yourself and sometimes even your closest friends. Your intuition leads you to this meridian to stimulate your love and business connections. It does ask you to be reasonable in what you ask of people. A brighter today or tomorrow is always possible to experience. This is the universe's way of showing you that there is much magic to tap into. All you have to do is tune in to the beauty and abundance of this dazzling meridian.

Shadow: Challenges

What could possibly go wrong in this meridian if everything sounds so wonderful? It is when you are too indecisive about making choices that you run into problems. You could hesitate in committing to a relationship, thinking you could find a better situation later. Or you have a pattern of attracting individuals who are afraid to commit to a long-term relationship. Neither scenario brings you happiness.

If you don't value your own life goals, you will settle for relationships and jobs that are far below your worth and ability. This causes you stress and anxiety, which you could do without. Better opportunities pass you by.

Your dedication to individuals and groups may go overboard. Serving others is rewarding, but being taken advantage of by a person or group is not in your best interest. In the end, you will feel used and abused.

Having a compulsive urge to want to be liked works against you. Your belief in yourself is missing in action. The equality you seek is not there. You are looking for too much attention due to insecurity.

Dawn: Maximizing Your Potential

The Venus meridian promotes self-confidence in your ability to create solid, rewarding relationships. When your intuition connects with Venus, there is another big payoff. Your work life is elevated to discover new opportunities. Tuning in to how to market your abilities increases your earning power. Your artistic talent gets very stimulated in expressing Venus energy. Your Pisces Sun sign forms a magical bond with the Venus meridian to potentially produce works of art.

Building stable partnerships is your path to relationship happiness. The equal give and take of a productive romance, friendship, or work connection is quite satisfying. Your intuition knows to drink from the fountains of this meridian to guide you to these wonderful experiences.

It is in having belief in your values that an evolutionary intuitive synchronicity manifests. Having the faith to pursue paths that reflect your highest beliefs attracts more abundance than you ever dared to dream about.

Initiating Action:
Mars Meridian Activating Your Pisces Intuition

Light: Strengths

If you are waiting for the right feeling to proceed with an idea, then perhaps it is time to make use of this fiery meridian. It is fueled up and ready to go. There is always ample fire in this Mars land to ignite your dreams into action. So you see there is no need to wait any longer to move full speed ahead.

Pisces is known for having strong emotions. This does not mean that you will be quick to reveal them to just anyone. When your intuition links to Mars, you will be more direct in letting your feelings be broadcast. Mars tends to encourage being upfront with your opinions.

This is the meridian associated with assertiveness. Mars brings out your courage. So if you are a watery Pisces with a longing to show the world your talents, this is the place to visit on a regular basis.

Career drive comes alive when you bring Mars into the picture. Your identity passionately desires to find work and a life mission that better symbolizes your beliefs. When you do this, it ignites self-confidence. A charisma colors your persona and people take notice. You magnetically attract support when you show your faith in a project or goal.

If you need a more direct approach in initiating romances and friendships, this is a meridian that gives you an edge. An introverted energy quickly is converted into an extroverted one. Letting go of shyness comes fast when Mars joins forces with you.

Your creative power is awakened when your intuition aligns with Mars. A revitalized sense of urgency takes over. The adrenalin is pumped. It is time to trust your intuitive instincts and make a bold statement.

Shadow: Challenges

If your intuition gets its wires crossed when trying to connect with Mars energy, it will show in a few different scenarios. One is you will procrastinate rather than being proactive. Treading water is the news of the day and not moving forward confidently. Losing momentum causes you to miss out on growth-promoting experiences.

Swallowing your anger on a regular basis produces emotional confusion. Your mind and body suffer the consequences. Your identity loses clarity. Your intuition is not functioning to full capacity. Your relationships get out of balance as well. Clear communication is absent.

Impatience with yourself and others is possible. This is a dynamo of an intense energy meridian. It will speed up your impulses. Hasty judgments and actions get you into trouble. Assertiveness could turn into misguided aggression. Power struggles result. Denying you have problems only makes it more difficult to find your way to clear perceptions and actions.

Dawn: Maximizing Your Potential

The warrior in you comes alive in a big way in the Mars meridian. This is a bold terrain asking you to step up to the plate and put your ideas into action. It is fine to be emotional. After all, you are a Pisces Sun sign and are supposed to be. But don't let your feelings keep you dwelling on what might have been possible. Your intuition knows the path to Mars to put your ideas to work so they will become a reality.

Proceeding with courage and believing in your ability brings an evolutionary intuitive synchronicity into your life. Overcoming a reluctance to let the world view your talents attracts abundance. Allowing your intuition to walk with a spirit of adventure launches the relationships and goals you hope to make come true.

Expanding Knowledge:
Jupiter Meridian Activating Your Pisces Intuition

Light: Strengths

You have an interesting relationship with this meridian. Before Neptune (the ruler of your Pisces Sun sign) was discovered, Jupiter was considered the ruling planet. It is as though you have a kinship connection with Jupiter more like a cousin. Both your sign Pisces and the planet Jupiter have a similar idealism about life. Jupiter is a fiery planet that encourages you to move forward confidently to fulfill plans for the future. Your intuition has its tank filled with optimism any time you visit this meridian.

Travel is a favorite Jupiter way of expanding your knowledge. Another one is increasing your opportunities for success by taking a courageous risk. Your intuition gets motivated to guide you to go to locations that offer stimulating experiences. You might feel an inner pull to visit places that you had not thought of exploring before. It is as though something deep inside of you feels an inclination to go there.

Education and experimenting with new skills are part of Jupiter's world. Your curiosity about people, places, and things gets awakened.

A desire to make a dream come true occurs often with the Jupiter influence. Your luck has an excellent chance to take a turn for the better when you link to this meridian. Making the effort to put your ideas into action gets the universe to respond to you with greater abundance. Keep positive mantras going in your thoughts, as this attracts relationship and work harmony. This is the magical force of the Jupiter meridian.

Shadow: Challenges

If your intuition misses the mark with this meridian, it will show up in various ways. One is that you will have problems focusing. The expansive wing span of this meridian is without rival. You must exercise caution in not becoming too overextended. Watch what you promise people. You will disappoint them if you don't follow through.

You could become too critical if people don't live up to your hopes and wishes. There is only so much others will be able to do to please you. Be reasonable in what you request. It will keep your relationships happier. You will become frustrated if you ask for the impossible.

Procrastination can surface. This occurs if you put off dealing with a problem. Running away from obstacles only makes them harder to face later.

If you don't believe in your ability, it is very challenging to find success. Abundance will always be out of reach. A positive attitude is missing. Your mind is seeing the world through self-doubt.

Dawn: Maximizing Your Potential

The Jupiter meridian raises your hopes to fulfill your most important goals. This is an optimistic meridian for your intuition to blend into. The world appears user-friendly when your mind soaks up this planet's energy. An expansive outlook is inspired by the creative power emanating from this terrain. Your mind can't help but feel like it is holding a handful of winning luck.

It is in venturing into adventurous learning that an evolutionary intuitive synchronicity is launched. Your perceptions gain new insights that replenish your drive for self-discovery.

You attract the people and work that satisfy your hope for harmony. Maintaining an open mind brings you the mental, emotional, physical, and spiritual wealth you hope to achieve.

Career and Ambition:
Saturn Meridian Activating Your Pisces Intuition

Light: Strengths

The Saturn meridian is the great focusing agent of the universe. The word "business" is synonymous with this planet's key symbolism. When your intuition joins with Saturn, you get a chance to put your beliefs to the test. The bonus here is that you will see in reality how sound your ideas are. Being determined to see a plan to its conclusion is the reward for putting Saturn to work for you.

If you are too idealistic, Saturn tries to guide you to become grounded. This does not mean that you have to give up on your decisions. It is only saying that you need to stay realistic and patient with your expectations. Finding the right balance is the key to success.

Your creativity finds discipline and concentration in this meridian. You are able to tap into great creative power when putting your best effort into your skills. Mastering difficult projects begins with a committed first step.

Wisdom comes through learning from past mistakes. Having a positive attitude allows you to get through any obstacle in your path. Letting go of your fear of making a mistake is liberating. This gives you the freedom to redefine the present that best matches who you have become and desire to express.

Your intuition leads you to start a business or make a career move. The Saturn meridian makes a great ally in connecting with those roles you currently want to embrace. Putting a work strategy together is part of utilizing this meridian energy effectively.

Tuning in to Saturn intuitively helps you conquer past-life patterns. It could be that in some previous lifetimes, you ran from challenges. In this incarnation, you are getting a chance to take responsibility for your actions. Dealing with conflict makes you intuitively stronger. There may have been past lives where you were too much the dreamer and lacked the willpower to accomplish your goals. This lifetime presents you with an opportunity to hone right in on a plan and get it done. Your mental and creative power multiplies when showing the world your ability. Your ambition gains clarity and confidence when you forge ahead knowing you will succeed.

Shadow: Challenges

What might happen if your intuition is not tuning in to Saturn accurately? Your self-confidence takes a dip. You feel a lack of energy. This might be due to feeling depressed or having a negative attitude. Your idealism and imagination are squashed. A Pisces like yourself finds this frustrating.

Your boundaries in relationships lack clarity. You are either leaning too heavily on others or allowing someone to do the same to you. The downside in these situations is that the harmony you seek with others is missing. Responsibility is not being evenly shared.

Commitments may appear scary. Fear of closeness shortens the lifespan of a relationship. You will never know the full potential of a romance or friendship if you don't give it a chance.

You might become too obsessed with being a success. A failure will be earth-shattering. If you are too attached to the results, life is not as much fun. This is ambition gone astray. The wonderful determination offered by Saturn is being misread when you become obsessed with getting ahead.

Past-life patterns can emerge once again. Escapism thwarts your dreams for success. Running away from challenges will cause you to miss out on finding the harmony you desire.

Dawn: Maximizing Your Potential

The Saturn meridian is well known for making its presence known in the world of business. It brings out your ambition instincts in a big way. There is nothing to fear according to Saturn. New challenges in work, family life, relationships, or even identity need not be reason for great concern. A cornerstone of this meridian is patience and practice. If you use these two tools, life will go smoother. This prepares you for the unexpected.

Your ideals and spirituality get tested in this land of Saturn. The idea is to make you a stronger person. This planet shows you how to follow through on your most serious life commitments.

Embracing love and your highest beliefs brings you to the doorway of an evolutionary intuitive synchronicity. You only need to walk through with a positive mental approach to find abundance. Your conscious mind may hesitate to turn the handle and open the door, but your intuition will give you the faith to enter. Being willing to adjust to change and not run away from making key decisions is your path to fulfillment and harmony.

Future Goals and Inventiveness:
Uranus Meridian Activating Your Pisces Intuition

Light: Strengths

There is an interesting fact concerning you and Uranus. When your ruling planet, Neptune, was discovered in 1781, it was moving through the sign of Aquarius at the time. This is the sign that Uranus rules. So there is a special connection between Pisces and Uranus because of this. It is as though your intuition can figure out in magical ways how to make contact with this unique meridian that is powered by Uranus.

A Pisces like yourself is known for strong emotions, whether you make them readily visible or not. Uranus and its mentally powerful meridian help you stay objective about your feelings. This is a terrain that propels your mind to stay clear about your goals no matter how emotionally charged you become.

This is an inventive world. Your intuition knows quickly that this is the right planetary influence to contact when looking for new insights.

It does not matter how long you have been working on a project. You may suddenly see a whole new way of operating. That is the gift of this meridian. It is constantly attempting to feed your mind with an alternative vision.

Separating yourself from old, familiar routines that have long served their purpose is encouraged by Uranus. Breaking new ground to prepare for a promising future is possible. You don't have to leave stable situations that are good for you. It is those circumstances that limit your potential to pursue your goals that you might need to say goodbye to.

Relationships begin suddenly when you embrace this planet that enjoys surprising you. This is the Uranus way of taking your mind into new experiences before you can say no. Love and friendship possibilities are increased when Uranus is permitted to come into your consciousness. Your intuition has an internal global positioning system that is guided by Uranus to take you into a reinvented reality.

Freedom is a Uranus word, as is rebelling. There are times when you feel like you have served others long enough and need to take some time to fulfill your own needs. This is Uranus calling. The message, when received loud and clear by your mind via your intuition, will motivate you to act with boldness. Speaking your mind magnifies in importance.

Your creativity is sparked in innovative directions when you respond to Uranus energy. Excitement is your response as you embark with renewed purpose full of magnificent energy. A new career, business, or hobby can capture your imagination. You may wonder why you did not think of this idea sooner. But don't criticize yourself. Just be grateful that you followed your intuition into an interesting frontier that is large enough to allow you to put your creative thinking to work.

Shadow: Challenges

What might be clues that you are not in harmony with this meridian? Your goals seem to disintegrate before you get to put them into action. Why? Perhaps your emotions are so powerful that your mental clarity is fogged. This is the meridian that helps you step back from troublesome problems to take a deep breath and then move on. But you are stuck in the mud and not getting any traction. Negative thinking keeps you glued to neutral and even reverse.

Remaining in relationships, jobs, or localities that no longer are growth-promoting is another strong indication that you are not making use of Uranus in a positive way. The spirit of freedom and equality featured in this meridian is not being properly used. As a matter of fact, it is dormant. Your creative drive is not operating at optimum speed if you are not giving yourself the chance to tap into this great energy.

If you become too self-absorbed, this is yet another wrong use of Uranus. You are too attached to your own ideas and not listening to input from others. This creates great tension in your relationships and causes you to miss out on some great information from others.

Instability is the result if you are not able to follow through on commitments. You may be spontaneously following your instincts but not really letting anyone else know when you suddenly do this. Your unpredictability causes a lot of confusion for people trying to understand you.

Dawn: Maximizing Your Potential

The Uranus meridian awakens your dreams so you can realize that now is the time to act on them. This is a goal-oriented landscape that your intuition enjoys latching on to. Your imagination becomes exhilarated when you visit this world of Uranus. Your mind finds it easier to develop unique perceptions when utilizing Uranus energy. Past negative thinking need not rule you in the present. A sense of feeling liberated from limiting ideas gives you the courage to dare to believe in a bright future.

Uranus manufactures inventive ideas at the speed of light. Your intuition knows this. Experimenting with new creative outlets spawns an evolutionary intuitive synchronicity quickly. This is the reward for letting your intuition join forces with Uranus. Your entire being feels a sense of wholeness. Your mind, body, and soul rejoice. The love you seek and the creative expression you hunger for are never more than a Uranus beat away.

Creative Imagination and Idealism:
Neptune Meridian Activating Your Pisces Intuition

Light: Strengths

Neptune is the ruler of your Pisces Sun sign, meaning this is your home meridian. The door is always open to you here should you choose to come. There is always room for your intuition to adopt the creative power of this meridian. It fits the emotional and soul-driven values you develop when understanding your true purposes for this lifetime. Your intuitive strength is constantly being nurtured by this meridian, although it likely is going on most of the time beyond your conscious awareness. How do you tap into this treasure chest? It takes your greatest faith in showing the world your abilities. Don't be timid when you have this ancient powerhouse ambassador of the collective unconscious willing to aid your quest for harmony.

Your search for a soul mate may have begun early. The yearning to find a special lover who shares your values and highest beliefs is an innate desire. Being reasonable in your expectations makes it easier to be content in a relationship. Your belief in a person gets them to want to give their best effort to secure their own goals. This is the best way to get the same in return.

It is vital to know your boundaries in all personal dealings when you are using Neptune energy. Why? Because it is easy to move that middle line too far one way or the other, either in your favor or very much away. Maintaining a fair sharing of emotions, wealth, and commitment to a partnership is the key to navigating a successful union.

Perfection will drive you to do great things. It motivates you to express your creative intensity and shine like a shooting star. Learning when to stop perfecting is just as important. This is true wisdom. The sooner you understand this, the happier you will be in life.

Symbols will likely come to inspire you in magical ways. It could happen in your sleep during a dream. Neptune often drops by for a visit in this manner. It likes to wait until your conscious mind is not as active. Meditation is another one of its favorite entry points. It is especially attracted to a Pisces like yourself because it knows you are on the same wavelength, whether you realize this or not. When Neptune pays you a visit, you may be communing with nature, such as being at the ocean, watching a sunrise or sunset, or simply taking a relaxing walk. Neptune may sneak into your mind during a movie that moves you emotionally, weaving its energy to get you to see something in a new light. You may be studying or practicing a metaphysical art and have an experience that transforms your mental processes.

You get healed in this ethereal land. Old inner wounds are resolved if you let Neptune do its work on you. Don't be afraid to express your feelings. Your intuitive power multiplies when you do this. If you are too emotional, then stay grounded in your favorite way. That balance between going with an inner flow and keeping your mind sharp is a winning formula.

Shadow: Challenges

How might this meridian get out of alignment for you? It usually goes something like this. You are too sensitive. Criticism stops you in your tracks. You fall into a canyon of self-doubt. You buy in too much to a negative opinion about yourself. Rather than take it in stride and move on, you stop. The end result is usually mental confusion.

Another area is getting lost in serving a mission or cause. Be realistic. You don't have to save the world and donate all of your time and resources. Your own key goals might get lost in the shuffle. Be sure that what you are giving most of your time to is worth it. You may lose a person or some wealth along the way and regret it later.

Let's get back to the subject of boundaries. As a Pisces, you have a natural capacity to go beyond the call of duty to help others. That is a good quality, but it can go overboard and take you with it. Your relationships lose their clarity if you enable others to exhibit negative behaviors too much of the time. It takes away from the love you really want. The other side of the coin is true as well. If you are acting helpless to get attention, this throws a partnership out of balance.

Being too emotional too much of the time is no better than hiding your feelings for fear of revealing them. Finding that middle ground is the best place to be. If you are always reacting with intense feelings, you and everyone else becomes drained. You need to find a grounding wire. If you don't ever show a feeling, you can't expect a great deal of closeness with others. It is difficult to get a read on where you are at in your mind if you don't express any emotions.

Dawn: Maximizing Your Potential

The Neptune meridian takes you into great intuitive depth. It teaches you how to trust your innermost instincts. It does take some sound reality testing to keep your goals on target. Your Pisces idealism is shown how to find a true purpose when you visit this terrain. This is the place that gives birth to dreams and leads you on paths to make them come true.

Your creativity grows immensely by making contact with Neptune. Having faith in your creative power is a foolproof way to tap into an evolutionary intuitive synchronicity. It is in experiencing the magic of your intuition as you allow it to perform spontaneously that new doors of opportunity open for you.

The love you hope to find in the world resides within you. That is a key message in this meridian, although finding a soul mate to share your life with is a special gift offered when you make use of this energy. You will move into the work that you feel will express your belief system when mixing with Neptune's influence. The life roles you choose have a quality that is hard to rival when your intuition becomes friends with Neptune.

Personal Empowerment and Passion: Pluto Meridian Activating Your Pisces Intuition

Light: Strengths

Are you looking to empower your intuition? Then come to this meridian with a humble request that Pluto become your ally. This planet will fill your intuitive gaze at the world with great passion. This is the gift of this meridian. You do have to reach out with a little bit of faith and not doubt yourself as you move to achieve a goal. Trust that the seeds will grow. Be patient. Be diligent. Do your research. This is one of the best methods to bring Pluto into your life. Don't back down when you run into the first sign of an obstacle. Shrug off this adversity and maintain a steady pace toward pursuing your quest to make a dream come true.

Business skills flourish under the watchful eye of Pluto. Your negotiation instincts are strengthened in this landscape. Your ideals merge with your professional aspirations when you make use of Pluto. There is a magical alchemy that takes place pointing you toward work that gives you an intuitive feeling as to where your skills will best be used. You may need to develop a tough skin to ensure that you don't give up on a plan too soon before it has had a real chance to be realized. This meridian showers you with survival instincts.

Emotions are intensified when your intuition links to Pluto. This means you must be honest with yourself when needing to communicate your deepest feelings to others. Why? Because this is part of the process of making an even stronger connection to a clear use of your intuition. Expressing your creative power is tied to a sincere evaluation of not projecting your problems onto others.

Pluto promises a rebirth when you are true to your ideals. When you courageously face your shortcomings and personal issues, you actually find empowerment. This is wisdom at its best. You find renewed courage to pursue the paths that best personify your desire for self-growth.

Your relationships are in a state of harmony when you share the power. You don't need to overpower someone else. This means you can't be a doormat either. It is in locating that middle ground that you enjoy relationship success when you are working with a partner or business associate to achieve shared rewards. Your romances discover greater love when there is a spirit of give and take, and your work connections flow with honest communication.

Shadow: Challenges

How will you know if you are not in sync with this meridian? You will either assume too much power in relationships or not enough. It is insecurity that drives both behaviors. You will not be happy if people fear you and will not be fulfilled if you are serving others and getting little in return. The happiness you could enjoy in balanced partnerships is absent.

Hiding your emotions will not deliver closeness if you want to establish a long-term intimate relationship. Your lover will always be trying to guess what you are really feeling . The trust will be missing. It is difficult to maintain a committed relationship without honest communication. Your fear of closeness is the problem here.

Running away from conflict will not get you the answers you are seeking. You lose your personal power when fleeing responsibility and not facing adversity. Thinking the grass will be greener elsewhere only means your issues keep following you until you deal with them.

Lacking faith in your ability to be a success causes you to settle for a lot less than you could accomplish. The other extreme of having blind faith that you can take unrealistic risks yields results that are just as bad. Reality testing is the answer to both of these type of patterns. It is a safer bet that you will reach your goals and find happiness if you stay grounded.

Dawn: Maximizing Your Potential

The Pluto meridian is a land that guides you to personal empowerment. It is not an easy place to tune in to but is well worth the effort. When you show Pluto that you are determined to put your most passionate ideals into practice, this planet comes to help in a hurry. Conquering your fear of taking that first step into a new venture brings great rewards in ways you never imagined. Business expertise and management ability are part of the Pluto package. You are able to increase your wealth by having faith that the universe will respond to your hard work.

Embracing your inner world with an honest self-evaluation attracts an evolutionary intuitive synchronicity. Overcoming your reluctance to try new experiences ignites your creative power. Self-confidence builds with each step you walk toward your most heartfelt goals. When your intuition partners with Pluto, you come to realize that there is a lot to gain by forming a trusted bond with a special lover. Having someone who truly knows your inner world and does not run away from it is the best friend you could have. Your friendships are highly valued as you proceed to put your creative efforts to work. Having the support of good people makes the ride pleasurable. You are a person who enjoys privacy, and Pluto is the planet that rules this dimension of life. Sharing your time with those you cherish and having a few sacred moments to yourself is the perfect balance.

CONCLUSION

My main intention in writing this book was to encourage you to enjoy experiencing your intuition. Your Sun sign has the potential to offer you a wonderful intuitive expression to help find inner peace and greater happiness in your relationships and work. The key thing to remember is that developing your intuition is a process of self-discovery. There is no need to worry about how you are doing in tuning in to your intuition. Your trust in knowing your intuition is working on your behalf comes with a lot of practice and patience.

You will likely find your own style or ways of learning to grow intuitively. There is no one formula that works for everyone. There is really no right or wrong way to become more intuitive. In reading your own sign chapter, I hope you were able to enhance your intuition and realize there are several paths available to you to tune in to your intuition. I wish you the best of luck in expanding your intuitive awareness!

To Write to the Author

If you wish to contact the author or would like more information about this book, please write to the author in care of Llewellyn Worldwide Ltd. and we will forward your request. Both the author and publisher appreciate hearing from you and learning of your enjoyment of this book and how it has helped you. Llewellyn Worldwide Ltd. cannot guarantee that every letter written to the author can be answered, but all will be forwarded. Please write to:

Bernie Ashman
⅟ Llewellyn Worldwide
2143 Wooddale Drive
Woodbury, MN 55125-2989

Please enclose a self-addressed stamped envelope for reply,
or $1.00 to cover costs. If outside the U.S.A., enclose
an international postal reply coupon.

Many of Llewellyn's authors have websites with additional information and resources. For more information, please visit our website at http://www.llewellyn.com.